Electoral System Design:

The New International IDEA Handbook

Electoral System Design:

The New International IDEA Handbook

Andrew Reynolds
Ben Reilly
and Andrew Ellis

With
José Antonio Cheibub
Karen Cox
Dong Lisheng
Jørgen Elklit
Michael Gallagher
Allen Hicken
Carlos Huneeus
Eugene Huskey
Stina Larserud
Vijay Patidar
Nigel S. Roberts
Richard Vengroff
Jeffrey A. Weldon

Handbook Series

The International IDEA Handbook Series seeks to present comparative analysis, information and insights on a range of democratic institutions and processes. Handbooks are aimed primarily at policy makers, politicians, civil society actors and practitioners in the field. They are also of interest to academia, the democracy assistance community and other bodies.

International IDEA publications are independent of specific national or political interests. Views expressed in this publication do not necessarily represent the views of International IDEA, its Board or its Council members. The map presented in this publication does not imply on the part of the Institute any judgement on the legal status of any territory or the endorsement of such boundaries, nor does the placement or size of any country or territory reflect the political view of the Institute. The map is created for this publication in order to add clarity to the text.

International IDEA encourages dissemination of its work and will promptly respond to requests for permission to reproduce or translate its publications.

Graphic design by: Magnus Alkmar
Cover photos: © Pressens Bild
Printed by: Trydells Tryckeri AB, Sweden
ISBN: 91-85391-18-2

Foreword

The Universal Declaration of Human Rights states that 'everyone has the right to take part in the government of his country, directly or through freely chosen representatives'. The United Nations has thus been involved in the field of electoral assistance since its founding in 1945, working to establish and advance the principles of democracy and political rights.

The work of the UN in elections is most often most associated with comprehensive modern peacekeeping and peace-building operations, for example, in Cambodia, El Salvador and Mozambique, and more recently in Afghanistan and Iraq. These efforts are, however, only the most visible part of UN electoral assistance activities that currently support democratic election processes in over 50 countries.

The design of electoral systems is a vital component of these processes. It cannot be considered in isolation from the wider context of constitutional and institutional design, and it can be critical for areas as diverse as conflict management, gender representation and the development of political party systems. Done well, electoral system design can add to the momentum of political change, encourage popular participation, and enable the emergence of legitimate representatives who are capable of handling a wide range of needs and expectations, immediately and in the future. Done badly, it can derail progress towards democracy or even political stability.

To be successful, electoral system design processes must build understanding and trust—not just among politicians and election administrators, but among civil society organizations, among commentators, and above all among the citizens of a country undergoing democratic reform. Electoral systems must be designed not only to work under current situations but also to accommodate future changes in attitudes and behaviour as electoral incentives change. They can contribute to the development of stable democracy or they can be a major stumbling block to it.

I am delighted therefore to welcome the publication of this new Handbook by International IDEA. It lays out essential knowledge about electoral systems and their consequences, presenting complex ideas with accessible clarity. It addresses key issues in the process of democratic transition and reform in a practical way. It is clear, simple and global in its approach, and will be a vital tool for those involved in the development of stable democracies. It should be made widely available and be widely read by electoral practitioners worldwide.

Carina Perelli
Director, United Nations Electoral Assistance Division

Preface

It is now 50 years since Maurice Duverger's work initiated the widespread study of electoral systems and their effects. For many years, however, the impact of this study on the real political world was limited. The worlds of political scientists and of electoral framework designers did not often connect, and the scope for institutional change was itself limited in many parts of the world of the Cold War.

The 1990s saw an explosion of innovation and reform in electoral systems, especially as the new democracies in Africa, Asia, Eastern Europe, Latin America and the former Soviet Union began actively reforming their political and electoral systems and looking for options and experiences from elsewhere. Responding to this need for comparative information and guidance, IDEA, as a newly established international organization specifically mandated to promote democracy and electoral assistance, drew upon these many and varied experiences to create its first published Handbook, the *International IDEA Handbook of Electoral System Design*, in 1997. Since then, this resource has been widely used and has received much positive feedback. It has been made available on IDEA's web site, distributed by CD ROM, and produced in French, Spanish, Arabic and Burmese editions.

Notwithstanding its continuing success, there have, in the period since the first edition was published, been many more innovations and developments in electoral system design. Several countries have changed their systems, and lessons have been learnt in the process. There is much more understanding about the relationship between electoral systems and party systems and the broader democratic institutional framework, especially in the newer democracies. There is clearer acknowledgement that electoral system change is not simply a technical matter, but a political process requiring public debate and careful consensus building. In this context, electoral system design can be a crucial tool in conflict management strategies, helping to lay firm foundations for sustainable democracy.

IDEA is publishing this new edition—*Electoral System Design: The New International IDEA Handbook*—as part of its tenth anniversary celebrations. While staying faithful to the original edition, the new Handbook features an updated core text, fresh material on the process of electoral system reform, new case studies, and several additional sections on particular issues such as the quality of representation, the challenge of post-conflict situations, and the use of direct democracy options. There is also a revised listing of the electoral systems of the world through the maps, annexes and tables. We hope the result is an accessible and useful volume which will assist those actively engaged in the process of democracy building. We would welcome your comments, suggestions and ideas on any aspect of this Handbook.

Karen Fogg
Secretary-General, International IDEA

Contents

4. ELECTORAL SYSTEMS, INSTITUTIONAL FRAMEWORKS AND GOVERNANCE...129

5. COST AND ADMINISTRATIVE IMPLICATIONS OF ELECTORAL SYSTEMS............153

6. ADVICE FOR ELECTORAL SYSTEM DESIGNERS..159

Case Studies

Annexes

Acronyms and Abbreviations

ANC	African National Congress
AV	Alternative Vote
BC	Borda Count
BV	Block Vote
EMB	Electoral management body
FPTP	First Past The Post
LV	Limited Vote
List PR	List Proportional Representation
MMD	Multi-member district
MMP	Mixed Member Proportional
MP	Member of Parliament
PBV	Party Block Vote
PR	Proportional Representation
SMD	Single-member district
SNTV	Single Non-Transferable Vote
STV	Single Transferable Vote
TRS	Two-Round System

CHAPTER 1

CHAPTER 1

1. Overview

Introduction

1. THE CHOICE OF ELECTORAL SYSTEM IS ONE OF THE MOST IMPORTANT INSTITUTIONAL decisions for any democracy. In almost all cases the choice of a particular electoral system has a profound effect on the future political life of the country concerned, and electoral systems, once chosen, often remain fairly constant as political interests solidify around and respond to the incentives presented by them. However, while conscious design has become far more prevalent recently, traditionally it has been rare for electoral systems to be consciously and deliberately selected. Often the choice was essentially accidental, the result of an unusual combination of circumstances, of a passing trend, or of a quirk of history, with the impact of colonialism and the effects of influential neighbours often being especially strong.

2. Any new democracy must choose (or inherit) an electoral system to elect its legislature. Equally, political crisis within an established democracy may lead to momentum for electoral system change, and even without political crisis campaigners for political reform may attempt to put electoral system change onto the political agenda. Decisions to change, or indeed to keep in place, an electoral system are often affected by one of two circumstances:

- either political actors lack basic knowledge and information so that the choices and consequences of different electoral systems are not fully recognized;
- or, conversely, political actors use their knowledge of electoral systems to promote designs which they think will work to their own partisan advantage.

The choices that are made may have consequences that were unforeseen when they are introduced, as well as effects which were predicted. These choices may not always be the best ones for the long-term political health of the country concerned, and at times they can have disastrous consequences for its democratic prospects.

3. The background to a choice of electoral system can thus be as important as the choice itself. Electoral system choice is a fundamentally political process, rather than a question to which independent technical experts can produce a single 'correct answer'. In fact, the consideration of political advantage is almost always a factor in the choice of electoral systems—sometimes it is the *only* consideration—while the menu of available electoral system choices is often, in reality, a relatively constrained one. Equally, however, calculations of short-term political interest can often obscure the longer-term consequences of a particular electoral system and the interests of the wider political system. Consequently, while recognizing the practical constraints, this Handbook attempts to approach the issue of electoral system choices in as broad and comprehensive a manner as possible.

4. This Handbook is aimed in particular at political negotiators, the designers of constitutions and those involved in debate on political institutions in new, fledgling, and transitional democracies. However, as the crafting of political institutions is a critical task not only for new democracies but also for those established democracies that are seeking to adapt their systems to better reflect new political realities, the Handbook also seeks to address the likely concerns of those persons in established democracies who may be designing or redesigning electoral systems. Given this target audience, much of the academic literature on the subject is necessarily simplified, while at the same time the Handbook attempts to address some of the more complex issues inherent in the area. If the Handbook appears to be sometimes overly simplistic and at other times unduly complex, the explanation will usually lie in the attempt to balance the two objectives of clarity and comprehensiveness.

While the contexts in which emerging and established democracies make institutional choices can vary enormously, their long-term purposes are usually the same: to adopt institutions which are strong enough to promote stable democracy but flexible enough to react to changing circumstances. Each type of democracy has much to learn from the experiences of the other.

Institutional design is an evolving process, and this Handbook seeks to distil the lessons learnt from the many actual examples of institutional design around the world.

5. Much constitutional design has taken place relatively recently: the global movement towards democratic governance in the 1980s and 1990s stimulated a new urgency in the search for enduring models of appropriate representative institutions, and a fresh evaluation of electoral systems. This process was encouraged by the realization that the choice of political institutions can have a significant impact on the wider political system. For example, it is increasingly being recognized that an electoral system can be designed both to provide local geographic representation and to promote proportionality; can promote the development of strong and viable national political parties, and ensure the representation of women and regional minorities; and can help to 'engineer' cooperation and accommodation in a divided society by the creative use of particular incentives and constraints. Electoral systems are today viewed as one of the

most influential of all political institutions, and of crucial importance to broader issues of governance.

6. While the focus of this Handbook is on electoral systems at national level, the options discussed are those available to any community seeking to organize a vote. The Handbook may therefore be of value not only to designers of national, local and supranational institutions but also, for example, to professional associations, trade unions and civil society organizations.

How to Use this Handbook

7. Through providing this detailed analysis of choices and consequences, and showing how electoral systems have worked throughout the democratic world, this Handbook aims to achieve two things: to expand knowledge and illuminate political and public discussions; and to give designers of constitutions, political frameworks and electoral legislation the tools to make an informed choice and thereby avoid some of the more dysfunctional and destabilizing effects of particular electoral system choices.

8. The Handbook begins with a discussion of what electoral systems actually are (and what they are not), and why they are important to a nation's political success and stability. It then suggests ten criteria to be used when trying to decide which electoral system is best for any given society (paragraphs 27–45) and discusses issues relating to the process of review and change. Having set up this framework, it describes in chapters 2 and 3 the different systems and their possible consequences. The advantages and disadvantages of each system are drawn from historical experience and the writings of scholars in the field.

9. There are a large number of different electoral systems currently in use and many more permutations on each form, but for the sake of simplicity we have categorized electoral systems into *three broad families:* plurality/majority systems, proportional systems, and mixed systems. Within these there are nine *'sub-families':* First Past The Post (FPTP), Block Vote (BV), Party Block Vote (PBV), Alternative Vote (AV), and the Two-Round System (TRS) are all plurality/majority systems; List Proportional Representation (List PR) and the Single Transferable Vote (STV) are both proportional systems; and Mixed Member Proportional (MMP) and Parallel systems are both examples of the mixed model. In addition, there are other systems such as the Single Non-Transferable Vote (SNTV), the Limited Vote (LV), and the Borda Count (BC) which do not fit neatly into any particular category (see figure 1) and can be regarded as three further sub-families.

10. This family tree is designed to provide a clear and concise guide to the choice among systems. While rooted in long-established conventions, it attempts to take account of all the electoral systems used for national-level legislative elections in the world today, regardless of wider questions of democracy and legitimacy. The systems are classified by the process on which each is based, rather than their outcome: while results in countries

that use a proportional system are normally more proportional than results in countries using a plurality/majority system, this is not always the case.

11. After describing the mechanics and consequences of each electoral system, chapter 3 moves on to address a number of issues which can relate to all electoral systems, such as the representation of women and minorities, communal representation, election timing, compulsory voting and absentee or out-of-country voting. The focus of this Handbook is on electing legislatures such as national assemblies or lower houses of parliaments or congresses, but electoral system options for choosing a president, for electing the upper house of a legislature in bicameral systems, and for electing local government bodies are also discussed in chapter 4, and we examine the particular issues facing elections to supranational bodies such as the European Parliament, as well as the electoral implications of different forms of federalism, both symmetrical and asymmetrical, and autonomous jurisdictions.

Chapter 5 deals with the important cost and administrative implications of electoral system choice, and we conclude in chapter 6 with some advice for electoral system designers, culled from the experience of a number of experts who have helped draft constitutions and electoral laws around the world. The annexes include a table listing the electoral system particulars of 213 independent countries and territories, a glossary of terms, a bibliography of further reading, and examples of the effects of electoral systems and boundary delimitation.

12. Interspersed throughout the text are 18 case studies which attempt to root the abstract theory of electoral system design in practical reality. The authors of these case studies, experts on the politics of their assigned country, were asked to address the following questions. What is the electoral system and how did it come into being? How does it work in practice? What aspects of the system work well? On what grounds is it criticized? And, if there was a change at some stage, why was there a change, and does the new system fulfil the requirements expected of it?

13. This Handbook does not aim to provide all the answers to electoral system design; instead, the hope is to provide enough information to allow for an informed choice, and to open windows to a much broader discussion of which electoral systems may work best in a given country. The Handbook is not prescriptive: no formula exists, or can exist, to tell the reader, for example, that a society which is 60 per cent Muslim and 40 per cent Christian and has a three-party system and a history of violent secessionism should have a particular type of electoral system. What it does do is to suggest parameters of the available choices and, in so doing, provide a structure for making an informed decision. Through the examples and case studies, the reader from one country should be able to identify how similar problems and needs have been addressed in other parts of the world. Every country is different, but the uniqueness usually rests on its particular concoction of basic socio-political factors, for example, the way in which a society and culture defines the concept of representation, the salience of ethnicity or the history of internal conflict. For this reason the would-be electoral system designer

is recommended to begin with the criteria for choice (see paragraphs 27–45) and try to prioritize the issues which are particularly important to his or her country; he or she can then move on to the options available and their likely consequences and the process of consultation and debate that will precede the adoption of a new electoral system. The quest for the most appropriate electoral system thus involves assessing the available choices against the chosen criteria (always with history, time and political realities in mind) in order to identify one or more options which will suit the needs of the country concerned. It also involves following a process through which the final choice will be accepted as legitimate.

What Electoral Systems Are

14. At the most basic level, electoral systems translate the votes cast in a general election into seats won by parties and candidates. The key variables are the electoral formula used (i.e. whether a plurality/majority, proportional, mixed or other system is used, and what mathematical formula is used to calculate the seat allocation), the ballot structure (i.e. whether the voter votes for a candidate or a party and whether the voter makes a single choice or expresses a series of preferences) and the district magnitude (not how many voters live in a district, but how many representatives to the legislature that district elects). It must also be stressed that, although this Handbook does not focus on the administrative aspects of elections (such as the distribution of polling places, the nomination of candidates, the registration of voters, who runs the elections and so on), these issues are of critical importance, and the possible advantages of any given electoral system choice will be undermined unless due attention is paid to them. Electoral system design also affects other areas of electoral laws: the choice of electoral system has an influence on the way in which district boundaries are drawn, how voters are registered, the design of ballot papers, how votes are counted, and numerous other aspects of the electoral process.

The Importance of Electoral Systems

15. Political institutions shape the rules of the game under which democracy is practised, and it is often argued that the easiest political institution to manipulate, for good or for bad, is the electoral system. In translating the votes cast in a general election into seats in the legislature, the choice of electoral system can effectively determine who is elected and which party gains power. While many aspects of a country's political framework are often specified in the constitution and can thus be difficult to amend, electoral system change often only involves new legislation.

16. Even with each voter casting exactly the same vote and with exactly the same number of votes for each party, one electoral system may lead to a coalition government or a minority government while another may allow a single party to assume majority control. The examples presented in annex D illustrate how different electoral systems can translate the votes cast into dramatically different results.

Electoral Systems and Party Systems

17. A number of other consequences of electoral systems go beyond this primary effect. Some systems encourage, or even enforce, the formation of political parties; others recognize only individual candidates. The type of party system which develops, in particular the number and the relative sizes of political parties in the legislature, is heavily influenced by the electoral system. So is the internal cohesion and discipline of parties: some systems may encourage factionalism, where different wings of one party are constantly at odds with each other, while another system might encourage parties to speak with one voice and suppress dissent. Electoral systems can also influence the way parties campaign and the way political elites behave, thus helping to determine the broader political climate; they may encourage, or retard, the forging of alliances between parties; and they can provide incentives for parties and groups to be broadly-based and accommodating, or to base themselves on narrow appeals to ethnicity or kinship ties.

Electoral Systems and Conflict Management

18. These different impacts underline the important role that electoral systems often have in terms of conflict management. It is clear that different electoral systems can aggravate or moderate tension and conflict in a society. At one level, a tension exists between systems which put a premium on representation of minority groups and those which encourage strong single-party government. At another level, if an electoral system is not considered fair and the political framework does not allow the opposition to feel that they have the chance to win next time around, losers may feel compelled to work outside the system, using non-democratic, confrontationalist and even violent tactics. And finally, because the choice of electoral system will determine the ease or complexity of the act of voting, it inevitably impacts on minorities and underprivileged groups. This is always important, but becomes particularly so in societies where there are a substantial number of inexperienced or illiterate voters (see chapter 5 on Cost and Administrative Implications).

Psychological and Mechanical Effects

19. Electoral systems are generally considered to have both 'mechanical' and 'psychological' effects. The mechanical impact is most apparent in the way different electoral systems tend to encourage different kinds of party system. Plurality/majority systems often tend to have a constraining effect on party numbers, while proportional systems tend to be more 'permissive', resulting in a greater diversity of parties. The psychological impact of electoral systems reinforces this mechanical effect: under FPTP rules, voters who wish to support a minor party are often faced with a dilemma as to how best to avoid 'wasting' their vote, as only one candidate can be elected from any single-member district. The result of this dilemma is that many voters will not express their sincere choice but rather will vote for another candidate (usually from a major party) who they believe has a realistic chance of winning the seat. The overall effect of

this is to strengthen larger parties at the expense of smaller ones. Proportional systems or systems that allow multiple ballot choices, by contrast, are more likely to facilitate the election of small parties, and hence the pressure to vote strategically is reduced.

The Importance of Context

20. It is important to realize that a given electoral system will not necessarily work in the same way in different countries. Although there are some common experiences in different regions of the world, the effects of a particular type of electoral system depend to a great extent on the socio-political context in which it is used. For example, while there remains general agreement that plurality/majority systems tend to restrict the range of legislative representation and PR systems encourage it, the conventional wisdom that plurality/majority rules will produce a two-party system and PR a multiparty system is looking increasingly dated. In recent years, FPTP has not facilitated the aggregation of the party system in established democracies such as Canada and India, nor has it led to the formation of strong and lasting parties in Papua New Guinea. PR has seen the election of dominant single-party regimes in Namibia, South Africa and elsewhere. More broadly, the consequences of the choice of electoral system depend on factors such as how a society is structured in terms of ideological, religious, ethnic, racial, regional, linguistic or class divisions; whether the country is an established democracy, a transitional democracy or a new democracy; whether there is an established party system, or parties are embryonic or unformed, and how many 'serious' parties there are; and whether a particular party's supporters are geographically concentrated or dispersed over a wide area.

The Broader Democratic Framework

21. It is also important not to see electoral systems in isolation. Their design and effects are heavily contingent upon other structures within and outside the constitution. Electoral systems are one square of an interrelated patchwork of government systems, rules and points of access to power. Successful electoral system design comes from looking at the framework of political institutions as a whole: changing one part of this framework is likely to cause adjustments in the way other institutions within it work.

22. For example, how does the chosen electoral system facilitate or encourage conflict resolution between party leaders and activists on the ground? How much control do party leaders have over the party's elected representatives? Are there constitutional provisions for referendums, citizens' initiatives or 'direct democracy' which may complement the institutions of representative democracy? And are the details of the electoral system specified in the constitution, as an attached schedule to the constitution or in regular legislation? This will determine how entrenched the system is or how open it may be to change by elected majorities (see paragraph 49).

23. There are two issues of this kind that are worth considering in more detail. The first is the degree of centralization. Is the country federal or unitary, and, if federal,

are the units symmetrical in their power or asymmetrical? The second is the choice between parliamentarism and presidentialism. Both systems have their advocates, and the traditions of different countries may influence which is chosen or even foreclose debate; but the different relationship between legislative and executive institutions has important implications for electoral system design for both. The frequent debates over the direct election of mayors and heads of the executive at local level combine both issues.

24. In most bicameral legislatures in federal systems of government, the two chambers are elected by different (or incongruent) methods. This makes sense for two prime reasons which have to do with the theory underpinning federalism. First, the second (or upper) house of a federal legislature is there to represent the regions or states of the country, and each state often receives equal representation regardless of population or territory size (e.g. the US Senate or South Africa's National Council of Provinces). Second, there is little point in creating a two-chamber legislature unless there is a degree of difference between the roles and possibly also of the powers of the two chambers, and using the same electoral system for both is more likely to repeat and reinforce the majority power that controls the lower chamber—particularly if the elections to both chambers are simultaneous. As noted below (see paragraphs 189–192), upper chambers provide the opportunity for some degree of electoral innovation to include communities of interest which may not be fully represented in national elections to a lower chamber. But when elections take place at three or more levels, to the upper chamber of the legislature, the lower chamber of the legislature, and the institutions of government at regional level, it is crucial that the systems used are considered together. It may for example be possible to promote representation of minorities at regional level while discouraging or even prohibiting it at national level. Whether this is or is not desirable is a matter of political debate and choice.

25. Until recent years there were few examples of enduring democracies using presidential systems. However, the commitment to presidentialism in for example Latin America and parts of South-East Asia means that the question now asked is: What aspects of institutional design help make presidentialism work? There is some evidence from the Latin American experience that stability can be problematic in countries with presidential constitutions and highly fragmented party systems, and that there are tensions between divided executive and legislative branches when the presidential electoral system is over two rounds, the legislative system is List PR and the elections are not held concurrently. However, it appears helpful to adopt an electoral system which makes it likely that the party or coalition supporting an elected president has a significant block, although not necessarily an absolute majority, of elected members of the legislature.

26. Plurality elections for the presidency and simultaneous presidential and legislative elections are often seen as helping to focus the party system into fewer and more viable challengers for power. However, there can be serious dangers in combining the great power that is vested in the hands of a directly elected president who is head

of the executive with the use of a plurality method in a diverse or ethnically divided country where no single group has an absolute majority. The result can be devastating for legitimacy or indeed for the success of a peace process. A presidential electoral system may complement a federal system by requiring a successful candidate to achieve a winning vote not only nationwide but also a significant fraction of the vote in a minimum number of the states of the federation (as in Indonesia or Nigeria: see paragraphs 187–188).

Criteria for Design

27. When designing an electoral system, it is best to start with a list of criteria which sum up what you want to achieve, what you want to avoid and, in a broad sense, what you want your legislature and executive government to look like. The criteria which follow cover many areas, but the list is not exhaustive and the reader may add a host of equally valid items. It is also true that some of the criteria outlined overlap and may appear contradictory. This is because they often are contradictory: it is the nature of institutional design that trade-offs have to be made between a number of competing desires and objectives.

For example, one may want to provide the opportunity for independent candidates to be elected, and at the same time to encourage the growth of strong political parties. Or the electoral system designer may think it wise to craft a system which gives voters a wide degree of choice between candidates and parties, but this may make for a complicated ballot paper which causes difficulties for less-educated voters. The trick in choosing (or reforming) an electoral system is to prioritize the criteria that are most important and then assess which electoral system, or combination of systems, best maximizes the attainment of these objectives.

Providing Representation

28. Representation may take at least four forms. First, *geographical* representation implies that each region, be it a town or a city, a province or an electoral district, has members of the legislature whom it chooses and who are ultimately accountable to their area. Second, the *ideological* divisions within society may be represented in the legislature, whether through representatives from political parties or independent representatives or a combination of both. Third, a legislature may be representative of the *party-political* situation that exists within the country even if political parties do not have an ideological base. If half the voters vote for one political party but that party wins no, or hardly any, seats in the legislature, then that system cannot be said to adequately represent the will of the people. Fourth, the concept of *descriptive* representation considers that the legislature should be to some degree a 'mirror of the nation' which should look, feel, think and act in a way which reflects the people as a whole. An adequately descriptive legislature would include both men and women, the young and the old, the wealthy and the poor, and reflect the different religious affiliations, linguistic communities and ethnic groups within a society.

Making Elections Accessible and Meaningful

29. Elections are all well and good, but they may mean little to people if it is difficult to vote or if at the end of the day their vote makes no difference to the way the country is governed. The 'ease of voting' is determined by factors such as how complex the ballot paper is, how easy it is for the voter to get to a polling place, how up-to-date the electoral register is, and how confident the voter will be that his or her ballot is secret.

30. Electoral participation—at least as a free choice—is also thought to increase when the outcome of elections, either at a national level or in the voter's particular district, is likely to make a significant difference to the future direction of government. If you know that your preferred candidate has no chance of winning a seat in your particular district, what is the incentive to vote? In some electoral systems the 'wasted votes' (i.e. valid votes which do not go towards the election of any candidate, as distinct from spoiled or invalid ballot papers, which are excluded from the count) can amount to a substantial proportion of the total national vote.

31. Lastly, the actual power of the body being elected helps determine whether its election has any meaning. Hollow elections in authoritarian systems which offer no genuine choice, where legislatures have little real influence on the formation of governments or on government policy, are far less important than elections to legislatures which actually have the power to determine central elements in people's everyday lives.

32. Even within democratic systems, the choice of electoral system can influence the legitimacy of institutions. For example, the Australian Senate between 1919 and 1946 was elected by a highly disproportional electoral system (the Alternative Vote in multi-member districts), which produced lopsided and unrepresentative results. This tended to undermine the actual legitimacy of the Senate itself in the eyes of both electors and politicians and, some observers argued, also undermined public support for the institutions of federal government in general. After the system was altered to a fairer proportional system (the Single Transferable Vote) in 1948 the Senate began to be perceived as more credible and representative, and thus respect for it and its relative importance in decision making increased.

Providing Incentives for Conciliation

33. Electoral systems can be seen not only as ways to constitute governing bodies but also as a tool of conflict management within a society. Some systems, in some circumstances, will encourage parties to make inclusive appeals for electoral support outside their own core vote base; for instance, even if a party draws its support primarily from black voters, a particular electoral system may give it the incentive to appeal also to white, or other, voters. Thus, the party's policy platform would become less divisive and exclusionary, and more unifying and inclusive. Similar electoral system incentives might make parties less ethnically, regionally, linguistically or ideologically exclusive. Examples of how different electoral systems have worked as tools of conflict

management are given throughout this Handbook.

34. On the other side of the coin, electoral systems can encourage voters to look outside their own group and think of voting for parties which traditionally have represented a different group. Such voting behaviour breeds accommodation and community building. Systems which give the voter more than one vote or allow the voter to order candidates preferentially provide the space for voters to cut across preconceived social boundaries. At the 1998 Good Friday agreement election in Northern Ireland, for instance, vote transfers under the STV system benefited 'pro-peace' parties while still providing broadly proportional outcomes. At the 2003 election, however, a shift in first-preference votes towards hard-line parties tended to outweigh such effects.

Facilitating Stable and Efficient Government

35. The prospects for a stable and efficient government are not determined by the electoral system alone, but the results a system produces can contribute to stability in a number of important respects. The key questions are whether voters perceive the system to be fair, whether government can efficiently enact legislation and govern, and whether the system avoids discriminating against particular parties or interest groups.

36. The perception of whether results are fair or not varies widely from country to country. Twice in the United Kingdom (UK) (in 1951 and 1974) the party winning the most votes in the country as a whole won fewer seats than its opponents, but this was considered more a quirk of a basically sound system (FPTP—see paragraphs 76–79) than an outright unfairness which should be reversed. Conversely, similar results in New Zealand in 1978 and 1981, in which the National Party retained office despite winning fewer votes than the Labour opposition, are credited as starting the reform movement which led to the change of electoral system (see the case study on New Zealand).

37. The question whether the government of the day can enact legislation efficiently is partly linked to whether it can assemble a working majority in the legislature, and this in turn is linked to the electoral system. As a general rule of thumb, plurality/majority electoral systems are more likely to produce legislatures where one party can outvote the combined opposition, while PR systems are more likely to give rise to coalition governments. Nevertheless, it has to be remembered that PR systems can also produce single-party majorities, and plurality/majority systems can leave no one party with a working majority. Much depends on the structure of the party system and the nature of the society itself.

38. Finally, the system should, as far as possible, act in an electorally neutral manner towards all parties and candidates; it should not openly discriminate against any political grouping. The perception that electoral politics in a democracy is an uneven playing field is a sign that the political order is weak and that instability may not be far around the corner. A dramatic example of this was the 1998 election in Lesotho, in which the

Lesotho Congress for Democracy won every seat in the legislature with only 60 per cent of the votes under an FPTP system. The public unrest that followed, culminating in a request for military intervention in the country by the Southern African Development Community, demonstrated that such a result was not merely unfair but also dangerous, and the electoral system was consequently changed for future elections (see the case study on Lesotho).

Holding the Government Accountable

39. Accountability is one of the bedrocks of representative government. Its absence may indeed lead to long-term instability. An accountable political system is one in which the government is responsible to the voters to the highest degree possible. Voters should be able to influence the shape of the government, either by altering the coalition of parties in power or by throwing out of office a single party which has failed to deliver. Suitably designed electoral systems facilitate this objective.

40. The conventional wisdom in this area may be simplistic. Traditionally, plurality/majority systems like FPTP were seen as leading to single parties taking office, while PR systems were associated with multiparty coalitions. While the broad logic of this association remains valid, there have been sufficient examples in recent years of FPTP elections leading to multiparty cabinets (e.g. in India) or of PR elections leading to the election of a strong single-party government (e.g. in South Africa) to raise doubts about the automatic assumption that one kind of electoral system will lead to particular governance outcomes. But clearly, electoral systems do have a major impact on broader issues of governance, for both presidential and parliamentary systems.

Holding Individual Representatives Accountable

41. Accountability at the individual level is the ability of the electorate to effectively check on those who, once elected, betray the promises they made during the campaign or demonstrate incompetence or idleness in office and 'throw the rascals out'. Some systems emphasize the role of locally popular candidates, rather than on candidates nominated by a strong central party.

Plurality/majority systems have traditionally been seen as maximizing the ability of voters to throw out unsatisfactory individual representatives. Again, this sometimes remains valid. However, the connection becomes tenuous where voters identify primarily with parties rather than candidates, as in the UK. At the same time, open and free list systems and STV are designed to allow voters to exercise candidate choice in the context of a proportional system.

Encouraging Political Parties

42. The weight of evidence from both established and new democracies suggests that longer-term democratic consolidation—that is, the extent to which a democratic regime

is insulated from domestic challenges to the stability of the political order—requires the growth and maintenance of strong and effective political parties, and thus the electoral system should encourage this rather than entrench or promote party fragmentation. Electoral systems can be framed specifically to exclude parties with a small or minimal level of support. The development of the role of parties as a vehicle for individual political leaders is another trend which can be facilitated or retarded by electoral system design decisions.

Most experts also agree that the electoral system should encourage the development of parties which are based on broad political values and ideologies as well as specific policy programmes, rather than narrow ethnic, racial or regional concerns. As well as lessening the threat of societal conflict, parties which are based on these broad 'cross-cutting cleavages' are more likely to reflect national opinion than those which are based predominantly on sectarian or regional concerns.

Promoting Legislative Opposition and Oversight

43. Effective governance relies not only on those in power but, almost as much, on those who oppose and oversee them. The electoral system should help ensure the presence of a viable opposition grouping which can critically assess legislation, question the performance of the executive, safeguard minority rights, and represent its constituents effectively. Opposition groupings should have enough representatives to be effective (assuming that their performance at the ballot box warrants it) and in a parliamentary system should be able to present a realistic alternative to the current government. Obviously the strength of the opposition depends on many other factors besides the choice of electoral system, but if the system itself makes the opposition impotent, democratic governance is inherently weakened. A major reason for the change to an MMP electoral system in New Zealand, for example, was the systematic under-representation of smaller opposition parties under FPTP. At the same time, the electoral system should hinder the development of a 'winner takes all' attitude which leaves rulers blind to other views and the needs and desires of opposition voters, and sees both elections and government itself as zero-sum contests.

In a presidential system, the president needs the reliable support of a substantial group of legislators: however, the role of others in opposing and scrutinizing government legislative proposals is equally important. The separation of powers between legislature and executive effectively gives the task of executive oversight to all legislators, not only the opposition members. This makes it important to give particular thought to the elements of the electoral system which concern the relative importance of political parties and candidates, alongside the relationship between parties and their elected members.

Making the Election Process Sustainable

44. Elections do not take place on the pages of academic books but in the real world, and for this reason the choice of any electoral system is, to some degree, dependent on the cost and administrative capacities of the country involved. Although donor countries often provide substantial financial support for the first, and even the second, election in a country in transition to democracy, this is unlikely to be available in the long term even if it were desirable. A sustainable political framework takes into account the resources of a country both in terms of the availability of people with the skills to be election administrators and in terms of the financial demands on the national budget.

For example, a poor country may not be able to afford the multiple elections required under a Two-Round System or be able easily to administer a complicated preferential vote count. However, simplicity in the short term may not always make for cost-effectiveness in the longer run. An electoral system may be cheap and easy to administer but it may not answer the pressing needs of a country—and when an electoral system is at odds with a country's needs the results can be disastrous. Alternatively, a system which appears at the outset to be a little more expensive to administer and more complex to understand may in the long run help to ensure the stability of the country and the positive direction of democratic consolidation.

Taking into Account 'International Standards'

45. Finally, the design of electoral systems today takes place in the context of a number of international covenants, treaties and other kinds of legal instruments affecting political issues. While there is no single complete set of universally agreed international standards for elections, there is consensus that such standards include the principles of free, fair and periodic elections that guarantee universal adult suffrage, the secrecy of the ballot and freedom from coercion, and a commitment to the principle of one person, one vote. Moreover, while there is no legal stipulation that a particular kind of electoral system is preferable to another, there is an increasing recognition of the importance of issues that are affected by electoral systems, such as the fair representation of all citizens, the equality of women and men, the rights of minorities, special considerations for the disabled, and so on. These are formalized in international legal instruments such as the 1948 Universal Declaration of Human Rights and the 1966 International Covenant on Civil and Political Rights, and in the various conventions and commitments concerning democratic elections made by regional organizations such as the European Union (EU) and the Organization for Security and Co-operation in Europe (OSCE).

Conclusions

46. The ten criteria outlined above are at times in conflict with each other or even mutually exclusive. The designer of an electoral system must therefore go through a careful process of prioritizing which criteria are most important to the particular political context before moving on to assess which system will do the best job. A

useful way forward is first to list the things which must be avoided at all costs, such as political catastrophes which could lead to the breakdown of democracy. For example, an ethnically divided country might want above all to avoid excluding minority ethnic groups from representation in order to promote the legitimacy of the electoral process and avoid the perception that the electoral system was unfair. In contrast, while these issues might still be important to it, a fledgling democracy elsewhere might have different priorities—perhaps to ensure that a government can enact legislation efficiently without fear of gridlock, or that voters are able to remove discredited leaders if they so wish. Establishing the priorities among such competing criteria can only be the domain of the domestic actors involved in the institutional design process.

The Process of Change

47. The process through which an electoral system is designed or altered has a great effect on the type of the system which results, its appropriateness for the political situation, and the degree of legitimacy and popular support it will ultimately enjoy.

Electoral systems are very rarely designed on a blank slate where no precedents exist. Even the design efforts in Afghanistan and Iraq have historical multiparty competitive precedents to draw on (albeit distant in time and casting little light on what may work in the future).

Some key questions of electoral system design are: Who designs? That is, who puts the idea of electoral system change onto the political agenda, and who has the responsibility for drawing up a proposed new or amended system and through what type of process? What are the mechanisms built into the political and legal framework for reform and amendment? What process of discussion and dialogue is necessary to ensure that a proposed new or amended system is accepted as legitimate? Once change has been decided upon, how is it implemented?

Who Designs?

48. There are several ways by which electoral systems come into being.

First, they can be inherited without significant alteration from colonial or occupying administrations (Malawi, Mali, the Solomon Islands and Palau being examples).

Second, they can result from peace process negotiations between communal groups seeking to bring an end to division or war (e.g. Lesotho, South Africa and Lebanon). In these circumstances the electoral system choice may not be open to full public scrutiny or debate.

Third, the system may be effectively imposed by the groups responsible for post-conflict political reconstruction (e.g. the Coalition authorities in Iraq and the appointed Transitional National Council in Afghanistan).

Fourth, elements of a previous authoritarian regime may have a strong role in designing a new electoral system during the period when they are being divested of power (as in Chile).

Fifth, an expert commission may be set up to investigate the electoral system alone (as in the UK or Mauritius) or as part of the broader constitutional context (as in Fiji). This may lead to recommendations being put to a national referendum (as was the case in New Zealand) or to a legislative vote on the commission's recommendations (as in Fiji).

Sixth, citizens may be involved more widely in the design process by the establishment of a non-expert citizens' assembly on the electoral system. This was the approach adopted by the Canadian province of British Columbia; it led to a recommendation for a change from FPTP to STV that would be put to a province-wide referendum for decision (see the case study on British Columbia).

British Columbia: Empowered Citizen Participation

The British Columbia Citizens' Assembly on Electoral Reform

The government of the Canadian province of British Columbia, with the full endorsement of the province's Legislative Assembly, has initiated a historic, unique and precedent-setting process on electoral reform by establishing the Citizens' Assembly on Electoral Reform. This is the first time that a government has given a randomly selected group of citizens the opportunity and responsibility to independently review the electoral system and have its recommendation submitted to the public for approval at a referendum.

The 1996 election for the British Columbia provincial legislature was conducted under an FPTP system. It resulted in the New Democratic Party (NDP), with 39 per cent of the popular vote, winning 39 seats in the Legislative Assembly—more than the 33 seats gained by the Liberal Party, which had won 42 per cent of the popular vote. The NDP, with less popular support than the Liberal Party, thus formed the government for the next five years. This result motivated the Liberal Party to make electoral reform a priority in its political campaign for the next election. At the 2001 election the Liberal Party promised to implement electoral reform through a Citizens' Assembly: following an election victory which gave it 97 per cent of the seats in the legislature with 58 per cent of the popular vote, it clearly had the mandate to pursue these objectives.

The typical approach used in Canada for the development of public policy issues where the government is seeking public review is to establish a commission or board of public inquiry, usually led by judges, experts or political leaders. After inviting submissions from the public, and following a period of wider consultation, the government makes a decision on the actions that will follow, taking into account the report produced by the commission.

The blueprint of the Citizens' Assembly and the framing of its terms of reference were prepared by Gordon Gibson, an author on democracy and former political party leader active in business and public affairs, and the new government in consultation with electoral reform experts. There were two unique and precedent-setting features for British Columbia: the people appointed would not be experts or specialists in the field of electoral reform, but would instead be randomly selected citizens from across the province; and, if a change were recommended, the question would be put directly to the citizens of the province at a referendum and would not be filtered through the government.

The Citizens' Assembly that resulted was a non-partisan and independent group of 160 men and women of all ages from across the province of British Columbia, chosen by random selection from the electoral register. The selection phase was designed to give a balanced list of men and women, reflective of the age distribution of the population of British Columbia as reported in the 2001 census, including two members from the aboriginal community, and representing the whole of the province. This was followed by an intense learning phase for the Assembly during which various electoral system experts produced learning materials (all also available to the general public) and held sessions with the members to inform them of the different systems available and discuss their advantages and disadvantages.

At the conclusion of the learning phase a report, *Preliminary Statement to the People of British Columbia*, was sent to various groups in society, including members of the Legislative Assembly, libraries, municipal district offices, schools and universities, to inform the public of the preliminary conclusions of the Citizens' Assembly. This report was followed by a phase of public hearings, during which about 3,000 people attended some 50 hearings held in all areas of the province. During the subsequent deliberation phase, plenary sessions and discussion groups were held at which the Assembly narrowed down the choice of electoral systems to two and, as a group, sketched out the details of each system. The first day of that phase featured a repeat of some of the best presentations heard during the public hearings—presentations that advocated a variety of electoral systems and features. The objectives of all these phases were to identify the elements essential to a British Columbian electoral system, review thoroughly all electoral system options in the light of these elements and, most importantly, to increase public awareness, inclusion and participation. The three essential elements arrived at in the end were voter choice, local representation and proportionality. Finally, in late October 2004, the Assembly presented its recommendation, in which it supported (by 146 in favour to seven against) changing the FPTP system to STV. The completion of the Citizens' Assembly process then required the publication of the formal final report and the submission of the recommendation to referendum.

This participatory model attracted significant interest from groups across Canada. The concept was recommended to other governments within Canada as a good way of involving citizens in issues that should be the domain of citizens, and a similar process to the one in British Columbia was initiated by the Ontario government.

Other elections in Canada have also contributed to the growing support for a review of electoral processes. Federal majority governments have often been elected with significantly less than 50 per cent of the popular vote. As a result, a number of initiatives for a change of the electoral system at federal level, including Fair Vote Canada (FVC), have emerged, as have many individual lobbyists and advocates.

There is reason to think that the experience with the British Columbia Citizens' Assembly will have significant impact on the future of the debate on electoral system change, and on the process of review and change in particular, on a federal level in Canada. Following pressure from both the NDP and the Conservative Party, the following amendment to the Speech from the Throne was unanimously accepted in October 2004: 'an Order of Reference to the Standing Committee on Procedure and House Affairs instructing the committee to recommend a process that engages citizens and parliamentarians in an examination of our electoral system with a review of all options'.

The future impact of the British Columbia Citizens' Assembly on the process of review and change of electoral systems on an international scale remains to be seen, but it is safe to say that its establishment and work have raised interest in and added to the empirical knowledge of participatory processes around the world.

What are the Mechanisms for Reform and Amendment?

49. While electoral systems are an extremely important institution affecting the way in which a country's system of government works, traditionally they have not been formally specified in constitutions, the highest source of law. In recent years, however, this has started to change.

Today, a number of countries have 'embedded' details about the electoral system in their constitution or in a separate schedule to the constitution. The significance of this for electoral reformers is that constitutionally entrenched laws are usually much harder to change than ordinary laws, usually requiring a special majority in the legislature, a national referendum or some other confirmatory mechanism, which shields such systems from easy alteration. For example, the South African constitution states that the electoral system for the National Assembly elections shall result 'in general in proportionality' and so reform options are limited to PR-type systems unless a constitutional amendment is made.

However, the details of the electoral system are still more often to be found in regular law and thus can be changed by a simple majority in the legislature. This may have the advantage of making the system more responsive to changes in public opinion and political needs, but it also contains the danger of majorities in a legislature unilaterally altering systems to give them political advantage.

50. The opportunities for reform rely on both the legal mechanisms for change and the political context within which calls for change are made. Not all movements for electoral system change are successful. Almost all recent examples of major change have occurred in one of two sets of circumstances. The first is in the course of a transition to democracy or shortly afterwards, when the whole political framework is 'up for grabs'. The second is when there is a crisis of governance in an established democracy. Two examples are the perceived illegitimacy of two successive majority governments elected with fewer votes than their major opponents in New Zealand, and the perception that high levels of corruption in Italy and Japan were endemic to the political system rather than the results of the actions of particular individuals. The cases of New Zealand and Japan are illustrated in case studies in this Handbook.

51. Even when there is huge popular distrust and dissatisfaction with the political system, change still needs to be agreed by the current holders of power. Political elites are only likely to act if they can see benefit to themselves from change or if they are frightened of the electoral consequences to themselves of failing to change. Even when convinced, they will, unsurprisingly and almost inevitably, seek to choose a system that maximizes the benefit to themselves. If they are unsure how this can be achieved or if different interests seek different solutions, negotiated compromises may be likely—perhaps involving mixed systems. However, agreements and changes may not turn out to have the effects intended by their proponents or may produce other, unintended effects. In Mexico, reforms in 1994 designed by the governing party to

make concessions to the opposition led to the most disproportional result in recent years (see the case study on Mexico).

52. The cases of South Africa and Chile illustrate the fact that political realities and the desire of ruling parties to maintain their power and influence can be just as much a block on electoral system reform as legal hurdles. In South Africa there have been widespread calls for an element of local accountability to be built in to the closed-list PR system of large electoral districts under which elected representatives are perceived as detached from their electors. These were reinforced by the majority findings of a presidential commission which reported in January 2003, but the government shied away from changes that would reduce its control over candidate selection and caucus voting behaviour, and declined to entertain reform (see the case study on South Africa). In Chile General Pinochet's legacy was to rig the electoral system to advantage his allies. More than a decade after his removal from power, that system remains effectively unchanged (see the case study on Chile).

53. In New Zealand (see the case study), the use of referendums during the process of change resulted initially from a political move—an attempt by the leader of one major party to wrong-foot the other major party during a general election campaign. In the first referendum, the electorate was asked whether it wanted change at all and to indicate its preferred new system from four options. In the second, the chosen new system was pitted against the retention of the previous system. As a result, the new multi-member proportional system was adopted with a clear expression of public legitimacy.

54. Electoral systems will inevitably need to adapt over time if they are to respond adequately to new political, demographic and legislative trends and needs. However, once a system is in place, those who have benefited from it are likely to resist change. Without a transition or a major political crisis as catalyst, it appears that change at the margins may well be more likely than fundamental reform. In post-conflict transitions, this creates a tension between the practical constraints that may affect the implementation of elections driven for example by the political imperatives of a peace agreement, and the desirability of getting the system right at the beginning.

To try to engineer improvements within existing systems, reformers may consider changing district magnitude (see paragraphs 113–118), threshold levels (see paragraph 119) or quota formulae (see annex B). Many significant reforms proposed in the past few years have involved adding a List PR element on to an existing FPTP system to create a mixed, more proportional system (e.g. the changes enacted in Lesotho and Thailand: see the case studies).

Advice on Debate and Dialogue

55. It is the task of reformers not only to understand the legal form of the technical arguments for and the implications of potential change but also to understand and be able to explain the political arguments and the implications for the wider political

framework of the country. Significant voices in civil society, academia and the media may contribute to developing a public perception that change is necessary. But a sufficient number of those in power will need to be convinced of the benefits, including the benefits to themselves.

56. Even with the current increased interest in electoral systems, the number of people, both in elite circles and in society generally, who understand the likely impact of changes may be very limited. This is further complicated by the fact that the operation of electoral systems in practice may be heavily dependent on apparently minor points of detail. Reformers may need not only to fully work through and explain the legal detail that would be necessary to implement change, but also to make technical projections and simulations (often using data from previous elections) to show, for example, the shape and implications of proposals on electoral districts or the potential impact on the representation of political parties. Technical simulations can also be used to ensure that all contingencies are covered and to evaluate apparently unlikely outcomes: it is better to answer questions while change is being promoted than in the middle of a crisis later!

57. Voter involvement programmes, for example, inviting members of the public to participate in mock elections under a potential new system, may attract media attention and increase familiarity with proposals for change. They may also help to identify the problems—for example, voter difficulty with ballot papers—which a new system may generate.

Advice on Implementation

58. Voters, election administrators, politicians and commentators all tend to be comfortable with what is familiar. Years of use may have smoothed the rough edges of established systems. A new system can thus be a leap into the unknown, and problems in implementation can arise from its unfamiliarity. This cannot be avoided completely, and the planners of change cannot sit back when legislative changes are in place. A process of change is complete only with intensive voter education programmes to explain to all participants how the new system works and with the design and agreement of user-friendly implementing regulations.

59. The most effective voter education—and election administrator education—takes time. However, time is often in short supply to an electoral management body (EMB) organizing an election under a new system. All good negotiators use time pressure before a final agreement is reached, and this is particularly true when the new system is the product of hard negotiation between political actors. An effective EMB will nonetheless prepare as much as possible as early as possible.

Assessing the Impact of Change

60. Having discussed the process of change in some depth, a word of caution is needed. Because electoral systems have psychological as well as mechanical effects, the long-term effect of changes may take some time to work through. Parties, candidates and voters may take two or three elections to fully observe and respond to the effects and incentives of particular changes. The tendency towards mixed systems may accentuate this, as the overall effect on candidates and voters of mixed incentives may be less clear.

Judgement may be necessary as to whether problems in a new or amended electoral system are merely transitional or whether they show that the system is fundamentally flawed and requires urgent amendment or replacement. In the aftermath of George Speight's 2000 coup, such a debate is currently taking place in Fiji: will the Alternative Vote settle down so that parties and voters respond to incentives for inter-ethnic moderation, or does the course of events since its adoption in 1997 indicate that it is fundamentally unsound in the Fijian context?

Trends in Electoral System Reform

61. The Italian referendum in 1993, leading to a change to a Mixed Member Proportional System for the elections the following year, marked the beginning of a series of significant changes in electoral systems all over the world. In the vast majority of the cases, changes have been made on the margins, with a new seat allocation formula, a new number of electoral districts, or an extra few appointed members in the legislature; but as many as 26 other countries have since followed Italy's example and gone through reform processes that have altered their electoral system completely (see Table 1).

As Table 1 shows, the trend is rather clear. Most countries that have changed electoral systems have done so in the direction of more proportionality, either by adding a PR element to a plurality system (making it a Parallel or MMP system) or by completely replacing their old system with List PR. The most common switch has been from a plurality/majority system to a mixed system, and there is not one example of a change in the opposite direction. The new plurality/majority systems all come from within the same family except for the case of Madagascar, which moved from a List PR system, not to a pure plurality/majority system, but to a hybrid where the FPTP share is larger than the List PR share.

Table 1: Recent Changes to Electoral Systems

Previous System (Family)	New System(Family)			
	Plurality/Majority	Mixed	Proportional Representation	Other
Plurality /Majority	Bermuda (BV to FPTP)	Lesotho (FPTP to MMP)	Iraq (TRS to List PR)	Jordan (BV to SNTV)
	Fiji (FPTP to AV)	Monaco (TRS to Parallel)	Rwanda (FPTP to List PR)	Afghanistan (FPTP to SNTV)
	Montserrat (FPTP to TRS)	New Zealand (FPTP to MMP)	Sierra Leone (FPTP to List PR)	
	Papua New Guinea (FPTP to AV)	Philippines (BV to Parallel)	South Africa (FPTP to List PR)	
	Mongolia (BV to TRS)	Thailand (BV to Parallel)	Moldova (TRS to List PR)	
		Ukraine (TRS to Parallel)		
		Russian Federation (TRS to Parallel)		
Mixed		Mexico (Parallel to MMP)	Macedonia (Parallel to List PR)	
			Croatia (Parallel to List PR)	
Proportional Representation	Madagascar (List PR to FPTP & List PR)	Bolivia (List PR to MMP)		
		Italy (List PR to MMP)		
		Venezuela (List PR to MMP)		
Other		Japan (SNTV to Parallel)		

Note: Independent countries' and related territories' reforms to electoral systems for national-level legislatures (for countries or territories with bicameral legislatures, the system for the lower house) over the period 1993–2004. Kyrgyzstan changed from a TRS to a Parallel system and back to TRS again within this period and is not included in the table.

Design Components

62. Once a decision has been made about the important goals to be achieved—and the important pitfalls to be avoided—in a new electoral system, there are a group of electoral system design tools which can be used to help achieve these goals. They include, among others, electoral system family and type, district magnitude, the relative role of political parties and candidates, the form of the ballot paper, the procedures for drawing electoral boundaries, the electoral registration mechanisms, the timing and synchronization of elections, and quotas and other special provisions.

These tools will work differently in different combinations. Their use may depend on the level of information that is or can be available within a society, for example the numbers, diversity and location of the population. Their effect will also depend on other institutional framework tools, such as the choice between parliamentarism and presidentialism, the requirements for registration and management of political parties, the relationship between political parties and elected members, and the role of instruments of direct democracy—referendums, citizens' initiatives, and recall. It is worth emphasizing again that there is never a single 'correct solution' that can be imposed in a vacuum.

CHAPTER 2

CHAPTER 2

2. The World of Electoral Systems

63. THERE ARE COUNTLESS ELECTORAL SYSTEM VARIATIONS, AS NOTED IN PARAGRAPH 9 above, but essentially they can be divided into 12 main systems, the majority of which fall into three broad families. The most common way to look at electoral systems is to group them according to how closely they translate national votes won into legislative seats won, that is, how proportional they are. To do this, one needs to look at both the votes-to-seats relationship and the level of wasted votes. For example, South Africa used a classically proportional electoral system for its elections of 2004, and with 69.69 per cent of the popular vote the African National Congress (ANC) won 69.75 per cent of the national seats. The electoral system was highly proportional, and the number of wasted votes (i.e. those which were cast for parties which did not win seats in the Assembly) was only 0.74 per cent of the total. In direct contrast, in Mongolia in 2000, a Two-Round System only requiring a plurality of 25 per cent of the votes for candidates to be elected resulted in the Mongolian People's Revolutionary Party (MPRP) winning 72 seats in the 76-member Parliament with around 52 per cent of the popular vote. This result was mirrored in Djibouti's Party Block Vote election of 2003 when all 65 legislative seats were won by the Rassemblement Populaire pour le Progrès with 62.7 per cent of the vote.

64. However, under some circumstances non-proportional electoral systems (such as FPTP) can give rise to relatively proportional overall results, for example, when party support is concentrated in regional fiefdoms. This was the case in another Southern African country, Malawi, in 2004. In that election the Malawian Congress Party won 30 per cent of the seats with 25 per cent of the votes, the United Democratic Front won 27 per cent of the seats with 25 per cent of the votes, and the Alliance for Democracy won a little more than 3 per cent of the seats with just under 4 per cent of the votes. The overall level of proportionality was high, but the clue to the fact that this was not inherently a proportional system, and so cannot be categorized as such, was that the wasted votes still amounted to almost half of all votes cast.

Equally, some design factors accentuate disproportionality. Systems with a high level of malapportionment often produce disproportional results, as do proportional systems with high thresholds—which can result in a high level of wasted votes, as in Turkey in 2002 where a 10 per cent threshold resulted in 46 per cent of votes being wasted.

65. If we take the proportionality principle into account, along with some other considerations such as how many members are elected from each district and how many votes the voter has, we are left with the family structure illustrated in figure 1.

Figure 1: The Electoral System Families

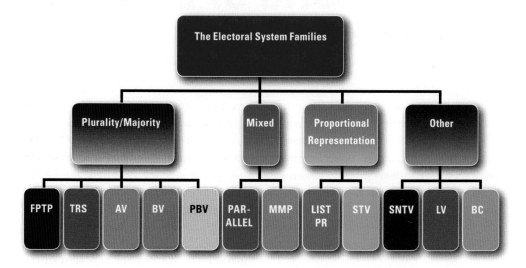

Plurality/Majority Systems

66. The distinguishing feature of plurality/majority systems is that they usually use single-member districts. In an FPTP system (sometimes known as a plurality single-member district system) the winner is the candidate with the most votes but not necessarily an absolute majority of the votes (see paragraphs 76–79). When this system is used in multi-member districts it becomes the Block Vote. Voters have as many votes as there are seats to be filled, and the highest-polling candidates fill the positions regardless of the percentage of the vote they achieve (see paragraphs 80–85). This system—with the change that voters vote for party lists instead of individual candidates—becomes the Party Block Vote (see paragraphs 86–88). Majoritarian systems, such as the Alternative Vote and the Two-Round System, try to ensure that the winning candidate receives an absolute majority (i.e. over 50 per cent). Each system in essence makes use of voters' second preferences to produce a winner with an absolute majority if one does not emerge from the first round of voting (see paragraphs 89–99).

Proportional Representation Systems

67. The rationale underpinning all PR systems is to consciously reduce the disparity between a party's share of the national vote and its share of the parliamentary seats; if a major party wins 40 per cent of the votes, it should win approximately 40 per cent of the seats, and a minor party with 10 per cent of the votes should also gain 10 per cent of the legislative seats. Proportionality is often seen as being best achieved by the use of party lists, where political parties present lists of candidates to the voters on a national or regional basis (see paragraphs 106–108), but preferential voting can work equally well: the Single Transferable Vote, where voters rank-order candidates in multi-member districts, is another well-established proportional system (see paragraphs 109–112).

Mixed Systems

68. Parallel systems use both a PR element and a plurality/majority (or other) element running independently of each other. Mixed Member Proportional (MMP) systems also use two elements (one of which is a PR system), with the difference that the PR element compensates for any disproportionality arising under the plurality/majority or other system, normally leading to a much more proportional outcome than a Parallel system. Parallel and MMP systems have been widely adopted by new democracies in Africa and the former Soviet Union (see paragraphs 128–137).

Other Systems

69. Three systems do not fit neatly under any one of the above-mentioned categories. The Single Non-Transferable Vote is a multi-member-district, candidate-centred system in which voters have one vote. Limited Vote is very much like SNTV but gives voters more than one vote (however, unlike Block Vote, not as many as there are seats to be filled). Borda Count is a preferential system in single- or multi-member districts (see paragraphs 138–144).

70. As Table 2 and the map which comes with this book illustrate, just under half (91, or 46 per cent of the total) of the 199 countries and territories of the world which have direct elections to the legislature use plurality/majority systems; another 72 (36 per cent) use PR-type systems; 30 (15 per cent) use mixed systems; and only six (3 per cent) use one of the other systems. When the different systems are classified by population size, the dominance of plurality/majority systems becomes even more pronounced, with legislatures elected by FPTP, Block Vote, PBV, AV or TRS methods representing collectively 2.65 billion people (54 per cent of the total population of these 199 countries). PR electoral systems are used in countries totalling 1.19 billion inhabitants, mixed systems are used to represent 1.07 billion people, and the population in countries using other systems is only 34 million.

Table 2: Electoral Systems for National Legislatures

	Number of Countries/Territories		Total Population		Established Democracies		Population		New Democracies		Population		Other Countries		Population	
	1		**2**		**3**	**4**		**5**	**6**	**7**		**8**	**9**	**10**		**11**
FPTP	47	23.6%	2 148 870 177	43.5%	22	32.4%	1 458 403 073	70.3%	4	13.0%	205 865	0.1%	21	21.0%	690 261 239	27.0%
BV	15	7.5%	32 102 545	0.6%	8	11.8%	1 515 622	0.1%	0	0	0	0	7	7.0%	30 586 923	1.2%
PBV	4	2.0%	30 423 015	0.6%	0	0	0	0	0	0	0	0	4	4.0%	30 423 015	1.2%
AV	3	1.5%	26 214 298	0.5%	2	2.9%	25 333 424	1.2%	0	0	0	0	1	1.0%	880 874	0.0%
TRS	22	11.1%	409 376 918	8.3%	3	4.4%	60 534 006	2.9%	2	6.5%	14708 102	4.8%	17	17.0%	334 134 810	13.1%
List PR	70	35.2%	1 181 718 922	23.9%	21	30.9%	195 051 175	9.4%	19	61.3%	168 528 219	55.0%	30	30.0%	818 139 528	32.%
STV	2	1.0%	4 366 409	0.1%	2	2.9%	4 366 409	0.2%	0	0	0	0	0	0.0%	0	0
MMP	9	4.5%	298 619 263	6.0%	4	5.9%	153 200 059	7.4%	1	3.2%	10 032 375	3.3%	4	4.0%	135 386 829	5.3%
Parallel	21	10.6%	773 091 334	15.7%	2	2.9%	175 931 177	8.5%	5	16.1%	112 701 569	36.8%	14	14.0%	484 458 588	18.9%
SNTV	4	2.0%	34 327 534	0.7%	2	2.9%	202 655	0.0%	0	0	0	0	2	2.0%	34 124 879	1.3%
Modified BC	1	0.5%	12 809	0.0%	1	1.5%	12 809	0.0%	0	0		0	0	0.0%	0	0
LV	1	0.5%	27 833	0.0%	1	1.5%	27 833	0.0%	0	0	0	0	0	0.0%	0	0
Total	199		4 939 151 057		68		2 074 578 242		31		306 176 130		100		2 558 396 685	

Note: As of November 2004. Includes only elections to national legislatures and lower houses. Based on the methodology used by Arend Lijphart in *Patterns of Democracy: Government Forms and Performance in Thirty-Six Countries* (1999). 'Established democracies' include all countries considered democratic now, and at least for the last 20 years, 'new democracies' include all countries that are considered democratic now and have been at least for the past 10 years, and 'others' are the ones which have not been considered democratic throughout the past 10 years by the Freedom House country ratings (2004) (see <http://www.freedomhouse.org/ratings/index.htm>). For countries and territories not included in the Freedom House country ratings (countries with a population less than 250,000) we have based our classifications on other sources. Fourteen countries are not included in this table because they do not have direct elections or have transitional governments. Countries which use two electoral systems running side by side (hybrids) are classified by the system under which the largest number of seats in the legislature is elected.

1 = Percentage of the 199 countries covered that have this type of electoral system.

2 = Percentage of the total population of the 199 countries that live in this type of electoral system.

3 = Number of countries/territories.

4 = Percentage of the established democracies that have this type of electoral system.

5 = Percentage of the population in the established democracies that live in this
      type of electoral system.

6 = Number of countries/territories.

7 = Percentage of the new democracies that have this type of electoral system.

8 = Percentage of the population in the new democracies that live in this
      type of electoral system.

9 = Number of countries/territories.

10 = Percentage of the 'other' countries that have this type of electoral system.

11 = Percentage of the population in the 'other' countries that live in this type of electoral system.

Sources: International IDEA databases; for the classification of democracies, Freedom House country ratings, <http://www.freedomhouse.org/ratings/index.htm>; and, for population, US Central Intelligence Agency *World Factbook* and additional estimates for countries and territories not included in the Factbook.

71. In terms of the number of countries which use them, List PR systems are the most popular, with 70 out of 199 countries and related territories, giving them 35 per cent of the total, followed by the 47 cases of FPTP systems (24 per cent of the 199 countries and territories). When it comes to numbers of people, however, FPTP systems are used in countries which contain almost twice as many people as List PR countries. The 2.1 billion figure in Table 2 is inflated by the size of India (population 1.1 billion) and the United States (293 million), but FPTP is also used by many tiny Caribbean and Oceanian islands as well. The largest country that uses List PR is Indonesia, with 238 million people, but it is predominantly a system used by middle-sized West European, Latin American and African countries. Next in order are Parallel systems (16 per cent of world population) and Two-Round systems (8 per cent of world population). While TRS systems are used in more countries, therefore, Parallel systems represent more people. This is largely because the Russian Federation (144 million inhabitants) and Japan (127 million) use classic Parallel systems.

Table 3: The Distribution of Electoral Systems across National Legislatures

	Africa	Americas	Asia	Eastern Europe	Western Europe	Oceania	Middle East	Total
FPTP	15	17	5	0	1	7	2	47
BV	1	3	2	0	3	2	4	15
PBV	3	0	1	0	0	0	0	4
AV	0	0	0	0	0	3	0	3
TRS	8	3	6	1	1	1	2	22
List PR	16	19	3	13	15	0	4	70
STV	0	0	0	0	2	0	0	2
MMP	1	3	0	2	2	1	0	9
Parallel	4	0	8	7	1	1	0	21
SNTV	0	0	1	0	0	2	1	4
BC	0	0	0	0	0	1	0	1
LV	0	0	0	0	1	0	0	1
Total	**48**	**45**	**26**	**23**	**26**	**18**	**13**	**199**

Note: As of 2004. Includes only elections to national legislatures; for countries with bicameral legislatures, system for the lower house.

Figure 2: Electoral System Families:
1 - Number of Countries and Territories

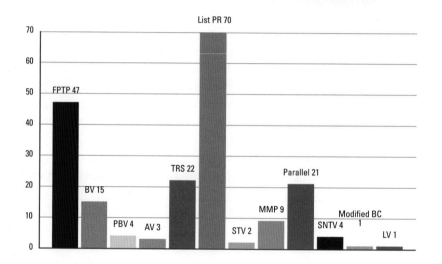

Other 6

Mixed 30

Plurality/ Majority 91

PR 72

2 - Electoral Systems:
Number of Countries and Territories

List PR 70

FPTP 47

BV 15

PBV 4   AV 3

TRS 22

STV 2

MMP 9

Parallel 21

Modified BC 1

SNTV 4

LV 1

3 - Total population (in millions)

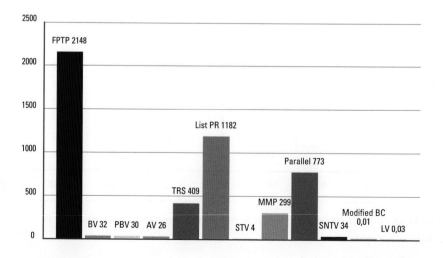

FPTP 2148

List PR 1182

Parallel 773

TRS 409

MMP 299

BV 32   PBV 30   AV 26

STV 4

SNTV 34

Modified BC 0,01

LV 0,03

72. The Block Vote is used in 15 countries and territories, 8 per cent of the countries included, but its 32 million people only represent 0.7 per cent of the total population of the 199 countries in Table 2. Conversely, Mixed Member Proportional systems are used in only nine countries—Albania, Bolivia, Germany, Hungary, Italy, Lesotho, Mexico, New Zealand and Venezuela—but their collective population of 299 million represents 6 per cent of the total population. The Single Transferable Vote, Limited Vote, Modified Borda Count, Alternative Vote, Party Block Vote and Single Non-Transferable Vote systems are the rarest electoral systems in use today, with only one to four examples of each. The use of AV in Australia, Fiji and Papua New Guinea means that 26 million people live under AV systems, while the SNTV systems of Afghanistan, Jordan, the Pitcairn Islands and Vanuatu represent 34 million people, and the Republic of Ireland and Malta's STV systems 4 million.

73. If we look at electoral systems in 'established democracies', then we find that PR systems are more numerous, with 21 (31 per cent) out of the 68 countries, but the size of India and the United States still means that 70 per cent of people living in these 68 countries live under FPTP systems. There are a disproportionate number of MMP systems among established democracies—6 per cent of the total, while worldwide MMP systems are found in only 4.5 per cent of all countries. Both the world's examples of STV, the Republic of Ireland and Malta, fall into the category of established democracies.

74. Across continents, the distribution of electoral systems is more mixed. As Table 3 and the attached map show, FPTP systems make up approximately 35 per cent of the total in Africa, the Americas and Oceania. The system is less common in Europe, Asia and Middle East. List PR systems are similarly spread throughout Africa and the Americas. However, List PR is more dominant in both Eastern and Western Europe, and together the two PR systems (List PR and STV) constitute almost two-thirds of all electoral systems in Europe. The Parallel System is primarily used in Asia and Eastern Europe.

CHAPTER 3

CHAPTER 3

3. The Systems and their Consequences

Plurality/Majority Systems

What Plurality/Majority Systems Are

75. The principle of plurality/majority systems is simple. After votes have been cast and totalled, those candidates or parties with the most votes are declared the winners (there may also be additional conditions). However, the way this is achieved in practice varies widely. Five varieties of plurality/majority systems can be identified: First Past The Post (FPTP), Block Vote (BV), Party Block Vote (PBV), Alternative Vote (AV), and the Two-Round System (TRS).

First Past The Post (FPTP)

76. The First Past The Post system is the simplest form of plurality/majority system, using single-member districts and candidate-centred voting. The voter is presented with the names of the nominated candidates and votes by choosing one, and only one, of them. The winning candidate is simply the person who wins most votes; in theory he or she could be elected with two votes, if every other candidate only secured a single vote.

> First Past The Post is the simplest form of plurality/majority electoral system. The winning candidate is the one who gains more votes than any other candidate, even if this is not an absolute majority of valid votes. The system uses single-member districts and the voters vote for candidates rather than political parties.

77. To date, pure FPTP systems are found primarily in the UK and those countries historically influenced by Britain. Along with the UK, the cases most often analysed are Canada, India and the United States. FPTP is also used by a number of Caribbean countries; in Latin America by Belize; in Asia by five countries, Bangladesh, Burma, India, Malaysia and Nepal; and by many of the small island countries of the South Pacific. In Africa 15 countries, mostly former British colonies, use FPTP systems.

In total, of the 213 countries listed in annex A (including transitional countries and countries with no direct elections) 22 per cent use FPTP systems.

78. *Advantages.* First Past The Post, like other plurality/majority electoral systems, is defended primarily on the grounds of simplicity and its tendency to produce winners who are representatives beholden to defined geographic areas. The most often cited advantages are that:

a. It provides a clear-cut choice for voters between two main parties. The inbuilt disadvantages faced by third and fragmented minority parties under FPTP in many cases cause the party system to gravitate towards a party of the 'left' and a party of the 'right', alternating in power. Third parties often wither away and almost never reach a level of popular support above which their national vote achieves a comparable percentage of seats in the legislature.

b. It gives rise to single-party governments. The 'seat bonuses' for the largest party common under FPTP (e.g. where one party wins 45 per cent of the national vote but 55 per cent of the seats) mean that coalition governments are the exception rather than the rule. This state of affairs is praised for providing cabinets which are not shackled by the restraints of having to bargain with a minority coalition partner.

c. It gives rise to a coherent opposition in the legislature. In theory, the flip side of a strong single-party government is that the opposition is also given enough seats to perform a critical checking role and present itself as a realistic alternative to the government of the day.

d. It advantages broadly-based political parties. In severely ethnically or regionally divided societies, FPTP is commended for encouraging political parties to be 'broad churches', encompassing many elements of society, particularly when there are only two major parties and many different societal groups. These parties can then field a diverse array of candidates for election. In Malaysia, for example, the Barisan Nasional government is made up of a broadly-based umbrella movement which fields Malay, Chinese and Indian candidates in areas of various ethnic complexions.

e. It excludes extremist parties from representation in the legislature. Unless an extremist minority party's electoral support is geographically concentrated, it is unlikely to win any seats under FPTP. (By contrast, under a List PR system with a single national-level district, a fraction of 1 per cent of the national vote can ensure representation in the legislature.)

f. It promotes a link between constituents and their representatives, as it produces a legislature made up of representatives of geographical areas. Elected members represent defined areas of cities, towns or regions rather than just party labels. Some analysts have argued that this 'geographic accountability' is particularly important in agrarian societies and in developing countries.

g. It allows voters to choose between people rather than just between parties. Voters can assess the performance of individual candidates rather than just having to accept a list of candidates presented by a party, as can happen under some List PR electoral systems.

h. It gives a chance for popular independent candidates to be elected. This may be particularly important in developing party systems, where politics still revolves more around extended ties of family, clan or kinship and is not based on strong party-political organizations.

i. Finally, FPTP systems are particularly praised for being simple to use and understand. A valid vote requires only one mark beside the name or symbol of one candidate. Even if the number of candidates on the ballot paper is large, the count is easy for electoral officials to conduct.

79. *Disadvantages.* However, FPTP is frequently criticized for a number of reasons. These include:

a. It excludes smaller parties from 'fair' representation, in the sense that a party which wins approximately, say, 10 per cent of the votes should win approximately 10 per cent of the legislative seats. In the 1993 federal election in Canada the Progressive Conservatives won 16 per cent of the votes but only 0.7 per cent of the seats, and in the 1998 general election in Lesotho the Basotho National Party won 24 per cent of the votes but only 1 per cent of the seats. This is a pattern which is repeated time and time again under FPTP.

b. It excludes minorities from fair representation. As a rule, under FPTP parties put up the most broadly acceptable candidate in a particular district so as to avoid alienating the majority of electors. Thus it is rare, for example, for a black candidate to be given a major party's nomination in a majority white district in the UK or the USA, and there is strong evidence that ethnic and racial minorities across the world are far less likely to be represented in legislatures elected by FPTP. In consequence, if voting behaviour does dovetail with ethnic divisions, then the exclusion from representation of members of ethnic minority groups can be destabilizing for the political system as a whole.

c. It excludes women from the legislature. The 'most broadly acceptable candidate' syndrome also affects the ability of women to be elected to legislative office because they are often less likely to be selected as candidates by male-dominated party structures. Evidence across the world suggests that women are less likely to be elected to the legislature under plurality/majority systems than under PR ones. The Inter-Parliamentary Union's study of Women in Parliament found that, as at June 2004, on average 15.6 per cent of the representatives in lower houses of legislatures were women. Comparing established democracies in 2004, those using FPTP averaged 14.4 per cent women in the legislature, but the figure was almost double that —27.6 per cent— in those countries that use some form of PR. This pattern has been mirrored in new democracies, especially in Africa.

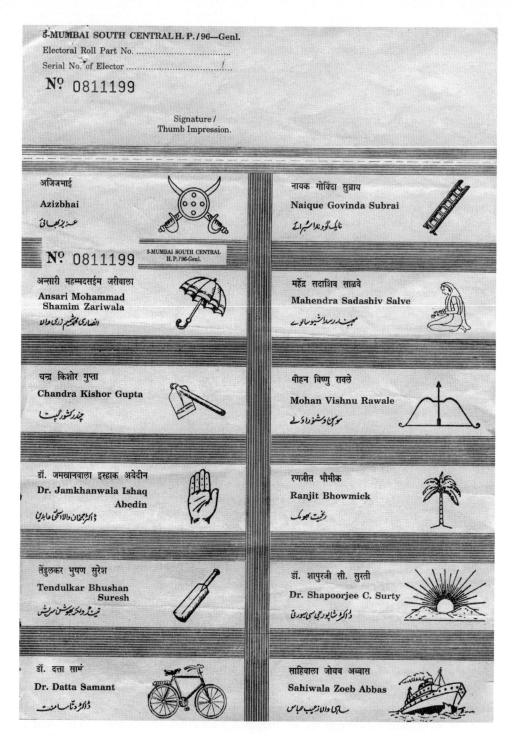

Indian FPTP ballot paper

INDIA: First Past The Post on a Grand Scale

Vijay Patidar

India remains by far the largest democracy in the world, with over 670 million electors in the parliamentary election of 2004. Its parliamentary government and FPTP electoral system are a legacy of British colonialism, which ended in 1947. The British introduced self-government to India in stages, and it was not until the end of colonial rule and the adoption of the Indian Constitution in November 1949 by a Constituent Assembly that universal suffrage was achieved. The Constituent Assembly, which comprised eminent jurists, lawyers, constitutional experts and political thinkers, and laboured for almost three years, debated at great length which electoral system would be best suited to India before finally choosing to retain the FPTP electoral system. Various systems of proportional representation were considered and attracted many advocates, given India's extremely diverse and multi-ethnic society, but FPTP was chosen, mainly to avoid fragmented legislatures and to help the formation of stable governments— stability being a major consideration in a country emerging from immediate post-colonial communal bloodshed and with widespread poverty and illiteracy.

Under the Indian Constitution, voters elect a 543-member Lok Sabha, or lower house, from single-member districts. By contrast, the upper house of Parliament, the Rajya Sabha or Council of States, and the corresponding upper houses of some states, are indirectly elected by members of the state legislative assemblies. There are also a president and vice-president who are indirectly elected by the members of parliament and state legislative assemblies.

General elections are held once every five years, but the president may dissolve the Lok Sabha on the advice of the prime minister before its term is over, as in the recent case of 2004, or if he or she is convinced that no stable government can be formed, as in 1991. The prime minister holds office for as long as he or she can command a majority in the Lok Sabha. All the successive Congress Party governments which ruled India continuously until 1977 served for almost five years, close to the maximum allowed in the constitution. From 1977 to 1997, governments were less stable, and a number of prime ministers had to resign as a result of party splits or votes of no confidence before completing their full term. Since 1997, a period of stability seems to be emerging again, now under coalitions of parties. All these political environments have arisen from the same FPTP electoral system.

The major effect of the electoral system until 1977 was to guarantee majority governments based on a minority of voter support. The FPTP electoral system initially resulted in the ruling Congress Party securing stable majorities in the Lok Sabha, usually against a fragmented opposition. This fragmentation was characterized by a rise in popularity for regional and state parties in some areas. When the opposition parties combined to form coalitions and started putting up common candidates against the Congress candidates (as was the case in the 1977 and 1989 general elections), the Congress majorities vanished. Moreover, the nature of the system meant that small changes in share of the vote often had a dramatic impact upon the number of parliamentary seats won, as the following table, relating votes for the Congress Party to the number of seats won at successive elections, illustrates.

The Congress Party's Performance in Indian General Elections: The dramatically large effect of the FPTP electoral system on the number of seats with slight changes in voting trend

Year of General Election	Percentage of Total Votes Polled by the Congress Party	Percentage Change in Votes Polled by the Congress Party	Number of Seats Obtained by the Congress Party	Percentage Change in Parliamentary Seats Held
1971 (won)	43.7%	-	352 (64.8%)	-
1977 (lost)	34.5%	−21.0%	154 (28.4%)	−56.2%
1980 (won)	42.7%	-	353 (65.0%)	-
1984 (won)	48.1%	-	405 (74.6%)	-
1989 (lost)	39.5%	−17.8%	197 (36.3%)	−51.4%
1991 (won)	36.5%	-	232 (42.7%)	-
1996 (lost)	28.8%	−21.1%	140 (25.8%)	−39.7%
1998 (lost)	25.8%	−10.3%	141 (26.0%)	+0.7%
1999 (lost)	28.3%	+9.6%	114 (21.0%)	−19.1%
2004 (won)	26.7%	-5.7%	145 (26.7%)	+27.2%

The same disproportionality between the share of votes obtained and the share of parliamentary seats won under the Indian FPTP electoral system can be seen in the case of the other major political party, the Bharatiya Janata Party (BJP), which led a coalition government up to 2004, from the following table:

The BJP's Performance in Indian General Elections

Year of General Election	Percentage of Total Votes Polled for the BJP	Number of Seats obtained by the BJP
1984	7.7%	2 (0.4%)
1989	11.5%	86 (15.8%)
1991	20.0%	121 (22.3%)
1996	20.3%	161 (29.7%)
1998	25.6%	182 (33.5%)
1999	23.6%	182 (33.5%)
2004	22.2%	138 (25.4%)

Thus the overall results of elections to the Lok Sabha have not been anywhere near proportional. Support can often be divided by setting candidates of the same caste, religion or region against each other. In this context, FPTP gives an incentive to electoral participants to encourage multiple candidacies by their opposition, and its effect can be to produce a winner who has much less than an absolute majority of the total vote. However, despite the divided nature of India's multi-ethnic democracy, the electoral system has retained a considerable degree of support, due in part to the practice of reserving seats for socially underprivileged and historically disadvantaged groups known as scheduled castes and scheduled tribes. These communities are thinly spread all over India, and the classical operation of FPTP would have resulted in them getting a comparatively very small number of parliamentary seats. The constitution, however, reserves districts for them in proportion to their numbers in the population, thus reserving 79 seats for the 15 per cent scheduled castes population and 41 seats for the 8 per cent scheduled tribes population. In these districts, although all electors have voting rights, only a member of the scheduled caste or tribe may stand for election. This has ensured that their parliamentary representation is in line with their proportion of the population.

A constitutional amendment which seeks to reserve 3 per cent of seats for women representatives at the national- and state-level legislatures has long been debated, but without any success so far, although 33 per cent of the seats have been reserved for women at the Panchayat (district) level, the third tier of government, since 1993.

The depth of popular support for the integrity of the electoral system became evident in 1977 when the election of the incumbent prime minister, Indira Gandhi, was set aside by a court after Congress had won a two-thirds legislative majority in 1971. She responded by curtailing fundamental constitutional rights for two years (1975–77), an authoritarian interlude in India's otherwise unbroken history of competitive democracy. In the 1977 elections, her government lost power through a fair poll, signalling the unwillingness of India's voters to accept undemocratic practices.

For a period of 20 years, from 1977 to 1997, the FPTP electoral system seemed to have ushered in an era of instability, principally because of the formation of coalitions without common principles and the pursuit of narrow self-interest by political parties. The non-Congress opposition parties (without the communists) took over in government in 1977 by uniting into a composite entity, the Janata Party. It split within two years. In December 1989, a successor party, the Janata Dal, came to power, supported by the communist parties and the Hindu revivalist Bharatiya Janata Party (BJP); this government lasted ten months. At the general election of 1996, no party was able to form a stable government. The BJP won 161 seats and the Congress 140. But the strength of the electoral system re-emerged in 1999 when a firm alliance of parties under the leadership of the BJP was able to form a government and almost complete its full term. Similarly, after the May 2004 general election, the Indian National Congress Party, along with left parties and others, formed a coalition government at the national level.

In 2000, the government of India established a National Commission to Review the Working of the Constitution. This commission's consultation process considered whether various provisions relating to the electoral process in the constitution should be amended or expanded. Its report, submitted to the government in 2002, recommended against any constitutional change in the electoral field, emphasizing that such changes as were needed could be brought about by amendments in the ordinary electoral legislation and even by subordinate legislation or executive instructions.

However, the National Commission also observed that, at the last three general elections at national level, an average of two-thirds of Indian MPs had been elected under FPTP without a majority of 50 per cent plus one and with a plurality only, and considered the questions this raises about the legitimacy of representation. As a consequence, and in the context of the nationwide introduction of electronic voting which then took place in 2004, the National Commission recommended that the government and the Election Commission of India conduct a careful and full examination of the introduction of a Two-Round system, with the second round conducted between the two leading candidates in each district on the day after the first round. The report of the Election Commission of India following the 2004 election did not follow up on this proposal, although it did recommend both the introduction of a 'none of these candidates' option on ballot paper and the abolition of the provision by which one person is able to stand in two different single-member districts.

The FPTP electoral system is often said to work best in countries where there are two major political parties. In India, by contrast, the Congress Party ruled continuously at the centre from 1952 to 1977 without any viable opposition. This monopoly ended in 1977. From single-party dominance, the pattern on the political arena changed, first to one of a competition between a single party and a coalition of parties, and from there to a competition between two coalitions of political parties—a trend that continued at the 2004 general election. The BJP started its upward mobility in the Indian Parliament with a shrill Hindu agenda, but after one full term in office the imperatives of electoral politics compelled it to scale down its ultra-rightist militant stance. It had to adopt an inclusive agenda, enabling it to appeal to Muslim, tribal, backward class and other Dalit (downtrodden) voters—who were once considered to be in the exclusive domain of the Congress Party.

d. It can encourage the development of political parties based on clan, ethnicity or region, which may base their campaigns and policy platforms on conceptions that are attractive to the majority of people in their district or region but exclude or are hostile to others. This has been an ongoing problem in African countries like Malawi and Kenya, where large communal groups tend to be regionally concentrated. The country is thus divided into geographically separate party strongholds, with little incentive for parties to make appeals outside their home region and cultural–political base.

e. It exaggerates the phenomenon of 'regional fiefdoms' where one party wins all the seats in a province or area. If a party has strong support in a particular part of a country, winning a plurality of votes, it will win all, or nearly all, of the seats in the legislature for that area. This both excludes minorities in that area from representation and reinforces the perception that politics is a battleground defined by who you are and where you live rather than what you believe in. This has long been put forward as an argument against FPTP in Canada.

f. It leaves a large number of wasted votes which do not go towards the election of any candidate. This can be particularly dangerous if combined with regional fiefdoms, because minority party supporters in the region may begin to feel that they have no realistic hope of ever electing a candidate of their choice. It can also be dangerous where alienation from the political system increases the likelihood that extremists will be able to mobilize anti-system movements.

g. It can cause vote-splitting. Where two similar parties or candidates compete under FPTP, the vote of their potential supporters is often split between them, thus allowing a less popular party or candidate to win the seat. Papua New Guinea provides a particularly clear example (see the case study).

h. It may be unresponsive to changes in public opinion. A pattern of geographically concentrated electoral support in a country means that one party can maintain exclusive executive control in the face of a substantial drop in overall popular support. In some democracies under FPTP, a fall from 60 per cent to 40 per cent of a party's share of the popular vote nationally can result in a fall from 80 per cent to 60 per cent in the number of seats held, which does not affect its overall dominant position. Unless sufficient seats are highly competitive, the system can be insensitive to swings in public opinion.

i. Finally, FPTP systems are dependent on the drawing of electoral boundaries. All electoral boundaries have political consequences: there is no technical process to produce a single 'correct answer' independently of political or other considerations (as illustrated in annex E). Boundary delimitation may require substantial time and resources if the results are to be accepted as legitimate. There may also be pressure to manipulate boundaries by gerrymandering or malapportionment. This was particularly apparent in the Kenyan elections of 1993 when huge disparities between the sizes of electoral districts—the largest had 23 times the number of voters the smallest had—

contributed to the ruling Kenyan African National Union party's winning a large majority in the legislature with only 30 per cent of the popular vote.

Block Vote (BV)

Block Vote is a plurality/majority system used in multi-member districts. Electors have as many votes as there are candidates to be elected. The candidates with the highest vote totals win the seats. Usually voters vote for candidates rather than parties and in most systems may use as many, or as few, of their votes as they wish.

80. The Block Vote is simply the use of plurality voting in multi-member districts. Voters have as many votes as there are seats to be filled in their district, and are usually free to vote for individual candidates regardless of party affiliation. In most BV systems they may use as many, or as few, of their votes as they wish.

81. The Block Vote is common in countries with weak or non-existent political parties. In 2004, the Cayman Islands, the Falkland Islands, Guernsey, Kuwait, Laos, Lebanon, the Maldives, Palestine, the Syrian Arab Republic, Tonga and Tuvalu all use Block Vote electoral systems. The system was also used in Jordan in 1989, in Mongolia in 1992, and in the Philippines and Thailand until 1997, but was changed in all these countries as a result of unease with the results it produced.

82. *Advantages.* The Block Vote is often applauded for retaining the voter's ability to vote for individual candidates and allowing for reasonably-sized geographical districts, while at the same time increasing the role of parties compared with FPTP and strengthening those parties which demonstrate most coherence and organizational ability.

83. *Disadvantages.* However, the Block Vote can have unpredictable and often undesirable impacts on election outcomes. For example, when voters cast all their votes for the candidates of a single party, the system tends to exaggerate most of the disadvantages of FPTP, in particular its disproportionality. When parties nominate a candidate for each vacancy in a Block Vote system and encourage voters to support every member of their slate, this is particularly likely. In Mauritius in 1982 and 1995, for example, the party in opposition before the election won every seat in the legislature with only 64 per cent and 65 per cent of the vote, respectively. This created severe difficulties for the effective functioning of a parliamentary system based on concepts of government and opposition. The use of 'best loser' seats in Mauritius (see paragraph 153) only partially compensates for this weakness.

84. In Thailand, the Block Vote was seen as having encouraged the fragmentation of the party system. Because it enables electors to vote for candidates of more than one party in the same district, members of the same party may be encouraged to compete against each other for support. The Block Vote is thus sometimes seen as being a contributor to internal party factionalism and corruption.

85. In recent years, a number of countries have therefore abandoned the Block Vote in favour of other systems. Thailand and the Philippines both changed from BV to a

PALESTINE: Political Realities Shape the System

Andrew Ellis

The Declaration of Principles or Oslo Agreement, reached in late 1993 between Israel and the Palestine Liberation Organization (PLO), contained a provision for an elected Palestinian Council to be established. The implementation of the Oslo Agreement required the negotiation of a further detailed agreement, the Interim Agreement. This was completed in Taba in September 1995 and included detailed provisions for holding elections to the Palestinian Legislative Council and, separately, for the head of its Executive Authority. The president (Raees) of the Palestinian Authority and the Palestinian Legislative Council were then elected on 20 January 1996.

Preparations for the elections began in 1994 in parallel with the negotiations for the Interim Agreement. The election law and the conduct of the elections were entirely the responsibility of the Palestinians, although some details of the election arrangements were required to be consistent with the provisions of the Interim Agreement. The final version of the law and the major regulations were put in place only in late 1995.

The political context of the election strongly influenced the available options for the electoral system. There was little doubt in anyone's mind that Yasser Arafat would be elected president, and for the presidential election a single-round FPTP system was adopted with little discussion. The assumption was borne out in practice when Arafat received over 80 per cent of the vote against one other candidate.

The choice of system for the Legislative Council elections was much less straightforward. First, agreement within the Palestinian community on accepting and participating in the Interim Agreement process was not unanimous. The emerging Palestinian Authority conducted lengthy discussions backstage with members of Hamas and other Islamic movements which included the question of their participation in elections. Second, the political party system was embryonic. Fatah had the character of a national liberation movement, a political form for which a continuing need was perceived because of the need for unity in moving into 'final status' negotiations with Israel (which were not successful). Some other small parties had formed, but many potential candidates were considering standing independently of Fatah. Third, there were some precedents to hand: local elections had been held in Gaza in the 1940s, using

Egyptian procedures, and in West Bank cities and towns in the 1970s, using Jordanian procedures inherited from traditions under the British Mandate. There was pressure in particular to follow Jordanian practice.

The choice of a candidate-based electoral system therefore emerged in response to three pressures: the wish to provide a channel for informal candidacies of persons linked to movements which formally rejected the process; the desire of a number of prominent figures to stand as independents; and the recollection of historic elections. The importance placed on simplicity, transparency, speed of counting and confidence in the results also led to a decision in favour of counting at the polling station, thus eliminating preferential systems such as the Alternative Vote (AV) or the Single Transferable Vote (STV) as options. The perception of where natural boundaries existed on the ground thus led to the choice of the Block Vote (BV), with districts which varied in magnitude from 12 in Gaza City down to one in the small towns of Jericho, Salfit and Tubas.

A further discussion centred on the representation of minorities, in particular the Christian community (which accounted for some 10 per cent of the electorate) and the Samaritans (a concentrated community of a few hundred people near Nablus). Six reserved seats were created within the Block Vote system for Christians in the four districts with the highest concentration of Christians (two each in Bethlehem and Jerusalem, and one each in Ramallah and Gaza City) and one reserved seat was created for Samaritans in Nablus. Christian candidates had the option to declare themselves as Christian. If the Block Vote count showed that there were not sufficient declared Christian candidates among those in the top positions, the candidate with the lowest vote of those who would otherwise have been elected would be replaced by the declared Christian candidate with the next—highest vote—as indeed happened in all four districts. This meant that there were representatives on the Legislative Council elected with fewer votes than some other candidates who were not elected. While there was some debate on this, it was accepted as legitimate in the context of wide representation and in the aftermath of a successful election.

In practice, the BV electoral system achieved much of what was expected of it. Eighty-seven candidates were nominated in Gaza City, but voters coped well with a ballot paper about a metre long. While few candidates associated with those who rejected the peace process stood, at least one member was elected who might be considered as a bridge to those movements. Candidates on Fatah slates gained an advantage, but voters made clear distinctions between more and less popular individuals. Leading independent figures were elected, as were representatives from minorities. Small towns with a fiercely independent identity gained their own representative. The president and the Legislative Council took office in 1996 with a wide degree of legitimacy within the Palestinian community.

mixed system in the late 1990s. In both cases, a major justification for the change was the need to combat vote-buying and strengthen the development of political parties (see the case study on Thailand).

Party Block Vote (PBV)

86. Under Party Block Vote, unlike FPTP, there are multi-member districts. Voters have a single vote, and choose between party lists of candidates rather than between individuals. The party which wins most votes takes all the seats in the district, and its entire list of candidates is duly elected. As in FPTP, there is no requirement for the winner to have an absolute majority of the votes. As of 2004, PBV was used as the only system or the major component of the system in four countries—Cameroon, Chad, Djibouti and Singapore.

87. *Advantages.* PBV is simple to use, encourages strong parties and allows for parties to put up mixed slates of candidates in order to facilitate minority representation. It can be used to help to ensure balanced ethnic representation, as it enables parties to present ethnically diverse lists of candidates for election—and may indeed be designed to require them to do so. In Djibouti each party list must include a mix of candidates from different ethnic groups. In Singapore, most members of Parliament (MPs) are elected from multi-member districts known as group representation constituencies. Of the candidates on each party or group list, at least one must be a member of the Malay, Indian or some other minority community. Singapore also uses 'best loser' seats for opposition candidates in some circumstances. Other countries, for example, Senegal and Tunisia, use the Party Block Vote as the plurality/majority part of their Parallel system (see the case study on Senegal).

> **Party Block Vote - A plurality/majority system using multi-member districts in which voters cast a single party-centred vote for a party of choice, and do not choose between candidates. The party with most votes will win every seat in the electoral district.**

88. *Disadvantages.* However, the Party Block Vote also suffers from most of the disadvantages of FPTP, and may indeed produce highly disproportional results where one party wins almost all of the seats with a simple majority of the votes. In Djibouti's 1997 election, the ruling Union for the Presidential Majority coalition won every seat, leaving the two opposition parties without any representation in the legislature.

The Alternative Vote (AV)

89. Elections under Alternative Vote are usually held in single-member districts, like FPTP elections. However, AV gives voters considerably more options than FPTP when marking their ballot paper. Rather than simply indicating their favoured candidate, under AV electors rank the candidates in the order of their choice, by marking a '1' for their favourite, '2' for their second choice, '3' for their third choice and so on. The system thus enables voters to express their preferences between candidates rather than simply their first choice. For this reason, it is often known as 'preferential voting' in the countries which use

it. (The Borda Count, STV and the Supplementary Vote are also preferential systems.)

90. AV also differs from FPTP in the way votes are counted. Like FPTP or TRS, a candidate who has won an absolute majority of the votes (50 per cent plus one) is immediately elected. However, if no candidate has an absolute majority, under AV the candidate with the lowest number of first preferences is 'eliminated' from the count, and his or her ballots are examined for their second preferences. Each ballot is then transferred to whichever remaining candidate has the highest preference in the order as marked on the ballot paper. This process is repeated until one candidate has an absolute majority, and is declared duly elected. AV is thus a majoritarian system.

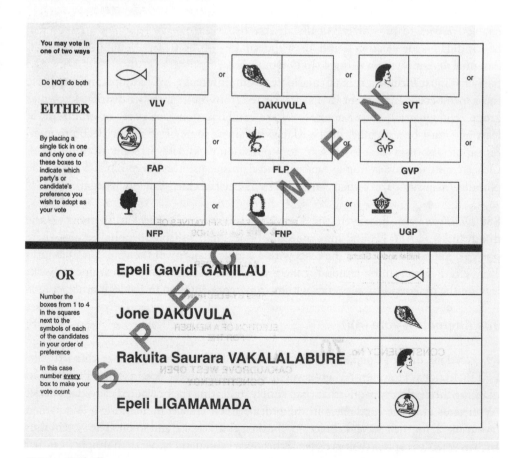

Fijian AV ballot paper

91. It is possible, but not essential, in preferential systems such as AV to require voters to number all, or most, of the candidates on the ballot paper. This avoids the possibility of votes becoming 'wasted' at a later stage in the count because they bear no further valid preferences. However, it can lead to an increase in the number of invalid votes, and it can sometimes give substantial importance to preferences between candidates to which the voter is indifferent or actively dislikes.

92. AV is used in Australia, Fiji and Papua New Guinea. It is thus a good example of the regional diffusion of electoral systems discussed above (see paragraph 74): all national-level examples of the Alternative Vote at present occur in Oceania. However, a number of sub-national jurisdictions in Europe and North America also use variants of AV, and it is used for presidential elections in the Republic of Ireland.

93. *Advantages.* One advantage of transferring ballots is that it enables the votes of several candidates to accumulate, so that diverse but related interests can be combined to win representation. AV also enables supporters of candidates who have little hope of being elected to influence, via their second and later preferences, the election of a major candidate. For this reason, it is sometimes argued that AV is the best system for promoting centrist politics, as it can compel candidates to seek not only the votes of their own supporters but also the 'second preferences' of others. To attract these preferences, candidates must make broadly-based appeals rather than focusing on narrower issues. The experience of AV in Australia tends to support these arguments: the major parties, for example, typically try to strike bargains with minor parties for the second preferences of their supporters prior to an election—a process known as 'preference swapping'. Furthermore, because of the majority support requirement, AV increases the consent given to elected members, and thus can enhance their perceived legitimacy.

The experience of AV in Papua New Guinea and in Australia suggests that it can provide significant incentives for accommodatory and cooperative politics. In recent years AV, or its variant the Supplementary Vote, has also been adopted for presidential and mayoral elections in Bosnia, London and San Francisco (see paragraphs 182–186).

94. *Disadvantages.* Nevertheless, AV also has a number of disadvantages. First, it requires a reasonable degree of literacy and numeracy to be used effectively, and because it operates in single-member districts it can often produce results that are disproportional when compared to PR systems—or even in some cases compared with FPTP. Also, the potential of AV for promoting centrist outcomes is very dependent on underlying social and demographic conditions: while it successfully promoted inter-ethnic accommodation in Papua New Guinea during the 1960s and 1970s and has now been reintroduced there (see the case study), it has been criticized in another Pacific country, Fiji, since it was implemented there in 1997. Moreover, as the earlier discussion of its use in the Australian Senate from 1919 to 1946 noted (see paragraph 32), AV does not work well when applied to larger, multi-member districts.

PAPUA NEW GUINEA: Electoral Incentives for Inter-Ethnic Accommodation

Ben Reilly

The South Pacific country of Papua New Guinea (PNG) has used two different electoral systems—the Alternative Vote (AV) from 1964 to 1975, when it was an Australian territory, and FPTP from 1975 to 2002. It has since reverted to the alternative vote again.

Its experience is interesting for a number of reasons. First, PNG is one of the few developing countries with an unbroken record of continuous competitive elections and numerous peaceful changes of government. Second, the change from one electoral system to another has had a series of unexpected consequences which illustrate the different effects apparently similar electoral systems can have. Third, PNG is one of the few countries to have adopted, abandoned, and then re-adopted a particular electoral system.

Papua New Guinea inherited the AV system from Australia and used it for three elections in 1964, 1968 and 1972. Unlike Australia, however, PNG is a highly ethnically fragmented society, with over 850 separate languages and several thousand competing clan and tribal groups.

Its experience lends support to the claims that AV can promote inter-ethnic accommodation and moderation in deeply divided societies by allowing voters to express not just their first choice of candidate but also their second and later choices. Because of the nature of PNG society, under AV most voters invariably gave their first preference to their own clan or 'home' candidate. In many seats, however, this was not enough for any single candidate to gain a majority of votes; they needed the second preferences of other groups as well. In order to gain a majority, candidates had to 'sell' themselves as a good 'second-best' choice to other clan groups—which meant, in general, someone who would be attentive to the interests of all groups, not just their own. It also meant that those candidates who formed alliances and cooperated with each other would often be more successful than candidates who attempted to win the seat from their own voter base alone.

This gave many candidates an incentive to act in an accommodating manner to other clans. The mechanics of the system also ensured that the winning candidate would have the support of an absolute majority of voters. In a substantial number of cases, the winning candidate was not the one who had the biggest 'bloc' of supporters but rather the one who could successfully build support across several groups.

Thinking that it would be a simpler system which would have similar effects to AV, Papua New Guinea changed to an FPTP electoral system at independence in 1975. However, the different incentives provided by the new FPTP system led to quite different results from those expected. Because candidates no longer needed an absolute majority of votes cast in order to be successful—just more votes than any other group—the candidate from the largest clan would often win the seat outright. There was no incentive to cooperate with anyone else. Electoral violence increased because it was in some candidates' interests to stop opponents' supporters from voting rather than to campaign for their second preferences as they had done under AV. Also, because there were so many clans all trying to win the seat, candidates learned that they could be successful with very limited support.

At the 2002 elections, over half of the MPs in the Parliament were elected with less than 20 per cent of the vote. Several candidates who won seats gained only 5 per cent. In an electoral cycle increasingly dominated by concerns about corruption, power and money politics, this led to a range of negative campaign tactics, such as encouraging rival candidates to stand in order to 'split' a dominant clan's voter base. This increased pressure for the reintroduction of AV. In 2003, the PNG Parliament re-adopted what it called 'limited' preferential voting for all future elections. Voters will be required to mark a minimum of three preferences.

The Papua New Guinea case illustrates just how dependent much of the accepted wisdom regarding electoral systems is on the structure of the society concerned. Despite having an FPTP electoral system, PNG had a very fluid party system, based on individuals rather than ideologies. All governments under FPTP were weak coalitions, which sometimes changed on the floor of the Parliament as well as at elections. The single-member system of representation resulted in high levels of turnover of politicians from one election to the next, as members could not both be in Port Moresby at sessions of the Parliament and be continually visible in their districts.

Accordingly, a strong sense of accountability on the part of many local members to their electorate developed: without it their chances of re-election would be slim. This matches a strong sense on the part of the electorate that the function of their member is to deliver direct benefits to the community, building on Melanesian tradition that a 'big man' ensures that his community shares in his wealth and good fortune. As one member has memorably put it, 'When people elect me to Parliament, they think I own the Bank of Papua New Guinea.'

Under the AV system, this sense of accountability tended to be spread across a number of groups, thus helping to manage inter-ethnic conflicts. However, this was itself a reflection of the extreme fragmentation of the country's society.

The Two-Round System (TRS)

95. The central feature of the Two-Round System is as the name suggests: it is not one election but takes place in two rounds, often a week or a fortnight apart. The first round is conducted in the same way as a single-round plurality/majority election. In the most common form of TRS, this is conducted using FPTP. It is, however, also possible to conduct TRS in multi-member districts using Block Vote (as in Kiribati) or Party Block Vote (as in Mali). A candidate or party that receives a specified proportion of the vote is elected outright, with no need for a second ballot. This proportion is normally an absolute majority of valid votes cast, although several countries use a different figure when using TRS to elect a president (see paragraph 179). If no candidate or party receives an absolute majority, then a second round of voting is held and the winner of this round is declared elected.

> The Two-Round System is a plurality/majority system in which a second election is held if no candidate or party achieves a given level of votes, most commonly an absolute majority (50 per cent plus one), in the first election round. A *Two-Round* System may take a majority-plurality form—more than two candidates contest the second round and the one who wins the highest number of votes in the second round is elected, regardless of whether they have won an absolute majority—or a majority run-off form—only the top two candidates in the first round contest the second round.

96. The details of how the second round is conducted vary in practice from case to case. The most common method is for it to be a straight run-off contest between the two highest vote-winners from the first round; this is called majority run-off TRS. It produces a result that is truly majoritarian in that one of the two participants will necessarily achieve an absolute majority of votes and be declared the winner. A second method, majority-plurality TRS, is used for legislative elections in France, the country most often associated with the Two-Round System. In these elections, any candidate who has received the votes of over 12.5 per cent of the registered electorate in the first round can stand in the second round. Whoever wins the highest number of votes in the second round is then declared elected, regardless of whether they have won an absolute majority or not. Unlike majority run-off, this system is not truly majoritarian, as there may be up to five or six candidates contesting the second round of elections.

97. Two-Round systems are used to elect 22 national legislatures and are the most common method used worldwide for the direct election of presidents (see paragraph 178). Alongside France, many of the other countries which use TRS were territorial dependencies of the French Republic or have been historically influenced in some way by the French. For elections to the legislature, TRS is used by the Central African Republic, Congo (Brazzaville), Gabon, Mali, Mauritania and Togo in francophone Sub-Saharan Africa, by Egypt in North Africa, by the Comoros Islands, Haiti, Iran, Kiribati, and Viet Nam, and by some of the post-Soviet republics (Belarus, Kyrgyzstan, Turkmenistan and Uzbekistan). A few other countries such as Georgia, Kazakhstan and Tajikistan also use TRS to elect district representatives as part of a mixed electoral system.

98. *Advantages*

a. First and foremost, TRS allows voters to have a second chance to vote for their chosen candidate, or even to change their minds between the first and the second rounds. It thus shares some features in common with preferential systems like the Alternative Vote, in which voters are asked to rank-order candidates, while also enabling voters to make a completely fresh choice in the second round if they so desire.

b. TRS can encourage diverse interests to coalesce behind the successful candidates from the first round in the lead-up to the second round of voting, thus encouraging bargains and trade-offs between parties and candidates. It also enables the parties and the electorate to react to changes in the political landscape that occur between the first and the second rounds of voting.

c. TRS lessens the problems of 'vote-splitting', the common situation in many plurality/majority systems where two similar parties or candidates split their combined vote between them, thus allowing a less popular candidate to win the seat. Also, because electors do not have to rank-order candidates to express their second choice, TRS may be better suited to countries where illiteracy is widespread than systems which use preferential numbering like the Alternative Vote or the Single Transferable Vote.

99. *Disadvantages*

a. TRS places considerable pressure on the electoral administration by requiring it to run a second election a short time after the first, thus significantly increasing both the cost of the overall election process and the time that elapses between the holding of an election and the declaration of a result. This can lead to instability and uncertainty. TRS also places an additional burden on the voter, and sometimes there is a sharp decline in turnout between the first round and the second.

b. TRS shares many of the disadvantages of FPTP. Research has shown that in France it produces the most disproportional results of any Western democracy, and that it tends to fragment party systems in new democracies.

c. One of the most serious problems with TRS is its implications for deeply divided societies. In Angola in 1992, in what was supposed to be a peacemaking election, rebel leader Jonas Savimbi came second in the first round of a TRS presidential election to Jose dos Santos with 40 per cent of the vote as opposed to dos Santos' 49 per cent. As it was clear that he would lose the run-off phase, he had little incentive to play the democratic opposition game and immediately restarted the civil war in Angola, which went on for another decade. In Congo (Brazzaville) in 1993, prospects of a government landslide in the second round of a TRS election prompted the opposition to boycott the second round and take up arms. In both cases, the clear signal that one side would probably lose the election was the trigger for violence. In Algeria in 1992, the candidate of the Islamic Salvation Front (Front Islamique du Salut, FIS) led in the first round, and the military intervened to cancel the second round.

KYRGYZSTAN: Electoral Manipulation in Central Asia

Eugene Huskey

In contemporary Central Asia, elections are as much political theatre as contests for office. After the break-up of the Soviet Union in late 1991, most of the countries in the region descended into one-man rule or civil war. The semi-competitive elections held in the last months of the Soviet order gave way to elections of acclamation in the first years of independence, with political power becoming increasingly centralized in the hands of the founding presidents of the republics. For a time it appeared that Kyrgyzstan might resist the temptation of authoritarianism; however, by the mid-1990s its president had begun to limit society's ability to hold the state and its representatives accountable.

The election that brought to power the country's first and only president, Askar Akaev, illustrates the role of changing rules in shaping electoral outcomes. In the late Soviet era, parliaments selected the head of state—the chair of the Supreme Soviet—in each republic. In Kyrgyzstan, the election law stipulated that if the Parliament failed to produce a winner after two rounds of voting all the candidates would be disqualified. In October 1990, this quirk in the electoral rules allowed Akaev—a little-regarded Gorbachev loyalist who was opposed to the dominant conservative forces in the Kyrgyz Communist Party—to win the next round of the parliamentary election for head of state of the Kyrgyz Republic. The following year, Kyrgyzstan, like most other Soviet republics, introduced popular direct elections for a newly-designed office of president whose powers supplanted those of the collapsing Communist Party. In October 1991, just weeks before Kyrgyzstan became an independent country, Akaev won the election for the presidency unopposed. He won the two subsequent presidential elections—in December 1995 and October 2000—by wide margins in the first round, although widespread violations were reported during both elections.

The rules governing presidential elections in Kyrgyzstan are a mixture of traditional and unconventional elements. Elections are held every five years and are decided by a two-round majority run-off system: if no candidate receives an absolute majority in the first round, the two candidates with the most votes proceed to a second round, where the candidate with the most votes wins. New elections must be called if less than half the electorate turns out for either the first or the second round. Presidents may serve for no more than two terms, although the Constitutional Court in Kyrgyzstan, unlike its counterpart in the Russian Federation, made an exception for the sitting president by ruling that his first term did not count because it began before the limit of two terms was adopted in the 1993 constitution.

To stand for president, a candidate must be at least 35 and not more than 65 years of age. Candidates must also satisfy several further requirements. First, they must undergo an examination by the Language Commission to ensure that they are fluent in the state language, Kyrgyz. This requirement, introduced to discourage Russians and Russified Kyrgyz from contesting the presidency, was used in the 2000 election to disqualify Akaev's most prominent challenger, Feliks Kulov. Second, they must pay from their personal funds a deposit equal to 1,000 times the minimum monthly wage—essentially the lifetime income of a poor person. For the deposit to be returned, a candidate must receive 10 per cent of the vote, and proposals now being debated by Parliament would increase that to 15 per cent. A further barrier to entry is the requirement that a candidate receive 50,000 signatures, of which at least 3 per cent must come from each of the country's eight territories—a provision designed to ensure that a president has adequate support in both the north and the south, whose elites have been at odds in recent years.

The relative stability of the rules governing presidential elections in Kyrgyzstan contrasts with the frequent changes made in the parliamentary electoral system. Perhaps the most dramatic have been to the size and structure of the Parliament. Independent Kyrgyzstan inherited from the Soviet era a unicameral Parliament of 350 deputies who had been elected in February 1990 in single-member districts using a two-round voting system. Following constitutional changes made in 1994 by referendum—the president's preferred means of enhancing his powers and reducing those of the Parliament—this unicameral assembly was replaced by a bicameral legislature, with 60 members in the Legislative Assembly and 45 in the Assembly of People's Representatives. In the parliamentary elections of February 1995 and February 2000, the entire Assembly of People's Representatives and 45 members of the Legislative Assembly were elected in 45 single-member districts using two-round voting. The remaining 15 members of the Legislative Assembly were elected by List PR using closed lists and a single nationwide district with a 5 per cent formal threshold, that is, parties must secure at least 5 per cent of the total vote nationwide to be represented in the Parliament. For the 15 PR seats, each party had the right to put forward a list of 30 persons, and in cases where candidates from the list also stood in single-member districts and won, their names were removed from the party list.

The reduction of the number of deputies from 350 to 105, ostensibly designed as a cost-saving measure, facilitated presidential control of the Parliament by trebling the size of the single-member districts and thus reducing the ability of smaller parties to win seats. The presence of a handful of List PR seats in the new Parliament did little to compensate for the disadvantages that a diminutive Parliament posed for small parties.

Moreover, the post-communist elections have returned parliaments whose composition differed dramatically from that of the rubber-stamp Soviet legislatures. Communist Party control of candidate nomination had worked in such a way as to create bodies in which those who had passed the approval process comprised a broad cross-section of society. In contrast, the post-communist assemblies in Kyrgyzstan were almost exclusively male and had a disproportionate number of executive officials and the newly rich.

Kyrgyzstan has recently changed the rules for parliamentary elections again. Revisions to the constitution adopted by referendum in February 2003 called for the 105-member bicameral assembly to be replaced at the next parliamentary election with a unicameral legislature of 75 members. The new election law of January 2004, which has been much criticized inside and outside Kyrgyzstan, provides that the 75 deputies will be elected in single-member districts using a two-round majority run-off voting system. Further reducing the size of the Assembly and abandoning the party list seats is likely to reduce the representation of minorities yet again, increase the executive branch's influence over the legislature and emasculate an already weak party system. It may also strengthen the political salience of the regions by giving the central party leaders less influence over the selection of candidates.

Because the smaller number of seats in recent parliaments produced larger electoral districts, it has been easier for ethnic Kyrgyz to win seats than for members of ethnic minorities. Where the ethnic Kyrgyz majority is now over-represented in the Parliament, the substantial Uzbek, Russian and German minorities are all significantly under-represented. In particular, the Uzbeks hold a share of the seats which is less than half of their share of the population.

In recent years, the political opposition in Kyrgyzstan has found it increasingly difficult to contest presidential and parliamentary elections. The deference of the judiciary, the Electoral Commission and the Language Commission to presidential authority has led to the selective prosecution and disqualification of electoral candidates. Moreover, presidential influence on the media has prevented the opposition from waging effective campaigns. In the 2000 presidential election, for example, President Akaev received almost ten hours of coverage on the national television channel, KTR, while his principal opponent received less than five minutes. One of the few sources of independent reporting on electoral campaigns, the foreign press, is threatened with legal sanctions if it criticizes establishment candidates. Voting irregularities are also widespread. The conduct of elections as well as the changing electoral rules has impeded the development of political competition in Kyrgyzstan.

For most of the first decade of independence, elections to representative assemblies below the national level were held in single-member districts using a two-round voting system. Since 1999, however, regional and local assembly elections have been conducted in multi-member districts using SNTV. Although the governors of the country's seven regions are still appointed by the president, the chief executives of cities, districts and villages are now selected by the members of the local assemblies. The sole exception to this pattern is the capital, Bishkek, where the mayor is directly elected.

As in Georgia and Ukraine, the manipulation of electoral rules and the conduct of elections ultimately delegitimized the elections themselves, which contributed to the March 24, 2005 revolution in Kyrgyzstan that overthrew the Akaev presidency and placed the newly elected parliament and the entire system of electoral rules under review.

Proportional Representation Systems

What Proportional Representation Is

100. The rationale underpinning all PR systems is the conscious translation of a party's share of the votes into a corresponding proportion of seats in the legislature. There are two major types of PR system—List PR and Single Transferable Vote (STV). PR requires the use of electoral districts with more than one member: it is not possible to divide a single seat elected on a single occasion proportionally. In some countries, such as Israel and the Netherlands, the entire country forms one multi-member district. In other countries, for example, Argentina or Portugal, electoral districts are based on provinces, while Indonesia lays down the range of permissible sizes for electoral districts and gives the task of defining them to its EMB.

101. PR systems are a common choice in many new democracies, and 23 established democracies use some variant of PR (see Table 2). PR systems are dominant in Latin America, Africa and Europe. Most of the 72 PR systems identified in this Handbook use some form of List PR; only two use STV.

102. There are many important issues which can have a major impact on how a PR system works in practice. The greater the number of representatives to be elected from a district (see paragraphs 113

> **Proportional representation requires the use of electoral districts with more than one member.**

–118 on district magnitude), the more proportional the electoral system will be. PR systems also differ in the range of choice given to the voter—whether the voter can choose between political parties, individual candidates, or both.

103. *Advantages.* In many respects, the strongest arguments for PR derive from the way in which the system avoids the anomalous results of plurality/majority systems and is better able to produce a representative legislature. For many new democracies, particularly those which face deep societal divisions, the inclusion of all significant groups in the legislature can be a near-essential condition for democratic consolidation. Failing to ensure that both minorities and majorities have a stake in developing political systems can have catastrophic consequences (see the case study on Lesotho).

104. PR systems in general are praised for the way in which they:
a. Faithfully translate votes cast into seats won, and thus avoid some of the more destabilizing and 'unfair' results thrown up by plurality/majority electoral systems. 'Seat bonuses' for the larger parties are minimized and small parties can gain access to the legislature by polling a small number of votes.

b. Encourage or require the formation of political parties or groups of like-minded candidates to put forward lists. This may clarify policy, ideology or leadership differences within society, especially when, as in Timor-Leste at independence, there is no established party system.

c. Give rise to very few wasted votes. When thresholds are low, almost all votes cast in PR elections go towards electing a candidate of choice. This increases the voters' perception that it is worth making the trip to the polling booth at election time, as they can be more confident that their vote will make a difference to the election outcome, however small.

d. Facilitate minority parties' access to representation. Unless the threshold is unduly high, or the district magnitude is unusually low, then any political party with even a small percentage of the vote can gain representation in the legislature. This fulfils the principle of inclusion, which can be crucial to stability in divided societies and has benefits for decision making in established democracies.

e. Encourage parties to campaign beyond the districts in which they are strong or where the results are expected to be close. The incentive under PR systems is to maximize the overall vote regardless of where those votes might come from. Every vote, even from an area where a party is electorally weak, goes towards gaining another seat.

f. Restrict the growth of 'regional fiefdoms'. Because PR systems reward minority parties with a minority of the seats, they are less likely to lead to situations where a single party holds all the seats in a given province or district. This can be particularly important to minorities in a province which may not have significant regional concentrations or alternative points of access to power.

g. Lead to greater continuity and stability of policy. The West European experience suggests that parliamentary PR systems score better with regard to governmental longevity, voter participation and economic performance. The rationale behind this claim is that regular switches in government between two ideologically polarized parties, as can happen in FPTP systems, makes long-term economic planning more difficult, while broad PR coalition governments help engender a stability and coherence in decision making which allow for national development.

h. Make power-sharing between parties and interest groups more visible. In many new democracies, power-sharing between the numerical majority of the population who hold political power and a small minority who hold economic power is an unavoidable reality. Where the numerical majority dominates the legislature and a minority sees its interests expressed in the control of the economic sphere, negotiations between different power blocks are less visible, less transparent and less accountable (e.g. in Zimbabwe during its first 20 years of independence). It has been argued that PR, by including all interests in the legislature, offers a better hope that decisions will be taken in the public eye and by a more inclusive cross-section of the society.

105. *Disadvantages.* Most of the criticisms of PR in general are based around the tendency of PR systems to give rise to coalition governments and a fragmented party system. The arguments most often cited against PR are that it leads to:

a. Coalition governments, which in turn lead to legislative gridlock and consequent inability to carry out coherent policies. There are particularly high risks during an immediate post-conflict transition period, when popular expectations of new governments are high. Quick and coherent decision making can be impeded by coalition cabinets and governments of national unity which are split by factions.

b. A destabilizing fragmentation of the party system. PR can reflect and facilitate a fragmentation of the party system. It is possible that extreme pluralism can allow tiny minority parties to hold larger parties to ransom in coalition negotiations. In this respect, the inclusiveness of PR is cited as a drawback of the system. In Israel, for example, extremist religious parties are often crucial to the formation of a government, while Italy endured many years of unstable shifting coalition governments. Democratizing countries are often fearful that PR will allow personality-based and ethnic-cleavage parties to proliferate in their undeveloped party systems.

c. A platform for extremist parties. In a related argument, PR systems are often criticized for giving a stage in the legislature to extremist parties of the left or the right. It has been argued that the collapse of Weimar Germany was in part due to the way in which its PR electoral system gave a toehold to extremist groups of the extreme left and right.

d. Governing coalitions which have insufficient common ground in terms of either their policies or their support base. These coalitions of convenience are sometimes contrasted with coalitions of commitment produced by other systems (e.g. through the use of AV), in which parties tend to be reciprocally dependent on the votes of supporters of other parties for their election, and the coalition may thus be stronger.

e. Small parties getting a disproportionately large amount of power. Large parties may be forced to form coalitions with much smaller parties, giving a party that has the support of only a small percentage of the votes the power to veto any proposal that comes from the larger parties.

f. The inability of the voter to enforce accountability by throwing a party out of power. Under a PR system it may be very difficult to remove a reasonably-sized centre party from power. When governments are usually coalitions, some political parties are ever-present in government, despite weak electoral performances from time to time. The Free Democratic Party (FDP) in Germany was a member of the governing coalition for all but eight of the 50 years from 1949 to 1998, although it never gained more than 12 per cent of the vote.

g. Difficulties either for voters to understand or for the electoral administration to implement the sometimes complex rules of the system. Some PR systems are considered to be more difficult than non-PR systems and may require more voter education and training of poll workers to work successfully.

List Proportional Representation (List PR)

> Under a List Proportional Representation system each party or grouping presents a list of candidates for a multi-member electoral district, the voters vote for a party, and parties receive seats in proportion to their overall share of the vote. In some (closed list) systems the winning candidates are taken from the lists in order of their position on the lists. If the lists are 'open' or 'free' the voters can influence the order of the candidates by marking individual preferences.

106. In its most simple form, List PR involves each party presenting a list of candidates to the electorate in each multi-member electoral district. Voters vote for a party, and parties receive seats in proportion to their overall share of the vote in the electoral district. Winning candidates are taken from the lists in order of their position on the lists.

The choice of List PR does not in itself completely specify the electoral system: more details must be determined. The system used to calculate the allocation of seats after the votes have been counted can be either a Highest Average or a Largest Remainder Method (see the glossary at annex B). The formula chosen has a small but sometimes critical effect on the outcomes of elections under PR. In Cambodia in 1998, a change in the formula a few weeks before polling day turned out to have the effect of giving the largest party 64 seats, instead of 59, in a 121-seat National Assembly. The change had not been well publicized, and it was with difficulty that the opposition accepted the results. This example clearly demonstrates the importance for electoral system designers of apparently minor details.

There are several other important issues that need to be considered in defining precisely how a List PR system will work. A formal threshold may be required for representation in the legislature (see paragraphs 119–121): a high threshold (for example 10 per cent, as used by Turkey) is likely to exclude smaller parties, while a low threshold (for example 1.5 per cent, as used by Israel) may promote their representation. In South Africa, there is no formal threshold, and in 2004 the African Christian Democratic Party won six seats out of 400 with only 1.6 per cent of the national vote. List PR systems also differ depending on whether and how the voter can choose between candidates as well as parties, that is, whether lists are closed, open or free *(panachage)*(see paragraphs 122 –126). This choice has implications for the complexity of the ballot paper.

Other choices include arrangements for formal or informal 'vote pooling'; the scope for agreements between parties, such as that provided by systems which use *apparentement* (see paragraph 127); and the definition of district boundaries.

107. *Advantages*
a. In addition to the advantages attached to PR systems generally, List PR makes it more likely that the representatives of minority cultures/groups will be elected. When, as is often the case, voting behaviour dovetails with a society's cultural or social divisions, then List PR electoral systems can help to ensure that the legislature includes members of both majority and minority groups. This is because parties can be encouraged by the system to craft balanced candidate lists which appeal to a whole spectrum of voters'

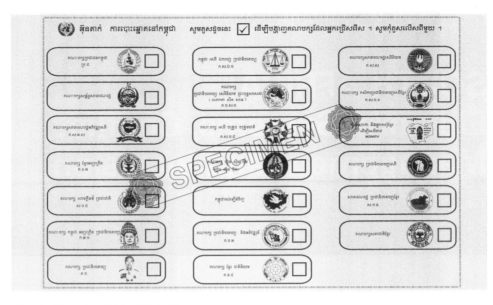

Cambodian closed List PR ballot paper

interests. The experience of a number of new democracies (e.g. South Africa, Indonesia, Sierra Leone) suggests that List PR gives the political space which allows parties to put up multiracial, and multi-ethnic, lists of candidates. The South African National Assembly elected in 1994 was 52 per cent black (11 per cent Zulu, the rest being of Xhosa, Sotho, Venda, Tswana, Pedi, Swazi, Shangaan and Ndebele extraction), 32 per cent white (one-third English-speaking, two-thirds Afrikaans-speaking), 7 per cent Coloured and 8 per cent Indian. The Namibian Parliament is similarly diverse, with representatives from the Ovambo, Damara, Herero, Nama, Baster and white (English- and German-speaking) communities.

b. List PR makes it more likely that women will be elected. PR electoral systems are almost always more friendly to the election of women than plurality/majority systems. In essence, parties are able to use the lists to promote the advancement of women politicians and allow voters the space to elect women candidates while still basing their choice on other policy concerns than gender. As noted above, in single-member districts most parties are encouraged to put up a 'most broadly acceptable' candidate, and that person is seldom a woman. In all regions of the world PR systems do better than FPTP systems in the number of women elected and 14 of the top 20 nations when it comes to the representation of women use List PR. In 2004, the number of women representatives in legislatures elected by List PR systems was 4.3 percentage points higher than the average of 15.2 per cent for all legislatures, while that for legislatures elected by FPTP was 4.1 percentage points lower.

108. *Disadvantages.* In addition to the general issues already identified relating to PR systems, the following additional disadvantages may be considered:

SOUTH AFRICA: Electoral Systems, Conflict Management and Inclusion

Andrew Reynolds

The National Assembly parliamentary and provincial elections held in South Africa in 1994 marked the high point of a period of tumultuous change from authoritarian rule to multiparty democracy in Southern Africa as a whole. At midnight on 27 April 1994 perhaps the most despised flag in Africa was lowered, heralding the end of 300 years of colonialism and four decades of apartheid. Those first multiparty democratic elections opened the stage to political movements which had been driven underground by the Pretoria regime's policy of racial divide and rule. Nelson Mandela's African National Congress (ANC) was poised on the threshold of power; the Pan-Africanist Congress of Azania (PAC) was challenging it within the same community, while Mangosotho Buthelezi's Inkatha Freedom Party (IFP) hoped to build on its hegemony in the north of the province of KwaZulu-Natal. These new parties joined F. W. De Klerk's National Party (NP), the liberal Democratic Party (DP) and the new Freedom Front (FF)—a descendant of the 'white right' parties of the old constitutional dispensation—in battling for the votes of millions of newly-enfranchised people.

Elections were conducted under List PR with half the National Assembly (200 members) being chosen from nine provincial lists and the other half being elected from a single national list. In effect, the country used one nationwide constituency (with 400 members) for the conversion of votes into seats, and no formal threshold for representation was imposed.

The Droop Quota was used to allocate seats, and surplus seats were awarded by an adaptation of the Largest Remainder Method. Early drafts of the electoral law put the threshold for parliamentary representation at 5 per cent of the national vote but, in a concession to the smaller parties, the ANC and the NP agreed in early 1994 to drop any 'mandatory' threshold. However, only those parties with 20 or more MPs, 5 per cent of the Assembly, were guaranteed portfolios in the first government's cabinet of national unity.

The fact that the 'Mandela liberation-movement juggernaut' would have won the National Assembly elections under almost any electoral system cannot diminish the importance of South Africa's choice of a List PR system for these first elections. The PR system, as an integral part of other power-sharing mechanisms in the new constitution, was crucial to creating the atmosphere of inclusiveness and reconciliation which precipitated the decline of the worst political violence and has made post-apartheid South Africa something of a beacon of hope and stability to the rest of troubled Africa.

Nevertheless, in 1990, upon Nelson Mandela's release from prison, there was no particular reason to believe that South Africa would adopt PR. The 'whites-only' Parliament had always been elected by an FPTP system, while the ANC, now in a powerful bargaining position, expected to be clearly advantaged if FPTP were maintained. As only five electoral districts, out of over 700, had white majorities, the ANC, with 50–60 per cent of the popular vote, expected to win 70 per cent or 80 per cent of the parliamentary seats easily due to the vagaries of FPTP voting. But the ANC did not opt for this course because it realized that the disparities of a 'winner-takes-all' electoral system would be fundamentally destabilizing in the long run for minority and majority interests. List PR also avoided the politically charged and controversial question of having to draw constituency boundaries and, furthermore, it fitted in with the executive power-sharing ethos which both the ANC and the Nationalists saw as a key tenet of the interim constitution.

It is probable that, even with their geographical pockets of electoral support, the Freedom Front (which won nine seats in the new National Assembly), the Democratic Party (seven seats), the Pan-Africanist Congress (five seats), and the African Christian Democratic Party (two seats) would have failed to win a single parliamentary seat if the elections had been held under a single-member district FPTP electoral system. While these parties together only had 6 per cent of the members of the new Assembly, their importance inside the structures of government far outweighs their numerical strength.

A reading of the detailed results reveals, somewhat surprisingly, that in 1994 List PR may not have particularly advantaged the medium-sized NP and the IFP over and above the number of seats they would have expected to win under an FPTP system. This was primarily due to the 'national referendum' nature of the campaign, which led to a two-party battle between the old and the new—the ANC versus the IFP in KwaZulu-Natal province, and the ANC versus the NP in the rest of the country. Furthermore, the ethnically homogeneous nature of constituencies and the strong geographical concentrations of support in South Africa meant that the NP and the IFP would have won only slightly fewer seats under a constituency system. However, FPTP would in all likelihood have given the ANC a small 'seat bonus', increasing its share of the seats in the National Assembly beyond its share of the popular vote (which was 62 per cent) and beyond the two-thirds majority needed to draft the new constitution without reference to other parties.

The practice of having one ballot for the National Assembly and one for the provincial parliament also proved to be an important innovation in the electoral system design. Until a few months before the election, the ANC was still insisting on a single ballot which would be counted for both the national and provincial elections. This was quite clearly a manoeuvre to advantage the larger, nationally-based parties and was only changed through the pressure of an alliance of business leaders, the Democratic

Party, and international advisers. The eventual results did show that large numbers of voters had split their national and provincial ballots between two parties, and it appears as though the major beneficiaries of separating the ballots were the small Democratic Party and the Freedom Front. Both polled more than 200,000 votes in the provincial elections over and above their national result, which went a long way to explain the 490,000 drop between the NP's national and provincial totals.

The choice of electoral system has also had an impact upon the composition of the Parliament along the lines of ethnicity and gender. The South African National Assembly sworn into office in May 1994 contained over 80 former members of the whites-only parliament, but that was where the similarities between the old and the new ended. In direct contrast to South Africa's troubled history, black sat with white, communist with conservative, Zulu with Xhosa, and Muslim with Christian. To a significant extent the diversity of the new National Assembly was a product of the use of List PR. The national, and unalterable, candidate lists allowed parties to present ethnically heterogeneous groups of candidates which, it was hoped, would have cross-cutting appeal. The resulting National Assembly was 52 per cent black (including Xhosa-, Zulu-, Sotho-, Venda-, Tswana-, Pedi-, Swazi-, Shangaan- and Ndebele-speaking), 32 per cent white (English- and Afrikaans-speaking), 8 per cent Indian, and 7 per cent Coloured—this compared to an electorate which was estimated to be 73 per cent black, 15 per cent white, 9 per cent Coloured, and 3 per cent Indian. Women made up 27 per cent of MPs.

In 1999 the proportion of black MPs rose to 58 per cent and that of Coloured MPs rose to 10 per cent, while whites made up 26 per cent and Indians 5 per cent. In 2004 the black proportion (65 per cent) came closer to their population share, while whites made up 22 per cent. Numbers of Coloured and Indian MPs held roughly steady. The proportion of women MPs rose to 30 per cent in 1999 and to 33 per cent in 2004. There is a widespread belief in South Africa that if FPTP had been introduced there would have been far fewer women, Indians and whites, with more black and male MPs.

Finally, more polarized forms of representation would be expected under FPTP, with whites (of different parties) representing majority white constituencies, Xhosas representing Xhosas, Zulus representing Zulus, and so on. While problems with lack of district accountability and of remoteness are perceived effects of the present South African List PR system, it has meant that citizens have a variety of MPs to approach when the need arises.

Nevertheless, there is a continuing debate in South Africa about how to increase democratic accountability and the representativeness of the MPs. It was widely accepted that the first non-racial election was more of a referendum about which parties should draw up the new constitution. But subsequent elections have been about constituting a representative Parliament, and many political actors and voters argue that the electoral system needs to be altered to take this into account.

Today, all the major political parties still support the principle of PR. Without greatly increasing the difficulty of the ballot, voters could be allowed to choose between candidates as well as parties, without the PR character of the Parliament being affected in any way. One option is to elect MPs in smaller multi-member constituencies in order to develop a stronger geographical tie between electors and their representatives. At the moment the regional lists represent areas so large that any form of local advocacy is entirely lost. A second option is to adopt the MMP system, with half the members elected from single-member districts while the other half come from compensatory PR lists. Both these options were considered by a 12-member Task Team, led by Frederick van Zyl Slabbert, a former leader of the Democratic Party, and briefed to consider reform options in 2002. This Task Team had an inbuilt ANC- Independent Electoral Commission (IEC) majority, and was appointed by the president to review the electoral system in the light of complaints that the List PR system did not include adequate geographical representation. It ultimately recommended that South Africa should retain its List PR system but change it to a two-tier system, splitting the country into 69 constituencies electing between three and seven MPs, and keeping 100 seats as 'compensatory' national seats. However, the ANC government rejected this reform for the 2004 general election and appears to be unwilling to implement a new system for 2009.

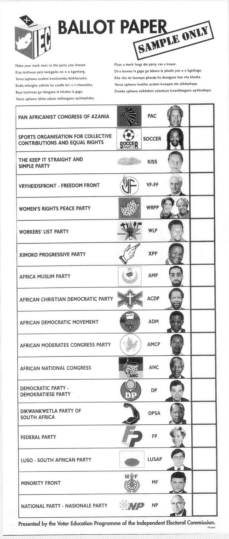

*South African closed
List PR ballot paper*

INDONESIA: Continuity, Deals and Consensus

Andrew Ellis

The development of political institutions able to provide stable and effective government has been a daunting challenge in Indonesia, a huge and ethnically diverse country of nearly 20,000 islands whose unity was based on common resistance to colonialism. Political identity in Indonesia is a complex subject, in the past often based on links to different strands of Islam, to a more secular nationalism, or in some areas to Christianity—to which assessment of leadership qualities and the impact of corruption now, in 2004, appear to have been added. Devising electoral systems that are inclusive and effective in the context of the Indonesian unitary state has never been easy.

The first general election in Indonesia after the 1945 proclamation of independence took place in 1955. A PR system using 15 regions was adopted without challenge. Seats were distributed in proportion to population, with a small extra allocation for Outer Island regions. The Largest Remainder Method using the Hare Quota was adopted. Parties or organizations could nominate lists, and individual candidates could also be nominated. Voters could vote either for a list or by writing in the name of one candidate.

The resulting legislature included representatives of 27 parties and lists, plus one individual member. The four largest parties all received between 16 per cent and 23 per cent of the vote. Not only was no single party able to command a majority in the legislature; not even two parties were. It was difficult to form governments, and their ability to retain the confidence of the legislature was limited. The Constituent Assembly, elected shortly afterwards to draw up a permanent constitution, had a similar political balance and failed to reach agreement.

General loss of confidence in political institutions and rebellions against the unitary state led President Soekarno to impose an authoritarian regime in 1959. This lasted until it was replaced by the New Order of President Soeharto in the mid-1960s, which established virtually complete dominance of the executive, legislative and judicial branches. Elections took place, but campaigns were heavily restricted, many candidates were disqualified, and the rules were applied disproportionately against opponents of the government. The desire for complete central control over the choice of candidates contributed to the choice of closed-list PR. Soeharto sought to allay fears of Javanese political domination, and Java received only just over half of the seats to be elected, despite having over 70 per cent of the registered electorate in 1955. Although this figure has fallen, it was still 61 per cent in 2004.

The Transition to Democracy: The 1999 Elections

After the Soeharto regime fell in 1998, new electoral legislation was finalized in late January 1999. The electoral system—described as a 'proportional system with district characteristics'—was unique. It was the clear product of incremental political negotiation against a time deadline. This agreement was reached in the legislature by the parties of the Soeharto era, which were under pressure from the new parties and others outside the negotiations, in addition to defending their own positions and coming under pressure from their own power bases. Given these pressures, it is unlikely that the end result of the negotiation could have been substantially different.

At the June 1999 election, each voter cast a single vote for a political party. The 27 provinces were retained as electoral districts, ranging in magnitude from four to 82 seats. The number of seats won by each party in each province was determined using the principles of PR, and each candidate on each party list was linked by the party to one of the second-tier districts (*kota*, city authorities, and *kabupaten*, authorities in non-city areas) within the province. Because of deep-rooted concern to maintain the unity of the state, there were provisions that made it impossible to register a specifically regional party. The law on political parties required all parties contesting the elections to be organized in at least nine provinces.

The legislation was not clear on essential detail. The method for converting votes cast into seats gained was not included. Nor were there rules for identifying which candidates from a party's list would occupy the seats gained by that party. These issues were resolved only at a very late stage.

The final seat allocation regulations retained the Largest Remainder Method using the Hare Quota. The allocation of candidates to seats won was much more complex. In practice, few central party leaderships even complied with the regulations, and leaderships took de facto powers simply to tell the Election Commission which candidates had been elected to the seats their party had won.

The 1999 elections were nonetheless judged to have been the first since 1955 to be acceptable overall, despite specific or localized concerns. Five parties gained more than 2 per cent of the vote: their relative strengths varied widely in the different parts of Indonesia. Sixteen other parties gained representation.

Reflection on the 1999 elections was rapidly overtaken by a full review of the 1945 constitution. The completion of this review in 2002 led to fundamental changes, including the introduction of the separation of powers, the principle of checks and balances, direct election of the president and vice-president, and the establishment of a regionally based elected second chamber with very limited powers. Four portmanteau amendments were passed to the constitution, completely changing the way in which the institutions will work in future, and five new laws—on elections, presidential elections, political parties, the structure of elected bodies, and the establishment of the Constitutional Court—were passed. Indonesia now falls recognizably within the mainstream of the family of presidential democracies.

Single-Member Plurality Fails to Find Favour for Elections to the Legislature

After 1999, there was considerable advocacy of a single-member district (SMD) plurality system among the media and in academia in particular, as the accountability of elected members was widely perceived to be lacking in the legislature elected in 1999. Even if the 1999 electoral system is viewed not as a political deal but as a brave attempt to marry the principles of List PR and the accountability of elected members to the electoral district, no constituency–member link was created in practice.

However, simulations made after the 1999 elections suggested that a plurality SMD system would be likely to produce results in Indonesia that were more disproportional than almost anywhere else in the world. Steadily worsening relations between the legislature elected in 1999 and many academic, media and civil society actors also meant that support for SMD systems by the latter became steadily less persuasive. It became evident that a plurality system would almost certainly fail to reflect the diversity of Indonesia, that introducing an acceptable districting process for the 2004 election would take time and involve considerable difficulty, and that plurality systems were not likely to favour the election of women.

The 2004 Electoral System

The new constitutional requirements agreed in 2002 state that the participants in elections to the lower chamber of the legislature (the National Assembly) are political parties, thus limiting the available options for the electoral system in the new electoral law. The government's draft election law provided for a PR system using multi-member districts, responding to the pressure for greater accountability by proposing open lists and the dividing up of larger provinces. This basic form was finally adopted, with multi-member districts of a magnitude of between three and 12 seats to be drawn up by the Election Commission. Subsequent debate led to multi-member districts whose magnitude is towards the higher end of this range. The restricted open-list system finally agreed requires voters to vote for one party and, if they wish, one candidate from that party. However, this will only result in the election of a particular candidate out of the order in which names appear on the party list if that candidate gains more than a full Hare Quota of individual votes—which made its likely effect minimal, as proved to be the case in practice in the 2004 elections to the legislature.

As a result of the creation of the regional chamber, some parties argued the case for 'one person, one vote, one value' (OPOVOV) for the legislature, with the same population for every seat, while others backed the retention of a representational bias in favour of the Outer Islands. The final compromise is a complex formula basing the number of seats for each province on a minimum of 325,000 population per seat in small provinces and a maximum of 425,000 population per seat in large ones, with a minimum of three seats per province.

The central party leaderships showed little inclination to relax their hold on their parties. The larger parties toughened the requirements for parties to participate in both the 2004 and subsequent elections.

The effective prohibition of regional parties has been strengthened. The issues of open or closed list, OPOVOV, the balance between Java and the Outer Islands, and party participation were all negotiated between the parties when the final deal was struck. A broadly-based campaign did, however, lead to the adoption of a 'maybe-quota' for gender representation: parties are required to 'bear in their hearts' the desirability of including at least 30 per cent women candidates on their lists. While there is no enforcement provision, this proved an important tool to encourage more women candidates, and 12 per cent of the members of the 2004 legislature are women- a significant improvement on 1999.

The 2004 legislative election results reflected both change and continuity. The same five parties that polled more than 3 per cent in 1999 did so again, and were joined by two more. Seventeen parties were represented altogether.

Elections to the Regional Chamber: SNTV Springs a Surprise

The constitution provides that candidates for the new regional chamber (the Regional Representatives' Council) should be individuals, not parties. Four members are to be elected per province. The draft law proposed the Block Vote system, clearly designed to advantage parties with support outside Java where provinces are smaller. SNTV was proposed as an alternative by the party that was strongest in Java, and was agreed as part of the final deal.

The first election to the regional chamber took place in 2004 and demonstrated a known weakness of SNTV: with an average of 30 candidates contesting the four seats in each province, many candidates were elected with less than 10 per cent of the vote. However, strong campaigns by women candidates meant that an unexpected 21 per cent of the members of the new chamber are women—a level unprecedented in a freely elected body in Indonesia.

Direct Presidential Elections

The president and vice-president are now directly elected, with candidates pairing up to form tickets. A two-round majority run-off system is used, with the aim of ensuring that the successful candidates have sufficient support across a large and diverse country. For a ticket to be elected on the first round, it must not only poll an absolute majority of votes cast but also meet a distribution requirement of 20 per cent of the vote in at least half the provinces. While a majority winner will almost certainly achieve this, the requirement prevents a ticket whose support is solid in Java and minimal elsewhere from winning an election in the first round. In the first direct presidential election in 2004, five tickets contested the first round in July, with none polling over 35 per cent; in the second round in September, Susilo Bambang Yudhoyono gained victory with 61 per cent of the votes.

The Political Reality: Negotiating a Deal

The 1999 electoral system agreement had to be acceptable both to the parties of the New Order, which still held the levers of power, and to the new parties outside on the street. The constitutional review that followed the 1999 election also required agreement across the political spectrum. The 2004 election law is yet another deal, similar in principle to that of 1999, but with important differences of detail. Each time, there were a limited number of practical solutions given the inherited traditions and the political background and positions of the actors. However, there are positive signs for democracy in the new Indonesian institutional framework: it is fortunate that some long-term vision existed alongside the inevitable perceptions of short-term political advantage among the parties and individuals who shaped the changes.

a. Weak links between elected legislators and their constituents. When List PR is used and seats are allocated in one single national district, as in Namibia or Israel, the system is criticized for destroying the link between voters and their representatives. Where lists are closed voters have no opportunity to determine the identity of the persons who will represent them and no identifiable representative for their town, district or village, nor can they easily reject an individual representative if they feel that he or she has performed poorly in office. Moreover, in some developing countries where the society is mainly rural, voters' identification with their region of residence is sometimes considerably stronger than their identification with any political party or grouping. This criticism, however, may relate more to the distinction between systems in which voters vote for parties and systems in which they vote for candidates.

b. Excessive entrenchment of power within party headquarters and in the hands of senior party leaderships—especially in closed-list systems. A candidate's position on the party list, and therefore his or her likelihood of success, is dependent on currying favour with party bosses, whose relationship with the electorate is of secondary importance. In an unusual twist to the List PR system, in Guyana parties publish their list of candidates not ranked but simply ordered alphabetically. This allows party leaders even more scope to reward loyalty and punish independence because seats are only allocated to individuals once the result of the vote is known.

c. The need for some kind of recognized party or political groupings to exist. This makes List PR particularly difficult to implement in those societies which do not have parties or have very embryonic and loose party structures, for example, many of the island countries of the Pacific.

The Single Transferable Vote (STV)

109. STV has long been advocated by political scientists as one of the most attractive electoral systems, but its use for legislative elections has been limited to a few cases—the Republic of Ireland since 1921, Malta since 1947, and once in Estonia in 1990. It is also used for elections to the Australian Federal Senate and in several Australian states, and for European and local elections in Northern Ireland. It has been adopted for local elections in Scotland and in some authorities in New Zealand. It was also chosen as the recommendation of the British Columbia Citizens' Assembly (see the case study on British Columbia).

The core principles of the system were independently invented in the 19th century by Thomas Hare in Britain and Carl Andræ in Denmark. STV uses multi-member districts, and voters rank candidates in order of preference on the ballot paper in the same manner as under the Alternative Vote system. In most cases this preference marking is optional, and voters are not required to rank-order all candidates; if they wish they can mark only one.

After the total number of first-preference votes are tallied, the count then begins by establishing the quota of votes required for the election of a single candidate. The quota

THE REPUBLIC OF IRELAND: The Single Transferable Vote in Action

Michael Gallagher

The Irish lower house of Parliament, Dáil Éireann, is elected by the STV system—proportional representation by means of the Single Transferable Vote. This relatively unusual system owes its origins to the circumstances of the Republic of Ireland's achievement of independence in 1922. The departing rulers, the British, wanted some form of PR in order to protect the Protestant minority, while the new state's political elite favoured PR in principle. With neither having much awareness of PR list systems, STV was adopted by agreement as the electoral system and has remained the electoral system ever since.

The Dáil is of central importance in the Irish political system. It elects the government, which needs to retain majority support in the Dáil in order to survive. Much less important is the presidency, although, unusually for a parliamentary system, the president is directly elected. Elections for the presidency take place under the Alternative Vote (AV) system.

The 166 members of the Dáil are elected from around 40 constituencies, each returning three, four or five members. Voting is straightforward: voters merely indicate their favoured candidate (by writing '1' beside that candidate's name on the ballot paper), and can go on to indicate their second and third choices and so on in the same way. Voters can rank candidates not only within but also across parties. Although most vote along party lines, it is not necessary to do so, and some vote along geographical lines, that is, they give their highest preferences, regardless of party, to the candidates from their own local area. The counting process, especially the distribution of 'surplus' votes, looks complicated to the uninitiated, but it is worth emphasizing that the voters do not have to be familiar with all the details; they need only to know how to cast their vote and to be satisfied that the counting process is 'fair' and transparent.

The electoral system is entrenched in the constitution and consequently cannot be changed without a referendum. On two occasions (1959 and 1968) the largest party, Fianna Fáil, instigated a referendum to replace STV by the British FPTP system, using the argument each time that any kind of PR was likely to create a problem of unstable coalition government. The proposed change was rejected by the voters on each occasion, by margins of 52 per cent to 48 per cent in 1959, and 61 per cent to 39 per cent in 1968.

On the basis of the criterion of stable government, anyone evaluating the record of STV in the Republic of Ireland would not, in fact, see its performance as a problem. Since the mid-1940s, governments (both coalition and single-party) have lasted three, four or five years, the only exception being a short-lived period of instability in the early 1980s. The voters, through their ranking of candidates of different parties, are able to indicate their wishes regarding potential coalition partners for their preferred party.

STV has generally delivered highly proportional outcomes, with Fianna Fáil receiving only a modest 'bonus' (around 48 per cent of the seats for 45 per cent of the votes at elections over the period 1945–92). However, the small size of the electoral districts (four seats per constituency on average) creates the potential for the largest party to reap a benefit if it can attract second- and third-preference votes from supporters of other parties, and this happened at the two most recent elections. These produced the least proportional results ever: in 2002, Fianna Fáil won 41 per cent of the votes and 49 per cent of the seats.

The system continues to allow representation to small parties and to independents, 13 of whom were elected in 2002. While many PR systems enable small parties to win seats in the Parliament, STV seems to give an unusual opportunity to independent candidates to do the same because of its essentially candidate-centred rather than party-centred nature.

Much of the praise and criticism of STV in the Republic of Ireland hinges on the same factor, namely the power it gives to voters to choose among candidates of the same party. This creates intense intra-party competition, especially among candidates of Fianna Fáil, which nominates between two and four candidates in each constituency. Statistics show that more incumbent Fianna Fáil MPs lose their seat to a running-mate than to a candidate of another party.

Critics argue that, as a result, incumbents become over-active at constituency level in order to curry favour with the voters and do not spend enough time on politics at national level, for example, on scrutinizing the government or discussing legislation in committees. They argue that this has an adverse effect on the calibre of Irish parliamentarians (in that individuals who could make a contribution at national level are discouraged by the likely casework load they would have to discharge if elected) and that it leads to short-termism and undue regard for localism in government thinking. They suggest that internal party competition for votes may lead to divided, incohesive political parties.

The defenders of the system, in contrast, see voters' opportunity to choose among candidates of their party as a virtue. They argue that it allows the voters to replace incumbents by more able and more active newcomers and that, at a time of decreasing interest in conventional politics, this gives MPs a strong incentive to keep in close contact with the voters and thus fulfil the role of linking citizens to the political system. They maintain that there is no evidence that Irish MPs are of lower calibre than those elsewhere and that the Republic of Ireland's recent record of impressive economic growth shows that there cannot be too much wrong with the behaviour of governments. They also point out that the Irish political parties are extremely cohesive and disciplined in their behaviour in Parliament, with no factions or recognizable subgroups.

In 2002 an all-party parliamentary committee considered the arguments for and against changing the system. It concluded that the public was strongly attached to STV, that a change to any other system would reduce the power of the individual voter, and that some of the alleged failings of the political system for which critics blamed STV were caused by other factors. As this conclusion indicates, there is no significant body of opinion in favour of amending or replacing the existing system.

Any evaluation of STV in the Republic of Ireland needs to take account of the characteristics of the country. It is a small country in terms of both area and population, and the ratio of MPs to population (about 1 : 20,000) is relatively high by international standards. This may foster closer links between MPs and their constituents, regardless of the electoral system, than are likely in a larger country. In addition, the Republic of Ireland is a prosperous, highly educated society where the political system as a whole is well established and is universally regarded as legitimate. Irish society does not have any significant cleavages (for example, ethnic, linguistic or religious).

For all these reasons we need to be careful about drawing firm conclusions about how STV would operate in other contexts. We can, though, say that there is no sign that the electorate in the Republic of Ireland would like to replace it by any other system.

BALLOT PAPER
HOUSE OF REPRESENTATIVES

WESTERN AUSTRALIA

ELECTORAL DIVISION OF

BRAND

Number the boxes from 1 to 10 in the order of your choice.

	BEAZLEY, Kim AUSTRALIAN LABOR PARTY
	GENT, Alan INDEPENDENT
	McCARTHY, Brian INDEPENDENT
	GOODALE, Bob THE GREENS (WA)
	McKERCHER, Mal AUSTRALIAN DEMOCRATS
	ANDERSON, Leone L INDEPENDENT
	GALLETLY, Clive Philip Arthur INDEPENDENT
	REBE, Phil AUSTRALIANS AGAINST FURTHER IMMIGRATION
	WALTON, Malcolm NATIONAL PARTY
	HEARNE, Penny LIBERAL

Remember...number <u>every</u> box to make your vote count

Australian Electoral Commission **/AEC**

Australian Senate Single Transferable Vote ballot paper

used is normally the Droop quota, calculated by the simple formula:

$$\text{Quota} = \frac{\text{votes}}{\text{seats} + 1} + 1$$

110. The result is determined through a series of counts. At the first count, the total number of first-preference votes for each candidate is ascertained. Any candidate who has a number of first preferences greater than or equal to the quota is immediately elected.

The Single Transferable Vote is a preferential system in which the voter ranks the candidates in a multi-member district and the candidates that surpass a specified quota of first-preference votes are immediately elected. In successive counts, votes are redistributed from least successful candidates, who are eliminated, and votes surplus to the quota are redistributed from successful candidates, until sufficient candidates are declared elected. Voters normally vote for candidates rather than political parties, although a party-list option is possible.

In second and subsequent counts, the surplus votes of elected candidates (i.e. those votes above the quota) are redistributed according to the second preferences on the ballot papers. For fairness, all the candidate's ballot papers are redistributed, but each at a fractional percentage of one vote, so that the total redistributed vote equals the candidate's surplus (except in the Republic of Ireland, which uses a weighted sample). If a candidate had 100 votes, for example, and their surplus was five votes, then each ballot paper would be redistributed at the value of 1/20th of a vote.

After any count, if no candidate has a surplus of votes over the quota, the candidate with the lowest total of votes is eliminated. His or her votes are then redistributed in the next count to the candidates left in the race according to the second and then lower preferences shown. The process of successive counts, after each of which surplus votes are redistributed or a candidate is eliminated, continues until either all the seats for the electoral district are filled by candidates who have received the quota, or the number of candidates left in the count is only one more than the number of seats to be filled, in which case all remaining candidates bar one are elected without receiving a full quota.

111. *Advantages.* The advantages claimed for PR generally apply to STV systems. In addition, as a mechanism for choosing representatives, STV is perhaps the most sophisticated of all electoral systems, allowing for choice between parties and between candidates within parties. The final results retain a fair degree of proportionality, and the fact that in most actual examples of STV the multi-member districts are relatively small means that a geographical link between voter and representative is retained. Furthermore, voters can influence the composition of post-election coalitions, as has been the case in the Republic of Ireland, and the system provides incentives for inter-party accommodation through the reciprocal exchange of preferences between parties. STV also provides a better chance for the election of popular independent candidates than List PR, because voters are choosing between candidates rather than between parties (although a party-list option can be added to an STV election; this is done for the Australian Senate).

112. *Disadvantages.* The disadvantages claimed for PR generally also apply to STV systems. In addition:

a. STV is sometimes criticized on the grounds that preference voting is unfamiliar in many societies, and demands, at the very least, a degree of literacy and numeracy.

b. The intricacies of an STV count are quite complex, which is also seen as being a drawback. This has been cited as one of the reasons why Estonia decided to abandon the system after its first election. STV requires continual recalculations of surplus transfer values and the like. Because of this, votes under STV need to be counted at counting centres instead of directly at the polling place. Where election integrity is a salient issue, counting in the actual polling places may be necessary to ensure legitimacy of the vote, and there will be a need to choose the electoral system accordingly.

c. STV, unlike List PR, can at times produce pressures for political parties to fragment internally because members of the same party are effectively competing against each other, as well as against the opposition, for votes. This could serve to promote 'clientelistic' politics where politicians offer electoral bribes to groups of defined voters.

d. STV can lead to a party with a plurality of votes nonetheless winning fewer seats than its rivals. Malta amended its system in the mid-1980s by providing for some extra compensatory seats to be awarded to a party in the event of this happening.

Many of these criticisms have, however, proved to be little trouble in practice. STV elections in the Republic of Ireland and Malta have tended to produce relatively stable, legitimate governments comprising one or two main parties.

PR-Related Issues

District Magnitude

113. There is near-universal agreement among electoral specialists that the crucial determinant of an electoral system's ability to translate votes cast into seats won proportionally is the district magnitude, which is the number of members to be elected in each electoral district. Under a system such as FPTP, AV or the Two-Round System, there is a district magnitude of one; voters are electing a single representative. By contrast, all PR systems, some plurality/majority systems such as Block Vote and PBV, and some other systems such as Limited Vote and SNTV, require electoral districts which elect more than one member. Under any proportional system, the number of members to be chosen in each district determines, to a significant extent, how proportional the election results will be.

114. The systems which achieve the greatest degree of proportionality will use very large districts, because such districts are able to ensure that even very small parties are represented in the legislature. In smaller districts, the effective threshold (see paragraph 121) is higher. For example, in a district in which there are only three members to be

CHILE:
A System Frozen by Elite Interests

Carlos Huneeus

Chile's electoral system can only be understood in the context of the long period of authoritarian rule under General Augusto Pinochet (1973–90), whose aim was to establish a regime of protected, authoritarian democracy, of which the electoral system was one component. The dictatorship abolished PR, which had been in force prior to the military coup of 11 September 1973. PR was the response to the cleavages in Chile's social structure since the 19th century and had produced a multiparty system. By the 1960s this had consolidated into six major parties—two on the left (the Socialists and the Communists), two in the centre (the Christian Democrats and the Radicals), and two on the right (the Liberals and the Conservatives, who merged in 1966 to form the National Party).

The Binomial System: a Legacy of Authoritarianism

In Chile's bicameral constitutional arrangements, the Chamber of Deputies, the lower house, consists of 120 members elected for a four-year term, two for each of the 60 electoral districts. The Senate has 38 elected members, two for each of the 19 districts, elected for an eight-year term: there are elections for half of the seats every four years, simultaneously with elections to the Chamber of Deputies. There are in addition nine non-elected members, the 'institutional' or 'designated' senators, named by the National Security Council (four), the Supreme Court (three) and the president (two), and one ex-officio life member, former President Eduardo Frei Ruiz-Tagle. (The original 13 senatorial districts of the 1980 constitution were expanded to 19 in the 1989 constitutional reforms to reduce the power of the non-elected senators.) These arrangements were negotiated by Pinochet and his supporters as they fell from power during the transition to democracy.

Parties, coalitions or independents present lists, normally containing a maximum of two candidates per district, in elections both for the Chamber of Deputies and for the Senate. Voters vote for the candidate of their choice. The first seat goes to whichever list receives the most votes in total: the representative elected is the individual candidate on that list who receives the highest vote. To take both seats, the most successful list must receive twice the number of votes of the second list. This system forces the parties to form electoral coalitions because the effective threshold is very high: 33.4 per cent of the total vote for the top list is required to win one seat. However, a list needs to receive 66.7 per cent of the total vote to be guaranteed both seats.

There are two major electoral coalitions, which in 2001 won all the seats in the Chamber of Deputies except one. The centre–left Concertación por la Democracia is formed by four parties opposed to the Pinochet regime (the Socialists, the Democracy Party, the Christian Democrats and the Radicals) and has ruled since the return to democracy in March 1990. The right-wing opposition Alliance for Chile (the Independent Democrat Union, UDI, and National Renewal, RN) supported the Pinochet regime. In practice the Concertación list contains one candidate from each of two groupings within the coalition, that is, one from the Christian Democrats and another from the Socialists, the Democracy Party and the Radicals. There is no district in which there is competition between the Socialists and the Democracy Party. On the opposition list, the UDI and National Renewal normally present one candidate each in all districts.

The result of this electoral system is that almost all districts return one representative from the Concertación and one from the Alliance for Chile. The system could create competition between the two candidates on a list for the one seat it will win, but in practice even this is severely limited by elite accommodation within both coalitions.

This electoral system is unique because in practice it favours the largest minority, not the majority. It is thus not a majoritarian system. It is a system which uses a proportional mechanism, but the results it produces are not proportional, since it allows an electoral list to take half the seats with only 34 per cent of the votes. The only reason why this distortion has not occurred in practice is the limits to electoral competition.

The electoral system was set up by the military regime following the plebiscite of 5 October 1988. The plebiscite had two goals: to approve the 1980 constitution and to elect General Pinochet as president for a further eight years. In this non-competitive election (there was no other candidate), Pinochet was defeated by the Concertación. This triggered the transition to democracy, with congressional and presidential elections in 1989, the presidential election being won by the opposition candidate Patricio Aylwin (Christian Democrat). The electoral system was designed to favour the two right-wing parties, which had backed Pinochet's candidacy, in the face of a predictable electoral victory for their opponents.

In the three presidential and four congressional elections held since 1990, the Concertación has received most votes, but has never controlled the Senate because the majority of the institutional senators have supported the opposition.

The Drawbacks of the Binomial System for the Parties and for Democracy

Several objections to the electoral system have been voiced. First, it forces the parties into electoral coalitions because of the high vote threshold required to win a seat. Second, it has a negative impact on representation because it has kept the Communist Party out of Congress, despite its relevance up to 1973 and its 5–7 per cent share of the national vote in the new democracy. Third, since each coalition will normally win one seat, the real contest takes place among the member parties, rather than between rival alliances and parties. These disputes endanger stability in the coalitions; in the 2001 senatorial elections the UDI and the RN avoided them and named a single consensus candidate in seven of the nine districts, or ran only a weak competitor who would not challenge the leadership's candidate. Fourth, the system hands enormous power to the party leaders, who virtually choose the winners when they make up the lists. With no real competition in many districts, the elections hold little interest for the voters, and even less so when there is no candidate of their own party to vote for.

The deficiencies have led the government to propose that there should be electoral reforms and to suggest that, instead of the two-member districts, larger districts that would yield more proportional results would be more appropriate. This has made little headway, however, because the Concertación parties fear the resulting uncertainty, and the opposition defends the current system because of the advantage it gives them.

Presidential Elections

The 1980 constitution establishes a two-round system for presidential elections. An absolute majority is required for victory in the first round, with a run-off round (*ballotage*) if this does not occur. The institution of *ballotage* tends to strengthen coalition politics. The winners of the presidential elections in 1989 and 1993—Christian Democrats Patricio Aylwin and Eduardo Frei, respectively—were elected with absolute majorities, but in 1999 there was only a scant 30,000-vote difference between Ricardo Lagos and his right-wing opponent, Joaquín Lavín. Lagos won with 50.27 per cent of the vote in the second round. (Under the previous (1925) constitution, when no candidate won an absolute majority, Congress decided the presidency, as occurred in 1946, 1958 and 1970. In each case it elected the candidate with the highest vote.)

Registration and Voting: Voluntary or Compulsory?

A further problem perceived in the current electoral system is that registration is voluntary but voting is compulsory. New electoral registers were opened in February 1987, when the military regime was preparing the October 1988 plebiscite, the old registers having been burned by the military in 1973. The democratic opposition mobilized strongly to get voters registered; its strategy was to defeat Pinochet at the polls in order to achieve democracy, and it succeeded in getting 92 per cent of eligible voters to register. Since then, however, the number of registered voters has not increased in line with the voting age population, as young people now show little interest in participating in elections. In the 2001 congressional elections 80 per cent of 10 million potential voters were registered; in the 2004 municipal elections the figure was 77 per cent.

Low registration among young voters led the government to propose automatic registration and voluntary voting. The Concertación parties support automatic registration, but there is no consensus on voluntary voting. They fear that overall participation will fall and that the financial costs of campaigning to mobilize voters will rise and rise, thus favouring the right-wing parties. The opposition, particularly the UDI, rejects automatic registration and supports voluntary voting.

Supporters of the binomial system claim that it has helped governability because there are two big coalitions, one in government and one in opposition. However, this view is mistaken: the Concertación as a coalition was created before the binomial system was introduced, as an alliance to work against authoritarian rule and promote a return to democracy by politicians who had learned from their past conflicts (which led to the crisis and breakdown of democracy in 1973) and had agreed on a strategy of elite cooperation within a political system somewhat comparable to a consociational democracy. The country is governable despite the binomial system, not because of it.

The system cannot last indefinitely because it damages the political parties and poses limitations to democracy, but it will be difficult to abolish because change would create uncertainty about the impact on party support. It would also require a constitutional amendment, because the binomial character of the Senate is in the constitution. There is consensus in Congress between the Concertación and the Alliance for Chile on eliminating the non-elected senators and former presidents as life members.

elected, a party must gain at least 25 per cent +1 of the vote to be assured of winning a seat. A party which has the support of only 10 per cent of the electorate would be unlikely to win a seat, and the votes of this party's supporters could therefore be said to have been wasted. In a nine-seat district, by contrast, 10 per cent +1 of the vote would guarantee that a party wins at least one seat.

The problem is that as districts are made larger—both in terms of the number of seats and often, as a consequence, in terms of their geographic size as well—so the linkage between an elected member and his or her constituency grows weaker. This can have serious consequences in societies where local factors play a strong role in politics or where voters expect their member to maintain strong links with the electorate and act as their 'delegate' in the legislature.

115. Because of this, there has been a lively debate about the best district magnitude. Most scholars agree, as a general principle, that district magnitudes of between three and seven seats tend to work quite well, and it has been suggested that odd numbers such as three, five and seven work better in practice than even numbers, particularly in a two-party system. However, this is only a rough guide, and there are many situations in which a higher number may be both desirable and necessary to ensure satisfactory representation and proportionality. In many countries, the electoral districts follow pre-existing administrative divisions, perhaps state or provincial boundaries, which means that there may be wide variations in their size. However, this approach both eliminates the need to draw additional boundaries for elections and may make it possible to relate electoral districts to existing identified and accepted communities.

116. Numbers at the high and low ends of the spectrum tend to deliver more extreme results. At one end of the spectrum, a whole country can form one electoral district, which normally means that the number of votes needed for election is extremely low and even very small parties can gain election. In Israel, for example, the whole country forms one district of 120 members, which means that election results are highly proportional, but also means that parties with only small shares of the vote can gain representation and that the link between an elected member and any geographical area is extremely weak. At the other end of the spectrum, PR systems can be applied to situations in which there is a district magnitude of only two. For example, a system of List PR is applied to two-member districts in Chile. As the case study indicates, this delivers results which are quite disproportional, because only two parties can win representation in each district. This has tended to undermine the benefits of PR in terms of representation and legitimacy.

117. These examples, from the opposite ends of the spectrum, both serve to underline the crucial importance of district magnitude in any PR electoral system. It is arguably the single most important institutional choice when designing a PR system, and is also of crucial importance for a number of non-PR systems as well. The Single Non-Transferable Vote, for example tends to deliver moderately proportional results despite not being in essence a proportional formula, precisely because it is used in multi-member districts. Similarly, the Single Transferable Vote when applied to single-member districts

becomes the Alternative Vote, which retains some of the advantages of STV but not its proportionality. In Party Block Vote and Block Vote systems, as district magnitude increases, proportionality is likely to decrease. To sum up, when designing an electoral system, district magnitude is in many ways the key factor in determining how the system will operate in practice, the strength of the link between voters and elected members, and the overall proportionality of election results.

118. On a related note, the party magnitude (the average number of successful candidates from the same party in the same electoral district) is an important factor in determining who will be elected. If only one candidate from a party is elected in a district, that candidate may well be male and a member of the majority ethnic or social groups in the district. If two or more are elected, balanced tickets may have more effect, making it likely that more women and more candidates from minorities will be successful. Larger districts (seven or more seats in size) and a relatively small number of parties will increase the party magnitude.

The Threshold

119. All electoral systems have *thresholds* of representation: that is, the minimum level of support which a party needs to gain representation. Thresholds can be legally imposed *(formal thresholds)* or exist as a mathematical property of the electoral system *(effective* or *natural thresholds)*.

120. Formal thresholds are written into the constitutional or legal provisions which define the PR system. In the mixed systems of Germany, New Zealand and Russia, for example, there is a 5 per cent threshold in the PR section: parties which fail to secure 5 per cent of the vote nationwide are ineligible to be awarded seats from the PR lists. This concept had its origins in the desire to limit the election of extremist groups in Germany, and is designed to stop very small parties from gaining representation. However, in both Germany and New Zealand there exist 'back-door' routes for a party to be entitled to seats from the lists; in the case of New Zealand a party must win at least one constituency seat, and in the case of Germany three seats, to bypass the threshold requirements. In Russia in 1995 there were no back-door routes, and almost half of the party-list votes were wasted.

Elsewhere, legal thresholds range from 0.67 per cent in the Netherlands to 10 per cent in Turkey. Parties which gain less than this percentage of the vote are excluded from the count. A striking example of this was the 2002 Turkish election, in which so many parties failed to clear the 10 per cent threshold that 46 per cent of all votes were wasted. In all these cases the existence of a formal threshold tends to increase the overall level of disproportionality, because votes for those parties which would otherwise have gained representation are wasted.

In Poland in 1993, even with a comparatively low threshold of 5 per cent for parties and 8 per cent for coalitions, over 34 per cent of the votes were cast for parties and coalitions which did not surmount it.

121. An effective, hidden or natural threshold is created as a mathematical by-product of features of electoral systems, of which district magnitude is the most important. For example, in a district with four seats under a PR system, just as any candidate with more than 20 per cent of the vote will be elected, any candidate with less than about 10 per cent (the exact figure will vary depending on the configuration of parties, candidates and votes) is unlikely to be elected.

Open, Closed and Free Lists

122. While the List PR system is based on the principle that parties or political groupings present candidates, it is possible to give voters a degree of choice within List PR between the candidates nominated as well as between the parties. There are essentially three options that can be chosen—*open, closed* and *free lists.*

123. The majority of List PR systems in the world are closed, meaning that the order of candidates elected by that list is fixed by the party itself, and voters are not able to express a preference for a particular candidate. The List PR system used in South Africa is a good example of a closed list. The ballot paper contains the party names and symbols, and a photograph of the party leader, but no names of individual candidates. Voters simply choose the party they prefer; the individual candidates elected as a result are predetermined by the parties themselves. This means that parties can include some candidates (perhaps members of minority ethnic and linguistic groups, or women) who might have difficulty getting elected otherwise.

The negative aspect of closed lists is that voters have no say in determining who the representative of their party will be. Closed lists are also unresponsive to rapid changes in events. In East Germany's pre-unification elections of 1990, the top-ranked candidate of one party was exposed as a secret-police informer only four days before the election, and immediately expelled from the party; but because lists were closed electors had no choice but to vote for him if they wanted to support his former party.

124. Many List PR systems in Western Europe use open lists, in which voters can indicate not just their favoured party but their favoured candidate within that party. In most of these systems the vote for a candidate as well as a party is optional and, because most voters plump for parties only rather than candidates, the candidate-choice option of the ballot paper often has limited effect. However, in Sweden over 25 per cent of the voters regularly choose a candidate as well as a party, and a number of individuals are elected who would not be if the list were closed.

125. In Brazil (see the case study) and Finland, voters *must* vote for candidates: the number of seats received by each party is determined by the total number of votes gained by its candidates, and the order in which the party's candidates are elected to these seats is determined by the number of individual votes they receive. While this gives voters much greater freedom over their choice of candidate, it also has some less desirable side effects. Because candidates from within the same party are effectively competing with each other for votes, this form of open list can lead to internal party

Danish open List PR ballot paper

Nicaraguan closed List PR ballot paper

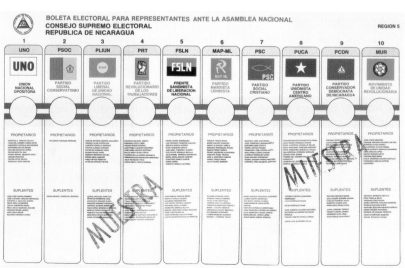

BRAZIL:
Candidate-Centred PR
in a Presidential System

José Antonio Cheibub

In 2002 Brazilians went to the polls to choose a new president, the members of the bicameral national legislature, governors for the component parts of the federation (26 states plus the Federal District of Brasília), and members of the unicameral state legislative assemblies. This was the fourth direct election since the end of the military regime in 1985 of the president and all other major legislative and executive posts.

Presidential elections in Brazil take place under a two-round majority run-off system, with candidates competing for votes throughout the country's 8,511,965 sq km area. Following a constitutional amendment approved in June 1997, presidents are now allowed to run for re-election once. Fernando Henrique Cardoso, the incumbent at the time the amendment was approved, won re-election in 1998 in the first round with 53.1 per cent of the vote. However, Luiz Inácio Lula da Silva polled 46 per cent in the first round in 2002 and was elected in the run-off round.

The rules governing legislative elections have remained essentially unchanged since they were first established in 1946. The Senate is the chamber where the regions of Brazil are represented: each of the 27 component parts of the federation is represented by three senators who are elected by plurality for an eight-year term. Membership is renewed every four years by one-third and two-thirds, in alternation: when two senators are to be elected, voters have two votes under a Block Vote (BV) system.

The Chamber of Deputies has 513 members who compete in 27 multi-member electoral districts, corresponding to the 26 states and Brasília. Their magnitude is determined by population, subject to the restriction that no state can have fewer than eight or more than 70 representatives. Elections take place under a system of open-list PR. Each voter has one vote to cast, which can be given to a political party or to an individual. Votes given to candidates from each party are pooled and added to the votes received by that party to give a total party vote, which is used to determine the number of seats to be allocated to each party. The candidates with the most votes on each party list win the seats allocated to that party. Seat allocation has been made under the D'Hondt Formula since 1950. Parties that do not gain a full quota in a district are, however, excluded from gaining a seat. Until 1998 the calculation of the quota was based on the total number of valid *and* blank votes, making the threshold for representation higher.

Deliberate Malapportionment

The rules for the Chamber of Deputies elections are probably the most controversial element of the Brazilian electoral system. The floor and the ceiling on the size of electoral districts mean that representation in the Chamber in terms of population is uneven across the states. This seriously violates the principle of 'one person, one vote, one value' (OPOVOV), as the number of votes necessary to elect one representative in São Paulo, which has over 25 million voters and 70 seats, is ten times higher than it is in Amapá, which has about 290,000 voters and eight seats. The resulting malapportionment benefits the less populous states, which tend to be poorer and more reliant on agriculture, and is disadvantageous to the larger states, which are richer and more industrialized. For this reason it has been blamed as one of the main mechanisms for reinforcing traditionalism in politics and thereby weakening political parties.

However, this needs to be qualified. The only significant loser from malapportionment is the state of São Paulo, where the number of representatives would increase by about 40 if the size of the electoral districts reflected population size strictly. Some other states are marginally under-represented, the second-biggest loss occurring in Minas Gerais (about four representatives). The losses due to malapportionment are therefore concentrated. They also reflect the goals of the makers of the 1946 constitution, who were concerned with finding a formula that would prevent São Paulo (and to a lesser extent Minas Gerais) from dominating the federation as they had done during the period known as the First Republic (1899–1930).

To the extent that malapportionment favours relatively poor states politically, it may help to promote a regional redistribution of wealth that is of no small consequence in a country with such high levels of regional inequality as Brazil.

In addition, the frequent assumption that over-represented states are capable of systematically blocking legislation of national scope remains to be proved. It is not necessarily the case that the pattern of politics that characterizes the over-represented states is any different from the one in the under-represented ones. Clientelistic practices exist in all states, and elections are mass phenomena that generate a high degree of competition. If clientelism characterizes Brazilian politics, malapportionment of the Chamber of Deputies is unlikely to be a significant cause.

Competition Between Parties—and Within Parties

One of the main features of the system of open-list PR for the Chamber of Deputies is that it induces both inter- and intra-party competition. These elections are quite competitive. For example, in 2002 a total of 4,901 candidates stood for the 513 seats in the Chamber. In only nine of the 27 districts were there fewer than 100 candidates; the lowest number was 66 for eight seats in Tocantins. There were 793 candidates for 70 seats from São Paulo, 602 for 46 seats from Rio, and 554 for 53 seats from Minas Gerais. Parties compete with each other. Candidates, seeking to be elected for the seats which their parties gain, compete among themselves for the votes their parties obtain. This is said to lead to personalism, which is considered to be at the root of the weakness of Brazil's political parties, to clientelistic ties between voters and their representatives, and to a national legislature that is primarily concerned with local rather than national, and clientelistic rather than programmatic, issues.

Again, this view needs to be qualified. First, the view that it is personalism that mainly drives voters' decisions in elections to the legislature in Brazil is far from well established. Although the proportion of preference votes (when the voter chooses a specific candidate, not simply the party) is far larger than the proportion of party votes, these figures say very little about how voters actually decide. If voters give greater relative weight to the individual than to the party, many voters who vote for a specific candidate would presumably also vote for that candidate even if he or she were to change parties. While no studies have tried to address this issue directly, scattered evidence indicates that representatives who switch parties in the middle of the legislative term are less likely to be re-elected, which suggests that they are not able to carry with them the votes that got them elected in the first place.

Voters and Their Representatives

Even less is known about the ties between voters and their representatives. A great deal of effort has been spent trying to uncover the pattern of clientelism and localized favours that must have served as the basis for a successful electoral campaign and legislative career. Successful candidates, it is said, are those who bring 'pork' to their 'constituency'. In Brazil's multi-member district system, however, the individual member is one of at least eight representing the district, which makes it difficult to establish the link between a particular member and a new spending project. Even though some candidates may and do try to carve de facto geographic constituencies for themselves, this is not the only, and may not even be the most effective, way of getting into the Chamber of Deputies. One study of the geographical distribution of the votes of successful candidates demonstrates that in 1994 and 1998 only about 17 per cent of representatives adopted such a strategy, that is, were able to obtain the largest share of votes in a cluster of geographically concentrated localities. The others adopted different strategies, such as sharing with competitors a relatively defined geographic area, dominating localities that were distant from each other, or obtaining relatively small shares of their total vote in geographically dispersed areas. Given the level of competition of elections and the lack of legally protected constituencies, it is unlikely that a representative will feel safe about his or her 'bailiwick'. Indeed, rates of re-election are not very high: estimates put it at around 60 per cent of those who seek re-election. Thus, clientelism does not characterize, at least not exclusively, the ties between representatives and voters.

Does the Electoral System Contribute to Party Fragmentation?

There is much we still need to know about the way in which the system of open-list PR with large electoral districts, such as the one that exists in Brazil, operates. We do know, however, that elections are extremely competitive, that the advantage of incumbency is relatively weak, and that deputies' relations with their electoral districts differ, so that there is no dominant strategy for a successful candidacy.

The extent in which the electoral system induces clientelism and individualism inside the Chamber of Deputies is at least questionable. While it is beyond the scope of this overview to discuss the mechanisms which the president and the party leaders may use to shape the behaviour of individual deputies, deputies face other pressures in addition to the demands of localized and particularistic constituencies. These pressures are a counterbalance to increased party fragmentation.

Party fragmentation in the Brazilian legislature has been held responsible for a number of the malaises the country has suffered from in the past 15 years. The high degree of fragmentation of the party system is usually attributed to a combination of factors, which include the electoral system and its individualistic tendencies, the characteristics of presidential systems, and the strong federalism adopted by the 1988 constitution.

The degree of fragmentation in the Chamber of Deputies has, however, remained constant, at around eight effective parties, since the 1990 election. Some aspects of the electoral law tend to favour the larger parties and work against fragmentation. Examples include the adding of blank votes to the base on which the electoral quota is calculated (which makes the quota larger and hence more difficult to achieve), and the exclusion of all parties that do not obtain one quota in a district from winning a remainder seat.

The links between presidentialism and party systems are not yet well enough understood. This leaves federalism as a possible cause of fragmentation of the party system. Some of the national parties in Brazil are de facto coalitions of regional parties. Smaller parties emerge out of these coalitions for purely local reasons, thus leading to a multiplication of parties at the national level. Whether this is the real or the only reason why new parties emerge, it remains unclear whether federalism is a cause of fragmentation or simply a reflection of the variety of regional interests that a country as large as Brazil must accommodate in order to operate democratically.

conflict and fragmentation. It also means that the potential benefits to the party of having lists which feature a diverse slate of candidates can be overturned. In open-list PR elections in Sri Lanka, for example, the attempts of major Sinhalese parties to include minority Tamil candidates in winnable positions on their party lists have been rendered ineffective because many voters deliberately voted for lower-placed Sinhalese candidates instead. In Kosovo a switch from closed to open lists actually enhanced the presence of more extremist candidates. On the same note, open lists have sometimes proved to be disadvantageous for the representation of women in highly patriarchal societies, although in Poland voters have shown themselves willing to use open list to elect more women than would have resulted from the nominations made by the parties if closed list had been used.

126. Other devices are used in a small number of jurisdictions to add additional flexibility to open-list systems. In Luxembourg and Switzerland, electors have as many votes as there are seats to be filled and can distribute them to candidates either within a single party list or across several party lists as they see fit. The capacity to vote for more than one candidate across different party lists (known as *panachage*) or to cast more than one vote for a single highly favoured candidate (known as *cumulation*) both provide an additional measure of control to the voter and are categorized here as free list systems.

Apparentement

127. High effective thresholds can serve to discriminate against small parties–indeed, in some cases this is their express purpose. But in many cases an inbuilt discrimination against smaller parties is seen as undesirable, particularly where several small parties with similar support bases 'split' their combined votes and consequently fall below the threshold, when one aligned grouping would have gained enough combined votes to win some seats in the legislature. To get around this problem, some countries which use List PR systems also allow small parties to group together for electoral purposes, thus forming a cartel—or *apparentement* or *stembusaccoord*—to contest the election. This means that the parties themselves remain as separate entities, and are listed separately on the ballot paper, but that the votes gained by each are counted as if they belonged to the entire cartel, thus increasing the chances that the combined vote total will be above the threshold and hence that they may be able to gain additional representation. This device is a feature of a number of List PR systems in continental Europe, in Latin America (where the umbrella parties are called *lema*) and in Israel. They are nevertheless a rarity within PR systems in Africa and Asia, and were abolished in Indonesia in 1999 after some small parties discovered that, although their cartel gained representation overall, they as parties actually lost seats.

Mixed Systems

128. Mixed electoral systems attempt to combine the positive attributes of both plurality/majority (or 'other') and PR electoral systems. In a mixed system there are two electoral systems using different formulae running alongside each other. The votes

are cast by the same voters and contribute to the election of representatives under both systems. One of those systems is a plurality/majority system (or occasionally an 'other' system), usually a single-member district system, and the other a List PR system. There are two forms of mixed system. When the results of the two types of election are linked, with seat allocations at the PR level being dependent on what happens in the plurality/ majority (or other) district seats and compensating for any disproportionality that arises there, the system is called a Mixed Member Proportional (MMP) system. Where the two sets of elections are detached and distinct and are not dependent on each other for seat allocations, the system is called a Parallel system. While an MMP system generally results in proportional outcomes, a Parallel system is likely to give results of which the proportionality falls somewhere between that of a plurality/majority and that of a PR system.

Mixed Member Proportional (MMP)

129. Under MMP systems, the PR seats are awarded to compensate for any disproportionality produced by the district seat results. For example, if one party wins 10 per cent of the vote nationally but no district seats, then it will be awarded enough seats from the PR lists to bring its representation up to 10 per cent of the seats in the legislature. Voters may get two separate choices, as in Germany and New Zealand. Alternatively, voters may make only one choice, with the party totals being derived from the totals for the individual district candidates.

Table 4: Countries Using MMP Systems

Country	No. of PR Seats	No. of Plurality/Majority (or Other) Seats	Plurality/Majority (or Other) System	Total No. of Seats
Albania	40 (29%)	100 (71%)	FPTP	140
Bolivia	62 (48%)	68 (52%)	FPTP	130
Germany	299 (50%)	299 (50%)	FPTP	598
Hungary	210 (54%)	176 (46%)	TRS	386
Italy	155 (25%)	475 (75%)	FPTP	630
Lesotho	40 (33%)	80 (67%)	FPTP	120
Mexico	200 (40%)	300 (60%)	FPTP	500
New Zealand	55 (46%)	65 (54%)	FPTP	120
Venezuela	65 (39%)	100 (61%)	FPTP	165

130. MMP is used in Albania, Bolivia, Germany, Hungary, Italy, Lesotho, Mexico, New Zealand and Venezuela. In all but one of these countries, the district seats are elected using FPTP. Hungary uses TRS and Italy's method is considerably more complicated: one-quarter of the seats in the lower house are reserved to compensate for wasted votes in the single-member districts.

LESOTHO:
Africa's First MMP Electoral System

Jørgen Elklit

The result of the ordinary National Assembly elections in Lesotho in May 1998 was very clear. The governing Lesotho Congress for Democracy (LCD) won an overwhelming electoral victory, taking 79 of the 80 seats in the National Assembly.

The only problem was that LCD had only received the support of slightly over 60 per cent of the electorate. The result in terms of number of seats won was yet another example of how the FPTP electoral system can lead to remarkable discrepancies between the share of the vote and the share of the seats won by political parties. A discrepancy of this kind should not come as a surprise—it had happened before—but it was followed by the losing parties, and especially the main opposition party, the Basotho National Party (BNP), crying 'Foul'. This was also nothing new, but it was a sad surprise that the accusations about the overall correctness of the 1998 election results (which were never seriously challenged), some time after they were published, incensed the public to such a degree that they started rioting in the streets of the capital, Maseru, setting fire to and demolishing public as well as private buildings.

The government called on the Southern African Development Community (SADC) to intervene, and the SADC did so, relying mainly on the armed forces of South Africa. When order was restored, an agreement was reached on 2 October 1998 (later guaranteed by the SADC) which called for the establishment of an Interim Political Authority (IPA) on which the 12 parties which had put up candidates in the elections were given two seats each, no matter how small their electoral support. The IPA's brief was to develop a new electoral system and suggest other political and administrative measures to strengthen Lesotho's peaceful democratic development. However, all recommendations would be submitted to the government, which would then take them to Parliament to be enacted in the ordinary way.

The ideas behind the establishment of the IPA were clearly inspired by the institutions of the negotiation process in South Africa during the early part of the transition process, but it was not taken into account that the two processes were so different that the institutional solutions also had to be different. The subsequent political process in Lesotho was not an easy one, and it can be no surprise that the opposition's overwhelming majority on the IPA—by 22 to 2 against the government of the day—was not conducive to a constructive climate of negotiation.

The IPA representatives, none of whom had been able to ensure a seat for themselves in the National Assembly, were eager to suggest an electoral system which would keep the single-member constituencies and at the same time provide for a much more proportional outcome at the next elections than had been the case in 1998. The obvious solution was either an MMP or a Parallel System. A German expert on electoral systems was invited to give a presentation, after which the IPA majority opted for the MMP solution, with some seats allocated in single-member districts and others allocated from party lists on a compensatory basis. The LCD—in complete control of the legislature—decided to opt for the alternative, the Parallel System, which would give it, on top of its expected massive share of the single-member district seats, an additional number reflecting its share of the votes cast for the seats not allocated in the single-member districts.

It soon transpired that the IPA was not aware of all the practical details that should be taken into consideration when deciding to go for MMP, such as the seat allocation formula, the issue of a formal electoral threshold, overhang mandates, one or two ballots, and so on. The number of seats in the two categories was also an issue, even though most IPA members seemed to agree that keeping the 80 single-member districts was a good idea and that it was only natural to have 50 compensatory seats. The basis for the latter suggestion was a little awkward: previously Lesotho had had 65 single-member districts. If it returned to that number and then added an identical number of compensatory seats (as in Germany), the National Assembly would have 130 seats altogether. However, if the size of the Assembly was to be 130, as the number of single-member districts for the time being was 80, and as it was difficult to imagine this number being changed in the immediate future, the number of compensatory seats had to be 50. The government challenged this number, among other reasons because Lesotho is a small and poor country which should only have a reasonable number of parliamentary seats.

The political conflict was easy to understand. The IPA, which was tasked with suggesting institutional solutions to the political impasse, was strongly in favour of MMP with 80 single-member districts and 50 compensatory seats, while the government—in complete control of the legislature, which had to pass all the IPA's suggestions—argued that the best solution was a Parallel system with the same 80 single-member districts and probably 40 seats to be allocated separately on the basis of (preferably) the same ballot as was used in the single-member districts, although a second ballot was also an option.

The political compromise over the electoral system took some time to reach, mainly because of the level of distrust between the two sides and some hesitation about the very idea of compromise. It was eventually agreed that the electoral system should be MMP (which was the main opposition objective), while the number of seats should be 120 (80 + 40), which was very important for the government side. While the government held all the cards through its huge parliamentary majority, it was clear that some concession had to be made in order to ensure wider acceptance and thus legitimacy of the revisions. The consequent constitutional amendment required strong support not only in the National Assembly but also in the Senate (made up mainly of chiefs), which was another reason why compromise was necessary. The reason for this was that, if the two houses of Parliament could not agree on the constitutional amendment, it had to be put to a popular referendum, and this was not really possible because of disagreement over the electoral register. Eventually, the constitutional amendment was formally adopted in May 2001. Only then could the necessary changes to the electoral law be considered.

The 1998 internationally guaranteed agreement had provided for early elections, to take place in May 2000. This was completely unrealistic, not least because the government and the opposition (the IPA) were not really on speaking terms, and a new Independent Electoral Commission had only been appointed in April. Agreement was then reached on delaying the election by a year, but further delays in reaching agreement about the electoral system, concerns about an adequate voter registration system and so on meant that a new general election was only possible in May 2002.

The election went reasonably well. The LCD, not entirely unexpectedly, won 55 per cent of the party (PR) votes but 65 per cent of all the seats. The reason for this was that the party won 77 of the 78 single-member districts contested on election day (elections in the remaining two were postponed because of the death of candidates, but eventually the LCD also won them). The system does not have overhang mandates, so the opposition got all 40 compensatory seats.

Seven of the eight opposition parties which won seats ended up being under-represented in terms of share of votes compared to share of seats. This under-representation was, however, very much smaller than it had been in 1998, and the National Assembly of Lesotho is now a fairly representative body in terms of political representativeness. Thus the main objectives of the efforts after the 1998 troubles have certainly been achieved.

It is clear that the combination of (a) one party taking almost all the single-member districts, (b) only 33 per cent of the seats being compensatory seats, and (c) the absence of surplus seats may continue to cause some degree of disproportionality in future elections as well. However, this seems a small price to pay for the various improvements in the system achieved during the protracted political compromise-seeking process of 1999–2001, when it was also a concern not to have too many members of Parliament in a small and poor country.

In Venezuela there are 100 FPTP seats while the rest are National List PR seats and extra compensatory seats. In Mexico (see the case study) 200 List PR seats compensate for imbalances in the results of the 300 FPTP seats, which are usually high. Lesotho's post-conflict electoral system contains 80 FPTP seats and 40 compensatory ones.

Mixed Member Proportional is a mixed system in which the choices expressed by the voters are used to elect representatives through two different systems—one List PR system and (usually) one plurality/majority system—where the List PR system compensates for the disproportionality in the results from the plurality/majority system.

131. Although MMP is designed to produce proportional results, it is possible that the disproportionality in the single-member district results is so great that the list seats cannot fully compensate for it. This is more likely when the PR electoral districts are defined not at national level but at regional or provincial level. A party can then win more plurality/majority seats in a region or province than its party vote in the region would entitle it to. To deal with this, proportionality can be closely approached if the size of the legislature is slightly increased: the extra seats are called overhang mandates or *Überhangsmandaten*. This has occurred in most elections in Germany and is also possible in New Zealand. In Lesotho, by contrast, the size of the legislature is fixed, and the results of the first MMP election in 2002 were not fully proportional (see the case study).

132. *Advantages and Disadvantages.* While MMP retains the proportionality benefits of PR systems, it also ensures that elected representatives are linked to geographical districts. However, where voters have two votes—one for the party and one for their local representative—it is not always understood that the vote for the local representative is less important than the party vote in determining the overall allocation of seats in the legislature. Furthermore, MMP can create two classes of legislators—one group primarily responsible and beholden to a constituency, and another from the national party list without geographical ties and beholden to the party. This may have implications for the cohesiveness of groups of elected party representatives.

133. In translating votes into seats, MMP can be as proportional an electoral system as pure List PR, and therefore shares many of the previously cited advantages and disadvantages of PR. However, one reason why MMP is sometimes seen as less preferable than straight List PR is that it can give rise to what are called 'strategic voting' anomalies. In New Zealand in 1996, in the constituency of Wellington Central, some National Party strategists urged voters not to vote for the National Party candidate because they had calculated that under MMP his election would not give the National Party another seat but simply replace an MP who would be elected from their party list. It was therefore better for the National Party to see a candidate elected from another party, providing that candidate was in sympathy with the National Party's ideas and ideology, than for votes to be 'wasted' in support of their own candidate.

MEXICO:
Democratization Through Electoral Reform

Jeffrey A. Weldon

Mexico has a presidential system with strong and independent legislative, executive and judicial branches. The doctrine of the separation of powers, which did not function in practice between 1929 and 1997, when the single official party, the Institutional Revolutionary Party (PRI), controlled both the executive and Congress, has been resurrected and is now the dominant feature of politics at the federal level.

The president is elected by plurality vote. In the 1988 and 1994 elections, the winner won about half of the votes cast, but in the 2000 election the winner, Vicente Fox, won only 42.5 per cent of the votes. Proposals exist to amend the constitution to introduce a run-off election between the two front-runners if no candidate wins an absolute majority in the first round. Their success will depend primarily on the electoral prospects of the major parties, as well as considerations of the cost of a second round.

The president is elected for a six-year term and can never be re-elected or reappointed. This prevents presidents from becoming entrenched in power, but it also diminishes their accountability because they never have to face the electorate again. Considering the ideological and symbolic roots behind the prohibition on presidential re-election (it was a focal point in the Mexican Revolution), it is unlikely that this clause will be repealed soon.

The Mexican Congress is bicameral, the Chamber of Deputies elected for three-year terms and the Senate elected for six years (synchronized with the presidential term). Both chambers are elected through mixed systems, using FPTP and List PR.

The Chamber of Deputies has 500 members, 300 elected by FPTP in single-member districts (SMDs) and 200 elected by List PR in five 40-member regional districts. The 300 FPTP seats are apportioned to the states in proportion to population, with the restriction that no state can have fewer than two seats. The Federal Electoral Institute (IFE), the independent electoral authority, uses the pure Sainte-Laguë Method to allocate seats among the states. The IFE then creates SMDs of roughly equal population within each of the states, generally favouring following municipal boundaries over achieving electoral districts with equal populations, and also divides the country into the five 40-member districts for the purpose of elections to the List PR seats. Each party nominates a candidate for each SMD and presents a rank-ordered list of 40 candidates for each of the five regional districts.

Parties may form total or partial coalitions for electoral purposes, running the same candidate in some districts or sharing PR lists. If they do they must submit agreements to the IFE specifying how the votes in the coalition are to be allocated. If parties form a coalition to elect the president, then they must form a coalition for all the Chamber of Deputies and Senate contests as well. In the 2000 election, two of the three presidential candidates were backed by coalitions. In the 2003 legislative elections, there was a partial coalition between the PRI and the Greens, which ran together in 97 single-member districts and separately in 203, and had separate PR lists (the parties had agreed on how to divide the votes from the 97 districts for the purposes of assigning seats to the List PR candidates).

Voters cast a single ballot for deputies. The sum of all of the votes from the district FPTP contests is then used to calculate the number of PR seats to be allocated to each party, using the Largest Remainder Method and the Hare Quota, and there is a 2 per cent threshold based on the total national vote included in the law. The number of PR seats assigned to a party is independent of the number of FPTP districts won, with two important exceptions: no party can ever win more than 300 seats, and no party's share of the 500 seats can be more than 8 percentage points higher than its share of the valid vote. A party must therefore win at least 42.2 per cent of the valid vote plus at least 167 districts to win 251 seats in the lower chamber. In 1997 and 2003, the PRI's share of the seats was limited by the 8 per cent rule. In 2000, the 8 per cent rule did not affect either the PRI or the National Action Party (PAN).

Seats are assigned to party list deputies in the five 40-member regional districts, also using the Hare Quota with largest remainders. The lists are rank-ordered and closed, so that the deputies higher on the list are elected first, and voters cannot modify the order of the list.

The move towards pluralism and multiparty politics in Mexico has been a slow process of evolution. Since 1979 there have been extensive reforms to the electoral formulas used to elect the Chamber of Deputies. The formula used in the 1979, 1982 and 1985 elections had 300 SMDs and 100 party list seats, which were restricted to parties that did not win more than 60 districts. The formula used in 1988 increased the number of party list seats to 200, but guaranteed that the party that won a plurality of districts would win a majority of seats, regardless of its share of the vote. A ceiling was established to the number of seats a single party could win, at 350 seats. The 1991 reforms maintained the ceiling and the majority-assuring clause, but required that the winning party win at least 30 per cent of the vote. It also created bonus seats for the winning party, so that it would not have to function with only a narrow majority in the Chamber. In return, the government ceded some control over the electoral process to a partially autonomous electoral management body (the IFE) and to a federal electoral court. The 1994 reforms eliminated the majority-assuring clause and created a Parallel system, in which the elections to the List PR seats were completely decoupled from the elections to the plurality seats. No party could win more than 60 per cent of the seats (300 of 500) in most circumstances. However, this led to the most disproportional result that Mexico has experienced under mixed systems, with the PRI winning 60 per cent of the seats with about 50 per cent of the vote. So in 1996 the electoral law was adjusted again to set the limit to the number of seats a party could win at 300 and the maximum level of over-representation, as described above, at 8 percentage points. This electoral rule has been as stable as any since multiparty representation was established in 1964, having been used in the 1997, 2000, and 2003 elections. No party has won an absolute majority of seats under this rule. The 1996 reform also made the IFE fully autonomous and enhanced the powers of the federal electoral court. Currently there are proposals to make the Chamber of Deputies either more or less proportional, decreasing or increasing the proportion of list deputies, and decreasing or eliminating the margin of over-representation. However, since no two parties have similar goals, reforms are unlikely to come about.

The Senate before 1994 had 64 members, two for each of the 31 states plus the Federal District. The senators were elected under various plurality rules. The result was that until 1988 all senators were members of the PRI. The PRI monopoly in the Senate allowed the government to make concessions to opposition, making the Chamber of Deputies more proportional.

By 1994, there were calls for the Senate to be made more widely representative as well. It was expanded to 128 members, with at least a quarter of the seats guaranteed to the opposition. For the 1997 election, a mixed system was established. Each state elects three senators, and in addition 32 are elected by PR on a single national list. In each state, a party nominates a ranked slate of two Senate candidates. Both candidates of the party that wins the most votes are elected as senators, and the first listed candidate of the party that is placed second wins the third Senate seat. Voters cannot adjust the order of the candidates. Each party also nominates a closed, ranked list of 32 candidates for the national PR list. All the votes for the Senate in each state are totalled at the national level. The formula used is a Largest Remainder Method using the Hare Quota and a 2 per cent threshold. Unlike the Chamber of Deputies, there is no linkage between the plurality and the PR seats; instead, the two systems run in parallel and the PR seats do not compensate for any disproportionality. This electoral formula would create a majority for the largest party if it wins around 40 per cent of the national vote, favourably distributed, and has a margin of three or four points over its nearest rival. Winning two-thirds of the seats in the Senate (important for constitutional reforms, electing Supreme Court justices, and internal procedural matters) requires two-thirds of the national vote. No party won an absolute majority of Senate seats in the 2000 election.

Several proposals have been submitted in Congress to eliminate the party list senators, with arguments that a national list is not appropriate for a chamber that represents the states. However, simply eliminating the PR list would benefit the PRI, which is placed either first or second in all but one of the states, and is thus likely to be opposed by other parties. Alternatives would have three or four senators per state, all elected by PR, most likely using the D'Hondt Formula.

Re-election for consecutive terms is prohibited for all federal deputies and senators (and also for governors, state legislators, mayors, and municipal councillors). Legislators can be elected to the other chamber when their term expires, and they can be re-elected to the same chamber after sitting out a term. The 'no re-election' reforms were implemented in 1932 to resolve problems in the PRI by increasing loyalty to the central committee and reducing the power of local party bosses. At the time, the reform was sold as the natural conclusion of the ideology of no re-election from the Mexican Revolution. However, it has served to reduce the autonomy of legislators, because their career prospects after their term of office depended on the party machinery, and for many years increased the power of the president because of his control over his party's machinery. Party discipline has thus been traditionally very high, approaching 100 per cent for the federal legislators of the PRI up to 2000. This has had profound effects on accountability and representation. Voters can neither reward good performance nor punish poor representation.

All the parties use relatively closed procedures to select candidates—elite designation, closed conventions, or closed or highly controlled primaries. In general, nominating procedures have been opening up in recent years, but candidates are still highly dependent on parties. Additionally, parties control most campaign expenditures, even in district and state contests, and closed lists reduce the incentive for candidates to campaign.

Mexico's slow democratization has seen frequent electoral system change as a series of concessions by the dominant party to defuse dissent, which has resulted finally in a multiparty presidential system with very strong parties. Further change may now be less likely, as different parties have different interests and any change is seen as a zero-sum game.

NEW ZEALAND: Learning to Live with Proportional Representation

Nigel S. Roberts

New Zealand used to be regarded as a prime example of a country with an FPTP electoral system. However, after two referendums in the early 1990s, New Zealand adopted a mixed member proportional (MMP) voting system in a unicameral Parliament with 120 members. Until the end of 2004, three general elections had been held using the new system.

Why did New Zealand change its electoral system? What led the country to do something that was extremely unusual for any long-established democracy, especially one with an Anglo-Saxon heritage?

For a start, the FPTP system produced highly distorted results in 1978 and 1981. On both occasions the National Party retained office with an absolute majority of the seats in the House of Representatives despite winning fewer votes throughout the country as a whole than the opposition Labour Party. In addition, both elections saw the country's then third party, Social Credit, win a sizeable share of the votes for very little return (16 per cent of the votes in 1978 and 21 per cent in 1981 won it only one seat and two seats, respectively, in a Parliament that then had 92 seats). The disquiet engendered by these results led the Labour government elected in mid-1984 to establish a Royal Commission on the Electoral System. Its 1986 report, *Towards a Better Democracy*, recommended the adoption of a voting system similar to Germany's. The commission argued strongly that, on the basis of the ten criteria it had established for judging voting systems, MMP was 'to be preferred to all other systems'.

Neither of New Zealand's major parties favoured the proposal and the matter might have died had the National Party's 1990 election manifesto not promised a referendum on the topic. In an initial referendum, held in 1992, nearly 85 per cent of voters opted 'for a change to the voting system'; 14 months later, the new electoral system was adopted after a second referendum in which 54 per cent favoured MMP (while 46 per cent voted to retain FPTP).

As in Germany, in parliamentary elections in New Zealand the electors have two votes—one for a political party (called the party vote in New Zealand) in a nationwide constituency, and one for a candidate in a single-member district. Whereas

YOU HAVE 2 VOTES

PARTY VOTE

Explanation
This vote decides the share of seats which each of the parties listed below will have in Parliament. Vote by putting a tick in the circle immediately after the party you choose.

OFFICIAL MARK

ELECTORATE VOTE

Explanation
This vote decides the candidate who will be elected Member of Parliament for the **WELLINGTON CENTRAL ELECTORATE.** Vote by putting a tick in the circle immediately before the candidate you choose.

Vote for only one party

Vote Here | Vote Here

Vote for only one candidate

Party Vote		Electorate Vote
AOTEAROA LEGALISE CANNABIS PARTY	○ ○	APPLEBY, Michael — AOTEAROA LEGALISE CANNABIS PARTY
CHRISTIAN HERITAGE PARTY	○ ○	BARTLETT, Matthew — CHRISTIAN HERITAGE PARTY
	○	CROSS, Colin — LIBERTARIANZ
ACT NEW ZEALAND	○ ○	FRANKS, Stephen — ACT NEW ZEALAND
NEW ZEALAND FIRST PARTY	○ ○	HARRIS, Rob — NEW ZEALAND FIRST PARTY
LABOUR PARTY	○ ○	HOBBS, Marian — LABOUR PARTY
GREEN PARTY	○ ○	KEDGLEY, Sue — GREEN PARTY
UNITED FUTURE	○ ○	MOODIE, Rob — UNITED FUTURE
NATIONAL PARTY	○ ○	PARATA, Hekia — NATIONAL PARTY
ALLIANCE	○ ○	REID, Robert — ALLIANCE
JIM ANDERTON'S PROGRESSIVE COALITION	○	
MANA MAORI MOVEMENT	○	
NMP	○	
ONENZ PARTY	○	
OUTDOOR RECREATION NZ	○	

Final Directions
1. If you spoil this ballot paper, return it to the officer who issued it and apply for a new ballot paper.
2. After voting, fold this ballot paper so that its contents cannot be seen and place it in the ballot box.
3. You must not take this ballot paper out of the polling place.

New Zealand MMP ballot paper

representatives for single-member districts (called electorates in New Zealand) are elected by FPTP, the overall share of the seats in Parliament allocated to political parties stems directly from and is in proportion to the number of party votes they receive. If a party wins 25 per cent of the party votes, it will be entitled to (roughly) a quarter of all the seats in the 120-member Parliament, that is, about 30 seats. If a party that is entitled to a total of 30 seats has already won 23 electorate seats, then it will be given another seven seats drawn from the rank-ordered candidates on its party list who have not already been elected in a single-member district. Likewise, if a party entitled to 30 seats has won only 11 single-member district seats, then it will acquire another 19 MPs from its party list.

There are two thresholds for MMP in New Zealand. To win a share of the seats in Parliament based on the party votes, a party must either win at least 5 per cent of all the party votes cast in a general election or win at least one single-member district seat. In the 1996 general election, five parties crossed the 5 per cent threshold and one won a single-member district seat but did not clear the 5 per cent threshold. Three years later, five parties again cleared the 5 per cent threshold. Two other parties failed to do so but won single-member district seats, which qualified one of them for an additional four seats in Parliament (it had won 4.3 per cent of the party votes cast in the election). In the 2002 general election, six parties cleared the 5 per cent party vote hurdle, and a seventh party won a single-member district seat that enabled it to bring one other person into Parliament from the party's list.

These figures point to one major change caused by the introduction of MMP. Established, at least in part, to ensure 'fairness between political parties', the new voting system has seen the index of disproportionality plummet from an average of 11 per cent for the 17 FPTP elections held between 1946 and 1993, to an average of 3 per cent for the first three MMP elections. Every FPTP election in New Zealand from 1935 until 1993 saw one of the country's two larger parties—Labour or National—gain an absolute majority in the House of Representatives. One consequence of MMP has been that, in the three elections to date, no single party has won more than half the seats in Parliament. In 1996, the largest party won 44 out of the 120 seats; in 1999 the largest party won 49 seats; and in 2002 the largest party won 52 seats.

Not surprisingly, then, New Zealand has changed from being a country accustomed to single-party majority governments to being a country governed by coalitions. After the first MMP election, two parties formed a coalition government that commanded a small majority (61 out of 120 seats) in Parliament. Since that coalition disintegrated in August 1998, New Zealand has had minority coalition governments that have had to rely on either formal or informal supporting arrangements (negotiated with other parties or, on occasion, with individual MPs) to ensure that their legislative programmes have been able to win majorities in Parliament. One of the other criteria used by the Royal Commission on the Electoral System was 'effective government'. The commission noted that electoral systems should 'allow governments ... to meet their responsibilities. Governments should have the ability to act decisively when that is appropriate'. In this regard it should be stressed that MMP governments in New Zealand have had little trouble governing: all have had their budgets passed without any real difficulty, and none has faced the likelihood of defeat in a parliamentary vote of no confidence. At the same time, New Zealand parliaments have fulfilled another of the royal commission's criteria by also becoming more effective. Governments can no longer rely on (indeed, they seldom have) majorities on parliamentary committees, and there is a far greater degree of consultation—of give and take—between government and opposition parties in MMP parliaments.

The Royal Commission on the Electoral System also envisaged that under MMP the Parliament would represent the Maori (New Zealand's indigenous Polynesian minority) and other special-interest groups such as women, Asians and Pacific Islanders more effectively. This has happened. In the last FPTP Parliament, Maori accounted for 7 per cent of the MPs. They now constitute 16 per cent of the members of the legislature. The proportion of female MPs has risen from 21 per cent in 1993 to an average of 29 per cent in the first three MMP parliaments. During the period 1993–2002, the proportion of Pacific Island MPs went up from 1 per cent to 3 per cent, and the number of Asian MPs rose from 0 to 2 per cent.

Discarding a long-established voting system is never an easy process politically, nor is it likely to appeal to entrenched interests or to most incumbent politicians. Leading electoral systems scholars have warned that major electoral reforms should not be undertaken lightly. Nevertheless, there is growing evidence that the parliamentarians of New Zealand and the public alike are learning to live with (if not necessarily love) proportional representation. The reforms adopted in New Zealand in the early 1990s and instituted in 1996 seem likely to last for a considerable time.

Parallel Systems

134. Parallel systems also use both PR and plurality/majority components, but unlike MMP systems the PR component of the system does not compensate for any disproportionality within the plurality/majority districts. (It is also possible for the non-PR component of a Parallel system to come from the family of 'other' systems, as in Taiwan.) In a Parallel system, as in MMP, each voter may receive either one ballot paper which is used to cast a vote both for a candidate and for his or her party, as is done in South Korea (the Republic of Korea), or two separate ballot papers, one for the plurality/majority seat and one for the PR seats, as is done for example in Japan, Lithuania and Thailand (see the case studies on Japan and Thailand).

> **A Parallel System is a mixed system in which the choices expressed by the voters are used to elect representatives through two different systems—one List PR system and (usually) one plurality/majority system—but where no account is taken of the seats allocated under the first system in calculating the results in the second system.**

Parallel systems are currently used in 21 countries and have been a feature of electoral system design over the last decade and a half—perhaps because they appear to combine the benefits of PR lists with those of plurality/majority (or other) representation. Armenia, Guinea (Conakry), Japan, South Korea, Pakistan, the Philippines, Russia, the Seychelles, Thailand, Timor-Leste and Ukraine use FPTP single-member districts alongside a List PR component, while Azerbaijan, Georgia, Kazakhstan, Lithuania and Tajikistan use the Two-Round System for the single-member district component of their systems.

Andorra, Senegal (see the case study) and Tunisia use the Party Block Vote to elect a number of their representatives. Monaco is the only country with a Parallel System to use BV, and similarly, Taiwan is unique in using SNTV alongside a PR system component.

135. The balance between the number of proportional seats and the number of plurality/majority seats varies greatly (see Table 5). Only in Andorra, Russia and Ukraine is there a 50 : 50 split. At one extreme, 81 per cent of South Korea's 299 seats are elected by FPTP, with only 56 members coming from PR lists. At the opposite extreme, 75 of Timor-Leste's seats are proportionally elected and only 13 are based on FPTP districts. However, in most cases the balance is much closer. For example, Japan elects just over 60 per cent of its representatives from single-member districts, with the rest coming from PR lists.

THAILAND: Combating Corruption through Electoral Reform

Allen Hicken

In 1997 Thailand adopted a new constitution which brought about sweeping changes to its political and electoral landscape. Reforms included the creation of an autonomous Electoral Commission to oversee and administer elections, new rules governing the relationship between the members of Parliament and the Cabinet, and the creation of an elected Senate—the first ever in Thailand. The constitution also replaced the Block Vote (BV) electoral system that had been in place for most of Thailand's electoral history with a Parallel system made up of FPTP and List PR elements.

Prior to the 1997 reforms Thailand used the BV system to elect the House of Representatives. The Senate was entirely appointed. The country's electoral districts were broken down into one-, two- and three-seat districts, with most districts having more than one seat. Seats were allocated by province in proportion to population. Voters cast their votes for candidates rather than parties, and were allowed to vote for as many candidates as there were seats in a district. They could not cast all their votes for a single candidate but could split their votes between candidates from different parties. They could also partially abstain by not casting all their available votes. Parties were required to field a full team of candidates for any district they wished to contest (for example, three candidates in a three-seat district). Seats were awarded to the one, two or three candidates who got the most votes on the basis of the plurality rule.

The BV system in Thailand had at least two major implications for the party system. These multi-seat districts had tended to produce multiple parties in each district, which in turn had contributed to the presence of a large number of parties in the House. The average effective number of national parties between 1975 and 1996 was more than six. Not surprisingly, no party ever commanded a majority, making large, multiparty coalition governments necessary. These coalition governments were generally indecisive and short-lived. Reformers hoped that by changing the electoral system they could bring about a reduction in the number of parties and a reduction in government inaction and instability.

Second, the system pitted candidates from the same party against one another in the same district. Although each party nominated a team of candidates, they often tended to campaign against each other rather than trying to get voters to support all of the party team with all of their votes. This intra-party competition undermined the value of party labels to candidates and voters and contributed to making the parties factionalized and incohesive. One reflection of this was the rampant party-switching prior to every election, with attendant allegations of money politics. Intra-party competition, the weakness of party labels and the relatively small districts also encouraged politicians to cultivate and respond to relatively narrow constituencies. During election campaigns vote-buying helped candidates build personal constituencies. In office politicians focused on providing 'pork' and particularistic goods and services to their constituencies, often to the neglect of broader policy concerns and thus to the coherence and consistency of government policy. The drafters of the 1997 constitution hoped that through electoral reform they could encourage the development of party cohesion and meaningful party labels, and bolster the incentives of candidates and politicians to respond to broad, national constituencies.

In 1996 the House of Representatives, responding to long-simmering demands from within civil society for political reform, organized a Constitutional Drafting Assembly (CDA). A year later, after a widespread popular consultation and in the midst of a severe economic crisis that quickly escalated into a political crisis, the CDA submitted and the House approved a new constitution. The cornerstones of this new constitution were an elected Senate and an overhauled system for electing the House of Representatives. Gone is the Block Vote system for the House. Following a growing trend, the drafters of the constitution established a Parallel electoral system in Thailand. Four hundred single-member districts replaced Thailand's multi-member districts. In these districts voters cast a single vote for their preferred candidate. The 1997 constitution also created a second tier of 100 seats elected from a single nationwide district by PR. A party must reach a threshold of at least 5 per cent of the party list votes in order to be eligible for seats in this tier. Each party is required to submit a list of candidates for voters to consider, and voters cast two votes, one for a district representative and one for a party list. Candidates must choose between running in a district and running on the party list. The two tiers are not linked: a party's seats in one tier are not in any way dependent on the number of seats it has in the other tier.

The 1997 constitution also provided for an elected Senate, the first in Thailand's history. Two hundred senators are elected using the SNTV system. The electoral districts range from one to 18 seats in size. The Thai version of SNTV also has an added twist. Constitutional reformers wanted to create a Senate that would remain above the messy partisan fray. As a result, senators are constitutionally prohibited from belonging to a political party and are not allowed to campaign for election.

What were the results of these constitutional reforms? As discussed above, one of the drafters' chief goals was to reduce the number of parties in Thailand—hence the move to single-member districts and the 5 per cent electoral threshold in the party list tier. It appears that this goal has largely been achieved. In the 2001 election for the House of Representatives, the effective number of parties in the legislature fell dramatically from an average of 6.2 before 1997 to 3.1, reflecting both a decline in the number of parties contesting each single-member district and better coordination of parties between districts. For the first time since 1957 a single party, the newly formed Thai Rak Thai party, nearly captured a majority of the seats. It later gained a majority after a smaller party disbanded and joined its ranks.

The drafters also hoped that adding a national party list tier and doing away with intra-party competition would encourage voters and candidates to focus more on party policy positions regarding national issues. This in fact began to occur in the 2001 election. For the first time in recent Thai electoral history, political parties, led chiefly by the Thai Rak Thai party, put significant effort into developing coordinated party-centred electoral strategies. Parties began to differentiate themselves in terms of their policy platforms and in some cases made those differences an important campaign issue.

However, there are reasons to be somewhat cautious in assessing the emerging changes in the Thai party system. First, the shift towards party-centred strategies was primarily confined to the campaign for party list seats, while contests in the 400 single-member districts generally remained candidate-centred affairs. This is certainly no surprise given the electoral system: single-member districts still generate incentives to cultivate personal support networks (although it appears somewhat less than under the Block Vote system). Second, the new electoral system has brought about a dramatic reduction in the average number of votes needed to win a seat. This is the combined effect of adding more seats to the legislature and switching from Block Vote to single-member districts. This weakens the incentives to abandon personal strategies: the smaller the number of votes required to be elected, the more likely it is that individual candidates will employ personal strategies. Finally, the presence of a non-partisan Senate, elected by SNTV, undermines somewhat the attempt to create a more party-oriented electorate.

Obviously, any assessment of the consequences of the 1997 reforms must still be tempered. With only limited data available, it is not possible to determine whether the outcomes of the 2001 and 2005 elections represent new trends or are a reflection of the 'one-off' personality of Prime Minister Thaksin Shinawatra, the leader of Thai Rak Thai. Nonetheless the 2001 and 2005 House elections already mark Thailand as an interesting case study of the consequences (sometimes unintended) of electoral system reform.

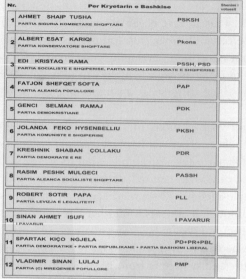

Albanian Parallel ballot paper

SENEGAL:
A Parallel System in Africa

Richard Vengroff

Senegal is one of only a handful of countries in Africa that have undergone a genuine democratic transfer of power as a result of the defeat of a sitting president. At the presidential level the electoral system is a two-round majority run-off system very similar to that used for elections for the president of France. Parties have incentives to put up candidates in the first round, and voters can freely vote for the candidate they really prefer while saving their 'strategic' vote for the second round. In 2000 the opposition parties denied President Abdou Diouf a first-round victory and, by previous agreement, united behind the leading opposition candidate, Abdoulaye Wade, to defeat the long-reigning Socialist Party (Parti Socialiste, PS) leader in the second round.

For the legislature, the electoral system was changed from a pure PR system by national list in 1978 to a mixed, Parallel system since 1983. Since then it has been modified numerous times. Most of the changes have been designed to provide for democratic legitimacy by ensuring that the system remains open to some opposition representation while maintaining the ruling party's majority of seats. Like many mixed systems, Senegal's relies on a national list for a part of the seats. Unlike most other Parallel systems, the plurality seats, rather than being decided in single-member electoral districts, are decided on the basis of Party Block Vote (PBV) in mostly multi-member electoral districts.

The PR seats (roughly half of the total) are allocated from the votes cast for the national list of each party, using a Largest Remainder Method with the Hare formula. The other seats are allocated by plurality vote in multi-member electoral districts in the 30 departments of the country, with between one and five seats each. The smaller parties and the opposition have always argued for a greater number of seats to be allocated from the national list, while the ruling party has always favoured a balance—ensuring that its domination of the plurality seats plus a proportion of the Parallel seats would enable it to retain power. For the 1998 election the ruling PS once again altered the distribution of seats, adding 20 new plurality seats. The PS won 18 of these and was easily able to maintain control of the legislature, despite the fact that it had only won a bare majority of the vote nationally (50.3 per cent).

President Wade, when he was leader of the opposition, argued for greater proportionality in the system and less reliance on the PBV seats, which heavily favour the party in power. For the 2001 elections, Wade, who had bitterly attacked the machinations by the PS, was in a position to alter this inequitable formula. Once in control of the presidency and with power to modify the electoral system, Wade could install a system designed either to be more representative of the voters' wishes or to maximize the opportunities for his coalition (the SOPI Coalition, led by the Democratic Party of Senegal (PDS)). Coupled with the greater resources now available to his party, including the full weight of the presidency, this made the highly inequitable system he had previously attacked seem suddenly attractive.

The PS and the Alliance of Forces of Progress (AFP), the only other large parties, also felt that they could profit from an emphasis on the plurality PBV side of the seat distribution by potentially winning a plurality in several districts. They too chose to argue for increased weight for the plurality side of the election. The smaller parties pushed for pure proportionality based on a national list system or some compromise that would provide greater opportunities for a better seat-to-vote distribution. The ruling PDS opted for reducing the size of the National Assembly from 140 to 120 and moving from a 70 : 70 plurality : proportional distribution to 65 plurality and 55 national list PR seats. The PDS calculated that as the new party in power it could win a plurality in many departments, thus increasing its share of seats relative to its voter support.

These calculations proved correct. Although the SOPI coalition received just under half of the votes (49.6 per cent), it won 89 of the 120 seats (74.2 per cent) in 2001. The former ruling party, the PS, finished second in terms of share of the vote, with 17.4 per cent, but garnered only ten seats, all in the proportional national list. In third place in the voting, the AFP of Moustapha Niasse (with 16.1 per cent of the vote), passed the PS in number of seats with 11, two of which it won on the plurality side by finishing first in one department. The Union for Democratic Renewal (URD), with 3.7 per cent of the vote, garnered three seats, one of which was a plurality seat in a single-member district in the small department which is the home of its leader. The African Party for Democracy and Socialism/Jef (AJ/PADS), with just over 4 per cent of the vote, won only two seats, both on the national list. Five additional parties were given one seat each on the national list by virtue of having the largest remainders, even though they did not achieve a full quota in votes. The remaining 15 parties which presented lists were excluded from the seat allocation.

The disproportionality in the 2001 election greatly exceeded even the high rates Senegal had experienced under PS rule. In the 1993 elections, 70 seats were allocated by the proportional formula on a national list and 50 in department-level districts using PBV; in 1998, seats were allocated 70 : 70 between the two electoral formulae, and disproportionality rose slightly. It rose sharply in the 2001 elections, the results of which were less proportional than the results of most elections in FPTP systems. As a consequence the legitimacy of the legislature is compromised. The SOPI coalition, which came to power in 2001 on the basis of arguments for democratic reform, has taken a major step backwards with its manipulation of the electoral system to its own advantage.

In Senegal, the objective of the then hegemonic ruling party in opting for a Parallel system was to ensure fragmentation of the opposition by discouraging coordination among parties, minimizing strategic voting and thereby providing an advantage to the largest party. The party furthered this objective by employing a ballot that offers a single choice that covers both the proportional and the plurality vote. Since the allocation of the proportional seats depends on the total number of votes a party or coalition receives, Senegal's opposition parties have an incentive to present candidates in as many plurality districts as possible. The fact that all votes cast at the district level are added together for the allocation of the proportional seats reduces any advantages of coordination between parties across constituencies, and provides incentives for sincere rather than strategic voting. Thus, the ruling party was able to ensure wins for itself in most plurality districts.

A Parallel mixed system is also used at the local (rural council) and municipal levels. To ensure an overwhelming majority for the winning party on every council, half of the seats are allocated in a single bloc for the whole municipality using the Party Block Vote. The other half of the seats are allocated by List PR using the whole rural community or municipality as one district.

Senegal illustrates the way in which short-term political advantage can be the overriding factor in debates about electoral system change. An opposition that clamoured for change became a government which defended a status quo which suddenly looked beneficial. The potential down side of this is that, if the electoral pendulum swings back to the PS, the heavier emphasis on the PBV part of the Parallel system is almost certain to ensure that this will be reflected in a more than proportional gain of seats for the opposition, leaving the forces in the SOPI coalition back where they were before 2001. Alternatively, this approach can be seen as moving towards a two-large-party system, in which the two beneficiaries ensure that any potential third political force has a huge task to break in.

Table 5: Countries Using Parallel Systems

Country	No. of PR Seats	No. of Plurality/Majority (or Other) Seats	Plurality/Majority (or Other) System	Total no. of Seats
Andorra	14 (50%)	14 (50%)	PBV	28
Armenia	56 (43%)	75 (57%)	FPTP	131
Azerbaijan	25 (20%)	100 (80%)	TRS	125
Georgia	150 (64%)	85 (36%)	TRS	235
Guinea	76 (67%)	38 (33%)	FPTP	114
Japan	180 (37.5%)	300 (62.5%)	FPTP	480
Kazakhstan	10 (13%)	67 (87%)	TRS	77
Korea, Republic of	56 (19%)	243 (81%)	FPTP	299
Lithuania	70 (50%)	71 (50%)	TRS	141
Monaco	8 (33%)	16 (67%)	BV	24
Pakistan	70 (20%)	272 (80%)	FPTP	342
Philippines	52 (20%)	208 (80%)	FPTP	260
Russia	225 (50%)	225 (50%)	FPTP	450
Senegal	55 (46%)	65 (54%)	PBV	120
Seychelles	9 (36%)	25 (74%)	FPTP	34
Taiwan	49 (22%)	176 (78%)	SNTV	225
Tajikistan	22 (35%)	41 (65%)	TRS	63
Thailand	100 (20%)	400 (80%)	FPTP	500
Timor-Leste	75 (85%)	13 (15%)	FPTP	88
Tunisia	52 (80%)	37 (20%)	PBV	189
Ukraine	225 (50%)	225 (50%)	FPTP	450

136. *Advantages.* In terms of disproportionality, Parallel systems usually give results which fall somewhere between pure plurality/majority and pure PR systems. One advantage is that, when there are enough PR seats, small minority parties which have been unsuccessful in the plurality/majority elections can still be rewarded for their votes by winning seats in the proportional allocation. In addition, a Parallel system should, in theory, fragment the party system less than a pure PR electoral system.

137. *Disadvantages.* As with MMP, it is likely that two classes of representatives will be created. Also, Parallel systems do not guarantee overall proportionality, and some parties may still be shut out of representation despite winning substantial numbers of votes. Parallel systems are also relatively complex and can leave voters confused as to the nature and operation of the electoral system.

Other Systems

138. In addition to the plurality/majority, proportional representation and mixed systems there are a number of other systems that do not fall neatly into any particular

category. Amongst these are the Single Non-Transferable Vote, the Limited Vote and the Borda Count. These systems tend to translate votes cast into seats in a way that falls somewhere between the proportionality of PR systems and the results of plurality/majority systems.

The Single Non-Transferable Vote (SNTV)

139. Under SNTV each voter casts one vote for a candidate but (unlike FPTP) there is more than one seat to be filled in each electoral district. Those candidates with the highest vote totals fill these positions.

SNTV can face political parties with a challenge. In, for example, a four-member district, a candidate with just over 20 per cent of the vote is guaranteed election. A party with 50 per cent of the vote could thus expect to win two seats in a four-member district. If each candidate polls 25 per cent, this will happen. If, however, one candidate polls 40 per cent and the other 10 per cent, the second candidate may not be elected. If the party puts up three candidates, the danger of 'vote-splitting' makes it even less likely that the party will win two seats.

> Under the Single Non-Transferable Vote system voters cast a single vote in a multi-member district. The candidates with the highest vote totals are declared elected. Voters vote for candidates rather than political parties.

Today, SNTV is used for elections to the legislative body in Afghanistan, Jordan, the Pitcairn Islands and Vanuatu, for second chamber elections in Indonesia and Thailand, and for 176 out of 225 seats in the Parallel system used for the Taiwanese legislature. However, its best-known application was for Japanese lower-house elections from 1948 to 1993.

140. *Advantages*
a. The most important difference between SNTV and the plurality/majority systems described earlier is that SNTV is better able to facilitate the representation of minority parties and independents. The larger the district magnitude (the number of seats in the constituency), the more proportional the system can become. In Jordan, SNTV has enabled a number of popular non-party pro-monarchist candidates to be elected, which is deemed to be an advantage within that embryonic party system.

b. SNTV can encourage parties to become highly organized and instruct their voters to allocate their votes to candidates in a way which maximizes a party's likely seat-winning potential. While SNTV gives voters a choice among a party's list of candidates, it is also argued that the system fragments the party system less than pure PR systems do. Over 45 years of SNTV experience, Japan demonstrated quite a robust 'one party dominant' system.

c. Finally, the system is praised for being easy to use and understand.

JAPAN: Adapting to a New Electoral System

Karen Cox

In 1993 the long-dominant Liberal Democratic Party (LDP) split and lost control of the main chamber of the Japanese Diet in the general election that followed. One of the achievements of the new coalition that formed in its place was reform of the electoral system, which had been widely viewed as a source of corruption and the basis of the LDP's long-standing dominance.

Under the old electoral system (SNTV), the 511 members of the House of Representatives (the lower house) were elected from 129 districts of between one and six seats each. This system had been in use since 1947 and had produced a distinctive approach to elections among the major parties, particularly the LDP. Under this system any party that hoped to win enough seats to obtain a majority or a significant minority of seats needed to put up multiple candidates in most districts. Thus, in order to maximize their representation, parties needed to find methods of ensuring that each candidate would poll the *minimum* number of votes required to be elected, rather than having each candidate follow his natural instincts by attempting to maximize his vote. A candidate who received more than his 'fair share' of the vote could actually hurt colleagues who received fewer votes: candidate A's 'unnecessary votes' could be enough to prevent candidate B of the same party from gaining a seat.

The LDP dealt with this problem through particularistic policies that targeted selected groups of voters and provided them with 'pork' and other benefits. As the first winning party under the SNTV system, the LDP controlled the spoils of office, making it difficult for the various opposition parties to mount an effective challenge. Not surprisingly, this system contributed to corruption. Furthermore, under such a personal and particularistic system, political choice and debate based on substantive policy issues were not given due importance.

By the early 1990s citizens' anger at the system had produced great pressure for electoral reform. The LDP's inability to agree on and pass reform legislation contributed to a split in the party that gave power to the opposition (including the LDP defectors) in 1993. The concept of a US-style two-party system and frequent alternation of parties in government had grown in popularity among politicians, scholars and the media, and had come to be seen as a 'magic bullet' that would solve the problems of the Japanese political system. As a result, many called for the establishment of a system of single-member districts (SMDs). However, members of the smaller parties in the new government feared that this would crowd them out of the system and thus opposed such a move. The resulting compromise created the two-tier system that is in use today.

The reformed electoral system is a Parallel system consisting of two tiers—List PR and FPTP single-member districts. Each voter casts one vote in each tier. For the first election under this system, in 1996, there were 200 seats in the PR tier divided between 11 regional districts, ranging in size from seven to 33 seats, and 300 SMDs in the second tier. Efforts at rationalization led the Diet to reduce the number of PR seats to 180 prior to the second election in 2000. The 11 PR districts now range in size from six to 29 seats.

In a Parallel system, there is no compensatory mechanism that adjusts the overall number of seats won by each party to better reflect the proportion of the vote actually received. The predominance of SMD seats over PR seats thus advantages larger parties that can win SMD seats. The two tiers of the Japanese electoral system are related in another, more unusual, way, however. Japan's electoral laws allow candidates to mount dual candidacies by standing both on a PR list and for an SMD seat.

While the PR tier is technically closed-list, there is also a provision that allows for some degree of voter influence over the ranking of candidates on the lists. Parties are allowed to present lists that give equal rankings to some or all of those candidates who are nominated both on a party list and for an SMD. After those who win in the SMDs are removed from consideration, the final ranking of the SMD losers on the PR list is determined by how well each polled in comparison to the winner in his or her district.

This provision has a number of benefits for parties. First, it allows them to abdicate the politically challenging job of ranking candidates. Second, it encourages candidates who are ranked equally on the PR lists to campaign more vigorously to win votes in their districts. While parties do make much use of equal ranking, they also retain the option to give some candidates firm rankings. This is also useful, as a higher or 'safe' ranking on the PR list can be used as an incentive to convince a candidate to run in a single-member district in which there is little chance of winning.

The first trial of the system came in 1996, and the results were largely seen as disappointing. In the years since the new electoral laws were passed, the LDP had re-established itself in power and the opposition parties had undergone a number of realignments. This instability led to the persistence of previous patterns, an overall win for the LDP, and little movement towards the hoped-for two-party system. The somewhat complicated nature of the system also produced dissatisfaction among the electorate, particularly regarding the phenomenon of losing SMD candidates being 'resurrected' in the PR tier. The results were especially counter-intuitive in cases in which the first- and third- (and occasionally fourth-) placed candidates from a single-member district won seats but the second-placed candidate (usually from the most competitive of the opposition parties) failed to win a place. It was also unclear that any significant decline in corruption and money politics had taken place.

By the time of the second election under the new system, in 2000, there had been a reduction in the number of competitive candidates vying for each SMD seat. However, the move towards a two-party system again made only slight progress as the non-communist opposition was still splintered and the centrist Komeito party had switched sides and joined the LDP-led coalition.

The third test of the new system took place in November 2003. In September, the small Liberal Party merged with the dominant opposition Democratic Party (DPJ). The merged party (which retained the DPJ name) gained an impressive 40 seats in an election that featured the use of party manifestos for the first time. The remaining opposition parties of significant size lost all but a few of their seats. On the government side, the LDP and the smaller of its two coalition parties also lost seats, leading to the smaller party being absorbed by the LDP. With most seats concentrated in the hands of the two leading parties, only Komeito remains as a significant small party. The LDP is still in coalition with Komeito, in part because it needs Komeito support in the upper house, but also because support from the well-organized Komeito played a large part in the victories of many of its SMD candidates.

The results of the legislative election of 2003 support the idea that the effects of electoral system reform are not felt immediately and that entrenched habits and processes require time to change. These outcomes also suggest that the mixed-member system may not be likely to produce a complete consolidation into a US-style two-party system, as the existence of the PR tier allows third parties to persist.

141. *Disadvantages*

a. Small parties whose votes are widely dispersed may not win any seats, and larger parties can receive a substantial seat bonus which turns a plurality of the vote nationally into an absolute majority in the legislature. Although the proportionality of the system can be increased by increasing the number of seats to be filled within the multi-member districts, this weakens the voter–MP relationship which is so prized by those who advocate defined geographical districts. Multi-member districts of up to 18 members in Thailand, for example, are at the very top end of what is manageable.

b. As with any system where multiple candidates of the same party are competing for one vote, internal party fragmentation and discord may be accentuated. This can serve to promote clientelistic politics where politicians offer electoral bribes to groups of defined voters.

c. Parties need to consider complex strategic questions of both nominations and vote management; putting up too many candidates can be as unproductive as putting up too few, and the need for a party to discipline its voters into spreading their votes equally across all a party's candidates is paramount.

d. As SNTV gives voters only one vote, the system contains few incentives for political parties to appeal to a broad spectrum of voters in an accommodatory manner. As long as they have a reasonable core vote, they can win seats without needing to appeal to 'outsiders'.

e. SNTV usually gives rise to many wasted votes, especially if nomination requirements are inclusive, enabling many candidates to put themselves forward.

The Limited Vote (LV)

142. Like SNTV, the Limited Vote is a plurality/majority system used in multi-member districts. Unlike SNTV, electors have more than one vote—but fewer votes than there are candidates to be elected. Counting is identical to SNTV, with the candidates with the highest vote totals winning the seats.

This system is used for various local-level elections, but its application at the national level is restricted to Gibraltar and to Spain, where it has been used to elect the Spanish upper house, the Senate, since 1977. In this case, with large multi-member districts, each voter has one vote less than the number of members to be elected.

143. *Advantages and Disadvantages.* Like SNTV, LV is simple for voters and relatively easy to count. However, it tends to produce less proportional results than SNTV. Many of the arguments relating to internal party competition, party management issues and clientelistic politics apply to LV in a similar way as to SNTV.

> Limited Vote is a candidate-centred electoral system used in multi-member districts in which electors have more than one vote, but fewer votes than there are candidates to be elected. The candidates with the highest vote totals win the seats.

Borda Count (BC)

144. A final—and unique—example of electoral system design is the modified Borda Count used in the tiny Pacific country of Nauru. The Borda Count is a preferential electoral system in which electors rank candidates as for the Alternative Vote. It can be used in both single- and multi-member districts. There is only one count, there are no eliminations and preferences are simply tallied as 'fractional votes': in the modified Borda Count devised by Nauru, a first preference is worth one, a second preference is worth half, a third preference is worth one-third and so on. These are summed and the candidate(s) with the highest total(s) are declared the winners.

Electoral System Tiers and Hybrid Systems

145. Many electoral systems, both plurality/majority and proportional, have a single tier of representation: each voter in the country votes once and there is one set of elected representatives. In one-tier List PR systems, the lists may be at national level, as in Namibia and the Netherlands, or at regional level, as in Finland and Switzerland.

In mixed systems, there are usually two tiers of representatives, those elected under the plurality/majority system and those elected under the proportional system. In Hungary, however, there are three tiers: plurality/majority representatives of single-member districts elected using TRS; and representatives at both regional and national levels elected using List PR.

It is also possible for an electoral system to have two tiers without being mixed in character. Two-tier proportional systems may have both national and regional lists (as in South Africa) or regional lists only (as in Denmark). In the two-tier plurality/majority system of the British Virgin Islands, there are representatives elected from single-member districts using FPTP and representatives elected from the Islands as a whole using Block Vote.

Table 6: Variations on Proportional Representation

	Voter Choice		
Tiers	**Closed List**	**Open List**	**Free List**
One: regional	e. g. Spain, Macedonia	e.g. Latvia, Indonesia	Switzerland, Luxembourg
One: national	e.g. Namibia, Moldova	Netherlands	-
Multiple	e.g. South Africa, El Salvador	e.g. Sweden, Iceland	-

146. Electoral systems with two or more tiers need to be distinguished from hybrid systems, in which one part of a country elects its representatives using one electoral system, and another distinct part of the country elects representatives using a different system. In Panama, about two-thirds of the representatives are elected from multi-member districts using List PR, while the remaining third are elected from single-member districts using FPTP.

147. Table 6 summarizes advantages and disadvantages of the principal electoral systems. It is important to keep in mind that the advantages and disadvantages presented here can vary from case to case and depend on a large number of factors. For example, turnout can in fact be high under an FPTP system, and a List PR system can produce strong legislative support for a president. Also, what is seen as an advantage in one context or by one party can be viewed as something negative in another context or by another party. However, the table does give an overview of some of the likely implications of the choice of electoral system. It can also give an indication of the relationship between electoral system choice and political/institutional outcome, even allowing for the effects of differences of detail within each type of electoral system.

Table 7: Five Electoral System Options: Advantages and Disadvantages

	Advantages	Disadvantages
List Proportional Representation (List PR)	• Proportionality • Inclusiveness • Minority representation • Few wasted votes • Easier for women representatives to be elected • No (or less) need to draw boundaries • No need to hold by-elections • Facilitates absentee voting • Restricts growth of single-party regions • Higher voter turnout likely	• Weak geographic representation • Accountability issues • Weaker legislative support for president more likely in presidential systems • Coalition or minority governments more likely in parliamentary systems • Much power given to political parties • Can lead to inclusion of extremist parties in legislature • Inability to throw a party out of power

	Advantages	Disadvantages
First Past The Post (FPTP)	• Strong geographic representation • Makes accountability easier to enforce • Is simple to understand • Offers voters a clear choice • Encourages a coherent opposition • Excludes extremist parties • Allows voters to choose between candidates • Strong legislative support for president more likely in presidential systems • Majority governments more likely in parliamentary systems	• Excludes minority parties • Excludes minorities • Excludes women • Many wasted votes • Often need for by-elections • Requires boundary delimitation • May lead to gerrymandering • Difficult to arrange absentee voting
Two-Round System (TRS)	• Gives voters a second chance to make a choice • Less vote-splitting than many other plurality/majority systems • Simple to understand • Strong geographic representation	• Requires boundary delimitation • Requires a costly and often administratively challenging second round • Often need for by-elections • Long time-period between election and declaration of results • Disproportionality • May fragment party systems • May be destabilizing for deeply divided societies
Parallel System	• Inclusiveness • Representation of minorities • Less party fragmentation than pure List PR • May be easier to agree on than other alternatives • Accountability • Few wasted votes	• Complicated system • Requires boundary delimitation • Often need for by-elections • Can create two classes of representatives • Strategic voting • More difficult to arrange absentee voting than with List PR • Does not guarantee overall proportionality
Mixed Member Proportional (MMP)	• Proportionality • Inclusiveness • Geographic representation • Accountability • Few wasted votes • May be easier to agree on than other alternatives	• Complicated system • Requires boundary delimitation • Often need for by-elections • Can create two classes of representatives • Strategic voting • More difficult to arrange absentee voting than with List PR

Considerations on Representation

Representation of Women

148. There are many ways to enhance the representation of women. As discussed in paragraph 107, proportional systems tend to result in the election of more women. Electoral systems which use reasonably large district magnitudes encourage parties to nominate women on the basis that balanced tickets will increase their electoral chances. Some List PR countries require that women make up a certain proportion of the candidates nominated by each party.

149. In addition to the choice of electoral system, there are also a number of other strategies that can be used to increase the number of women representatives.

a. First, there are reserved seats, where a certain number of seats are set aside for women in the legislature. These seats are filled either by representatives from regions or by political parties in direct proportion to their overall share of the national vote. Reserved seats typically exist in plurality/majority electoral systems, and are often entrenched in a country's constitution. This happens in a handful of countries, including Afghanistan (two women for each of the 32 provinces or roughly 25 per cent of seats), Uganda (one woman for each of the 56 districts, or roughly 18 per cent of seats) and Rwanda (24 women are elected by a women's-only ballot, accounting for 30 per cent of the seats). In India, seats on local authorities in some states are divided into three groups: at each election, only women may be nominated for one group of seats, thereby guaranteeing a minimum of one-third women elected, with the side effect of a two-term limit for elected men.

b. Second, the electoral law can require political parties to field a certain number of women candidates for election. This is most often done in PR electoral systems, for example in Namibia (30 per cent of candidates at the local level) and Peru (30 per cent of candidates). It is also required in the List PR component of Bolivia's MMP system (30 per cent of candidates). However, the laws do not always guarantee that the target will be met unless there are strict placement mandate and enforcement mechanisms guaranteeing that women are placed in electable positions on party lists. This is the case in Argentina (30 per cent in winnable positions), Belgium (the top two candidates must be one of each sex) and Costa Rica (40 per cent of winnable positions).

c. Third, political parties may adopt their own internal quotas for women as legislative candidates. This is the most common mechanism used to promote the participation of women in political life, and has been used with varying degrees of success all over the world: by the ANC in South Africa, the Peronist Party (PJ) and the Radical Civic Union (UCR) in Argentina, CONDEPA (the Conscience of the Fatherland) in Bolivia, the Party of the Democratic Revolution (PRD) in Mexico, and the Labour parties in Australia and the UK, and throughout Scandinavia. The use of women-only candidate short-lists by the Labour Party at the 1997 UK elections almost doubled the number of female MPs, from 60 to 119.

In 2004, 14 countries had quotas entrenched in the constitution (including most recently Afghanistan), 32 countries had quotas provided for by legislation, and at least 125 parties in 61 countries had adopted their own voluntary party quotas. In terms of electoral system type, 17 countries with plurality/majority systems have quotas, and there are 15 in mixed electoral systems and 45 in PR systems. Two of the 'others'—Afghanistan and Jordan—have quotas.

150. Systems that guarantee women representation in the legislature vary where both their success and their consequences are concerned. For example, reserved seats may help guarantee that women make it into elected positions of office, but some women have argued that quotas end up being a way to appease, and ultimately sideline, women. Being elected to a legislature does not necessarily mean being given substantive decision-making power, and in some countries women legislators, particularly those elected from reserved or special seats, are marginalized from real decision-making responsibility. Yet in other countries women have used the position afforded to them by quotas to make significant contributions to policy making and influence 'traditional' policy making.

For further details and data see the IDEA/Stockholm University Global Database of Electoral Quotas for Women at www.quotaproject.org.

Representation of Minorities

151. There are also many ways to enhance the representation of minorities and communal groups. Again, electoral systems which use reasonably large district magnitudes encourage parties to nominate candidates from minorities on the basis that balanced tickets will increase their electoral chances. A very low threshold, or the complete elimination of a formal threshold, in PR systems can also facilitate the representation of hitherto under-represented or unrepresented groups. In plurality/majority systems in particular, seats are sometimes set aside in the legislature for minorities and communal groups.

152. Reserved seats can be used to ensure the representation of specific minority groups in the legislature. Seats are reserved for identifiable ethnic or religious minorities in countries as diverse as Colombia ('black communities'), Croatia (the Hungarian, Italian, Czech, Slovak, Ruthenian, Ukrainian, German and Austrian minorities), India (the scheduled tribes and castes), Jordan (Christians and Circassians), Niger (Tuareg), New Zealand (Maori), Pakistan (non-Muslim minorities), Palestine (Christians and Samaritans), Samoa (non-indigenous minorities), Slovenia (Hungarians and Italians) and Taiwan (the aboriginal community).

Representatives from these reserved seats are usually elected in much the same manner as other representatives, but are sometimes elected only by members of the particular minority community designated in the electoral law. This requires a communal roll (see paragraphs 155–157). While it is often deemed to be a normative good to represent small communities of interest, it has been argued that it is a better strategy to design structures which give rise to a representative legislature without overt manipulation of the electoral law or legal obligation, and that quota seats may breed resentment on the part of majority populations and shore up mistrust between various cultural groups.

153. Instead of formally reserved seats, regions can be over-represented to facilitate the increased representation of geographically concentrated groups. In the UK, Scotland and Wales have more MPs in the British House of Commons than they would be entitled to if population size alone were the only criterion. The same is true in the mountainous regions of Nepal. Another possibility is the 'best loser' system currently used in Mauritius, whereby some of the highest-polling losing candidates from a particular ethnic group are awarded seats in the legislature in order to balance overall ethnic representation.

154. Electoral boundaries can also be manipulated to promote the representation of particular groups. The Voting Rights Act in the United States has in the past allowed the government to draw weirdly shaped districts with the sole purpose of creating majority Black, Latino or Asian-American districts; this might be called 'affirmative gerrymandering'. However, the manipulation of any electoral system to promote or protect minority representation is rarely uncontroversial.

Communal Representation

155. A number of ethnically heterogeneous societies have taken the concept of reserved seats to its logical extension. Not only are seats divided on a communal basis, but the entire system of representation in the legislature is similarly based on communal considerations. There is a separate electoral register for each defined community, which elects only members of its 'own group' to the legislature.

In Lebanon, multi-member districts are defined, in each of which an allocation of seats between confessional groups is determined. Representatives are elected by Block Vote from communal rolls separately to the seats allocated for each confessional group. In Fiji, electors are able to vote both for their own communal candidates and for candidates in 'open' districts.

156. Most communal roll arrangements were abandoned after it became clear that communal electorates, while guaranteeing group representation, often had the perverse effect of undermining the path of accommodation between different groups, since there were no incentives for political intermixing between communities. The tasks of defining a member of a particular group and distributing seats fairly between them were also full of pitfalls. In India, for example, the separate districts which had existed under colonial rule for Muslims, Christians, Sikhs and others were abolished at independence, although some reserved seats remain in order to represent the scheduled tribes and castes (see the case study). Similar communal roll systems used at various times in Pakistan, Cyprus and Zimbabwe have also been abandoned. Despite a controversial history of use, Fiji continues to elect part of its legislature from separate communal rolls for indigenous Fijian, Indian, Rotuman and 'general' electors.

157. While some communal roll arrangements give the task of determining who falls into which category to some form of registration body, others give this choice to the individual. The predominant example of a communal roll system still in place among contemporary democracies is the optional separate roll for Maori voters in New Zealand. Maori electors can choose to be on either the national electoral roll or a specific Maori roll, which now elects seven Maori representatives to the legislature. The results of New Zealand's first PR elections since 1996 could, however, be said to have weakened the rationale for the communal system: twice as many Maori representatives have been elected from the general rolls as from the specific Maori roll.

The Timing of Elections

158. Elections, whether they be for national, executive, legislative, state-wide or local bodies, may not necessarily be held on a single day (or specific days) but can instead be staggered. The reasons for separating elections over a significant period of time can be both practical and political. Staggering of elections usually occurs when there are major logistical preparations involved (e.g. elections to the lower house of India, the Lok Sabha) or when security concerns require it. Administrative and security considerations mean that it is far easier for the Indian Electoral Commission to sequence the holding of legislative votes across both time and states. Legislative elections from state to state can be weeks apart. The difficulties facing staggered elections include ballot security. In order for areas voting later not to be influenced by areas voting earlier, ballot papers need to be held at a secure centralized point until all voting has taken place.

159. More common is the staggering over time of presidential, legislative and federal state elections. There is evidence to suggest that holding presidential and legislative elections on the same day can advantage the president's party, and can make executive-legislative fragmentation less likely and thus make government more coherent—especially in embryonic democracies. However, if there is a desire to accentuate a separation of powers or there are logistical capabilities to consider then it may be necessary to separate presidential and legislative elections.

Remote Voting

160. Remote voting is used in many countries, both old and new democracies, around the world, to broaden participation. Remote voting may take place in person somewhere other than an allotted polling station or at another time, or votes may be sent by post or cast by an appointed proxy. When the requirements to qualify as a remote voter are minimal, remote voting can make up a significant proportion of the total vote. In Finland it has been as high as 37 per cent of all votes cast and in the 2003 legislative elections in the Marshall Islands it was 58 per cent. In Sweden, where it is commonly about 30 per cent, voters can also change their pre-cast vote if they subsequently travel to their allocated polling station on election day. However, its use may have implications for electoral system design, with issues of election integrity being salient.

161. Remote voting is easiest to administer under a nationwide List PR system with only one list per party, and most complicated under a system using single-member districts. Particularly if out-of-country voting is to be implemented, the practicalities of getting the right ballot paper to each elector need to be considered carefully. Requiring a country's embassies to issue ballot papers may not sit easily with a system with a significant number of electoral districts, because of the logistic challenge of ensuring that each embassy receives the right selection of ballot papers and gives the right ballot paper to each elector. If ballot papers are to be despatched by post, there will be an impact on the election timetable.

162. Once cast, out-of-country votes can be included in the absentee voter's home district (as in New Zealand); counted within single (or multiple) out-of-country districts (as in Croatia); attached to one or more particular districts (as in Indonesia); or merely added to the national vote totals when seats are allocated under a nationally-based List PR system (as in the Netherlands).

Turnout Issues

163. There is an established relationship between the level of turnout in elections and the electoral system chosen. PR systems are in general linked with higher turnout. In plurality/majority systems, turnout tends to be higher when national election results are expected to be close than when one party looks certain to win, and also higher in individual districts where results are expected to be closer.

164. As a measure to improve electoral legitimacy, some countries, notably several of the post-communist former republics of the USSR, introduced mandatory minimum turnout levels: if the turnout in an electoral district did not reach, for example, 50 per cent, the election would not be valid. However, the use of mandatory turnout levels can create administrative nightmares if repeated elections consistently fail to achieve the required turnout levels, leaving electoral districts in limbo. Ukraine, for example, abolished mandatory turnout provisions for the 1998 elections after the experience of repeated by-elections failing to reach the required turnout.

165. Several countries address the issue of participation by using compulsory voting, including Australia, Belgium, Greece and many countries in Latin America. Many other countries, however, reject compulsory voting on principle. While it is probably equally compatible with any electoral system, its use can be considered simultaneously with other turnout-related issues.

Additional Issues Relevant to Post-conflict and Transitional Elections

166. In post-conflict and transitional situations, there is often little time for debate and reflection. The political momentum generated by a peace agreement or by the fall of an authoritarian regime can lead to pressures for elections to take place quickly. While a general discussion of the political desirability and constraints surrounding transitional elections is outside the scope of this Handbook, there are some particular issues and pressures which relate to electoral system design.

167. The time needed to set up the infrastructure for different electoral systems varies. For example, electoral registration and boundary delimitation are both time-consuming exercises which can lead to legitimacy problems. At one extreme, if all voters vote in person and voters are marked at the polling station, List PR with one national district may be feasible without either. At the other extreme, a plurality/majority system with single-member districts may require both if no acceptable framework is in place. In any event, the system adopted for a first transitional election may not be the most suitable in the longer term—although a process of continual change in which voters and parties are never able to adapt to the effects of the system may also be undesirable.

168. Those negotiating a new institutional framework or electoral law may wish to be as inclusive as possible and therefore be impelled to make entry to elections easy both by setting relaxed criteria for nomination and by adopting an electoral system in which any threshold—either formal or effective—is low. Conversely, there are often concerns about the fragmentation of the party system driven by the politics of personality and ethnicity, and the negotiators and designers may thus want to set the bar for representation higher. The flowering of a multiplicity of parties is, however, a feature of elections in countries emerging from authoritarianism, and unsuccessful parties usually disappear of their own accord.

169. Arguments are sometimes offered suggesting that, when building democracy in a fragile or divided political environment, it may be politically desirable to start with local elections and build over time to provincial and national elections as the infrastructure and political situation allow—as has been proposed in Sudan. If such a strategy is chosen, it is important that the system is both designed to meet the political requirements of the local elections and feasible to organize given the timetable.

170. Provisions for voting by refugees and displaced persons may be particularly significant in post-conflict elections. The influence and importance of out-of-country voting is well illustrated by Bosnia and Herzegovina. 314,000 voters, out of a total of some 2 million, were registered to vote outside the country's borders in 1998, over half of them in Croatia and the former Federal Republic of Yugoslavia (now Serbia and Montenegro), the remainder in 51 other countries. Of these 66 per cent cast valid ballots.

CHAPTER 4

CHAPTER 4

4. Electoral Systems, Institutional Frameworks and Governance

171. ELECTORAL SYSTEMS HAVE LONG BEEN CONSIDERED TO HAVE SPECIFIC EFFECTS ON issues of governance, policy making and political stability. Different electoral systems have marked implications for governance in parliamentary systems. In particular, there is an inbuilt tension between electoral systems which maximize the potential for one-party government (e.g. plurality/majority systems) and those which make multiparty coalitions more likely (e.g. proportional systems). Both constellations have clear policy impacts: single-party government makes decisive policy making and clarity of responsibility much easier, while coalitions are more likely to produce more representative policies and more inclusive decision making. Similarly, major shifts in government policy are easier to achieve under single-party government, while coalitions are more likely to see issues discussed and debated before any changes are made.

172. Almost all countries which have a presidential or semi-presidential constitution elect the president directly. In addition, some republics which have parliamentary constitutions nevertheless elect their head of state directly.

In presidential systems, the extent to which an elected president can claim a popular mandate and legitimacy depends significantly on the means by which he or she is elected. Presidents who have clear majority support are likely to have much greater legitimacy and be in a stronger position to push their own policy agenda than those elected on a small plurality of the vote. This has an important impact on relations between the president and the legislature. A president elected by a clear absolute majority of the population can command a great deal of legitimacy in any conflict with the legislature. By contrast, Salvador Allende's election in Chile in 1970 on 36 per cent of the vote, and opposed by a right-wing Congress, helped create the conditions for the 1973 military coup.

173. The relationship between the legislature and the executive differs between parliamentary, semi-presidential and presidential systems. In a presidential or semi-

presidential system, the president's position does not depend on maintaining the confidence of the legislature: such a president cannot be removed from office on purely policy grounds. However, experience in Latin America in particular indicates that a directly elected president without a substantial block of support in the legislature will find successful government difficult.

In presidential and semi-presidential democracies, the electoral systems for the presidency and the legislature therefore need to be considered together, although the different roles of the president and the legislature bring different factors into play in making the two choices of system. The synchronization or otherwise of the elections and the provisions which may encourage or discourage fragmentation of parties and the relationship between parties and elected members should be considered at the same time.

Electing a President

174. In principle, any of the single-member district systems can be used for the direct election of a president. When a president is to be elected as the executive head of state, there is often a strong normative and practical preference for systems which ensure a victory by an absolute majority. The majority of all countries that have direct presidential elections use a Two-Round system.

175. The separation of the two rounds leads to efforts by the leading candidates to attract second-round support and endorsement from those eliminated after the first round. Such agreements are sometimes driven primarily by the desire for victory. They are thus perhaps less likely to reflect compatibility of policies and programmes than are pre-poll preference-swapping agreements reached between candidates in preferential systems with a single polling day. In addition, presidential elections held under TRS increase the cost of elections and the resources needed to run them, and the drop-off in turnout between the first and second rounds of voting can often be severe and damaging. For this reason, other options such as the Alternative Vote and the Supplementary Vote are increasingly being examined.

First Past The Post

176. The most straightforward way of electing a president is to simply award the office to the candidate who wins a plurality of the votes, even if this is less than an absolute majority. This is the case for presidential elections in Bosnia and Herzegovina, Cameroon, the Comoros Islands, Equatorial Guinea, Guyana, Honduras, Iceland, Kiribati, South Korea, Malawi, Mexico, Palestine, Panama, Paraguay, the Philippines, Rwanda, Singapore, Taiwan, Tunisia, Venezuela and Zambia. Clearly, such a system is simple, cheap and efficient, but in a strongly competitive multi-candidate contest it leaves open the possibility that the president will be elected with so few votes that he or she is not seen as the choice of a substantial majority of the electorate—and indeed may specifically be opposed by a substantial majority: the majority voted against him

لجنـــة الإنتخابات المركزية

انتخابات رئيس السلطة الوطنية الفلسطينية

١٩٩٦/١/٢٠

لا تقترع لصالح أكثر من مرشح واحد (ضع إشارة X بجانب المرشح الذي تختار)

إسم المرشح	الرقم	X
محمد ياسر عبد الرؤوف عرفات (أبو عمار)	١	
سميحة يوسف مصطفى القبج خليل (أم خليل)	٢	

Palestinian FPTP presidential ballot paper

BALLOT PAPER No. 000000

PRESIDENTIAL ELECTION, 1992

In the .... NORTH MUGIRANGO BORABU .... Constituency

Candidate's Name	Party Symbol	Voter's Mark
GEORGE ANYONA MOSETI		
DR. ANDERSON CHIBULE WA TSUMA		
DAVID MUKARU NG'ANG'A		
AJUMA OGINGA ODINGA		
KENNETH STANLEY NJINDO MATIBA		
DANIEL TOROITICH ARAP MOI		
MWAI KIBAKI		
JOHN HARON MWAU		

Constituency .... **NORTH MUGIRANGO BORABU**

Constituency No. **188**

Elector's Serial No.
in register
....

INSTRUCTIONS TO VOTER

1. Mark the paper by placing the mark X in the right-hand column above opposite the name of the candidate you wish to elect.
2. Do NOT place a mark opposite more than one candidate.

Kenyan FPTP presidential ballot paper

or her. Examples include Venezuela in 1993, when Rafael Caldera won the presidency with 30.5 per cent of the popular vote, and the May 1992 election in the Philippines, when Fidel Ramos was elected from a seven-candidate field with only 24 per cent of the popular vote. Taiwan experienced a major political shift in 2000 when the challenger Chen Shuibian won the presidency with just 39 per cent of the vote, less than 3 per cent ahead of the next candidate.

177. The United States is unique in conducting its national presidential election by FPTP at federal state level. The FPTP winner in each federal state gains all the votes of that state in an electoral college, with two exceptions, Maine and Nebraska, where the votes of the state are allocated two to the FPTP winner state-wide, and one to the FPTP winner of each individual congressional district in the state. The electoral college then elects the president by absolute majority. This can lead to a situation in which the winning candidate polls fewer votes than the runner-up—as in 2000 when the Republican candidate George W. Bush won despite polling some half a million fewer votes than the Democrat candidate, Al Gore.

Two-Round Systems

178. As in legislative elections, one way to avoid candidates being elected with only a small proportion of the popular vote is to hold a second ballot if no one candidate wins an absolute majority on the first round. This can either be between the top two candidates (majority run-off) or between more than two candidates (majority-plurality), as described above (see paragraph 96). France, most Latin American countries, all the five post-Soviet Central Asian republics, and many countries in francophone Africa use TRS to elect their presidents. Elsewhere in Africa the system is used by Angola, Cape Verde, Gambia, Ghana, Guinea-Bissau, Kenya, Mozambique, Namibia, Nigeria, São Tomé and Principe, the Seychelles, Sierra Leone, Sudan, Tanzania, Uganda and Zimbabwe; in Europe, apart from France, it is used by Armenia, Azerbaijan, Austria, Belarus, Bulgaria, Croatia, Cyprus, Finland, Georgia, Lithuania, Macedonia, Poland, Portugal, Romania, Russia, Slovakia, Slovenia and Ukraine; and it is found in Afghanistan, Haiti, Indonesia, Iran, Timor-Leste and Yemen.

179. There are a number of adaptations to straight majority run-off and majority-plurality rules. In Costa Rica a candidate can win on the first round with only 40 per cent of the vote; conversely, in Sierra Leone a second round is only avoided if one candidate gets 55 per cent in the first. In Argentina, a successful candidate must poll 45 per cent, or 40 per cent plus a lead of more than 10 per cent over the second-placed candidate. A similar 40 per cent threshold with a 10 per cent margin exists in Ecuador.

180. A number of countries also have minimum turnout rates for their presidential elections, typically 50 per cent, as is the case in Russia and many of the former Soviet republics; this is an additional mechanism for ensuring the legitimacy of the result.

Afghan TRS presidential ballot paper

134

181. Apart from those countries where parties could create winning pre-election alliances so that presidential candidates could be elected in the first round (e.g. in Brazil in 1994 and Chile in 1989 and 1994), the experience of TRS has appeared problematic in Latin America. For example, in the 1990 elections in Peru, Alberto Fujimori obtained 56 per cent of the votes in the second round, but his party won only 14 of 60 seats in the Senate and 33 seats of 180 in the Chamber of Deputies. In Brazil in 1989, Fernando Collor de Melo was elected in the second round with just under half of the votes, but his party won, in non-concurrent legislative elections, only three of the 75 Senate seats and only 40 of 503 seats in the Chamber of Deputies. No president in Ecuador has had majority support in the legislature since TRS was introduced for presidential elections in 1978.

The problems of governance which have resulted demonstrate the importance of considering interlinked institutional provisions together. Although TRS produced presidents who had the second-round support of a majority of the electorate, it existed alongside systems for election to the legislature which did not guarantee those presidents significant legislative support. In Brazil in particular it encouraged party fragmentation. While the successful candidates gathered the support of other parties between the first and second rounds, there was little to enable them to keep that support in place after the elections.

Preferential Voting

182. One way of getting around the disadvantages of TRS is to merge the first and second round into one election. There are several ways of doing this. AV is one obvious solution; it is used to elect the president of the Republic of Ireland. A lower-placed candidate who picks up many second-preference votes can overtake higher-placed candidates. The most recent example of a president winning through the transfer of preferences in this manner was the 1990 election of Mary Robinson to the Irish presidency.

183. A second possibility is the preferential system used for presidential elections in Sri Lanka and for London mayoral elections, known as the Supplementary Vote. Voters are asked to mark not only their first-choice candidate but also their second (and, in Sri Lanka, their third) choices. The way in which this is done differs: in Sri Lanka, voters are asked to place the numbers '1', '2' and '3' next to the names of the candidates, in the same manner as under AV and STV. In London, no numbers are required; the ballot paper contains two columns, for a first-choice vote and a second-choice vote, respectively. Voters are asked to mark their first-choice and second-choice candidates accordingly. This means that voters do not have to write in any numbers themselves.

184. Counting is the same in both cases: if a candidate gains an absolute majority of first-preference votes, he or she is immediately declared elected. However, if no candidate gains an absolute majority, all candidates other than the top two are eliminated and their second- (or, in Sri Lanka, second- and third-) choice votes are passed on to one or

ජනාධිපතිවරණය 1994 சனாதிபதித் தேர்தல் 1994 Presidential Election 1994	චන්ද්‍රිකා බණ්ඩාරනායක කුමාරතුංග சந்திரிகா பண்டாரநாயக குமாரதுங்க **Chandrika Bandaranaike Kumaratunga**		
—— උප පත්‍රිකාව அடிப்பிதழ் **Counterfoil**	ගලප්පත්ති ආරච්චිගේ නිහාල් கலப்பத்தி ஆரச்சிகே நிஹால் **Galappaththi Arachchige Nihal**		
	ගාමිණී දිසානායක காமினி திசாநாயக **Gamini Dissanayake**		
අංකය இல. } **CM** No.	ඒ. ජේ. රණසිංහ ஏ. ஜே. ரணசிங்க **A. J. Ranasinghe**		
	හරිශ්චන්ද්‍ර විජයතුංග ஹரிஸ்சந்திர விஜயதுங்க **Harischandra Wijayatunga**		
රජුදයකයාගේ අංකය வாக்காளரின் இல. **No. of Voter**	හඩ්සන් සමරසිංහ ஹட்சன் சமரசிங்க **Hudson Samarasinghe**		
B 034001-අ. මු. 94-රජයේ මුද්‍රණය CM/1	B 034001-අ. මු. 94-රජයේ මුද්‍රණය CM/1		

Sri Lankan preferential presidential ballot paper

the other of the two leading candidates, according to the preference ordering marked. Whoever achieves the highest number of votes at the end of this process is declared elected. This system thus achieves in one election what TRS achieves in two, with significant cost savings and greater administrative efficiency.

185. The disadvantages of the Supplementary Vote system include its additional complexity and the fact that voters are effectively required to guess who the top two candidates will be in order to make full use of their vote.

186. Despite these differences, both AV and the Supplementary Vote have the same core aim: to make sure that whoever wins the election will have the support of an absolute majority of the electorate. The use of preference votes to express a second choice means that a second round of voting is not required, and this results in significant cost savings as well as benefits in administrative, logistics and security terms.

Distribution Requirements

187. Three countries—Indonesia, Kenya and Nigeria—combine their presidential elections with a so-called 'distribution requirement', which requires candidates to gain a regional spread of votes, in addition to an absolute majority, before they can be declared duly elected. In Indonesia, which held its first direct presidential elections in 2004, a successful presidential and vice-presidential candidate team needed to gain an absolute majority of the national vote and at least 20 per cent of the vote in over half of all provinces to avoid a second round of voting. This requirement was inspired by Nigeria, another large and regionally diverse country, where presidential candidates need not only to win an absolute majority of the vote nationally but also to secure at least one-third of the vote in at least two-thirds of the country's provinces.

188. Distribution requirements do have the benefit of encouraging presidential candidates to make appeals outside their own regional or ethnic base, and if appropriately applied can work very well. However, the specification of two requirements for victory always carries the possibility that no candidate will fulfil both. It is important that designers note this possibility and include provisions to resolve it, because a system which produces no winner and no method of finding a winner could create a vacuum of power fraught with the dangers of instability.

The second round in Indonesia merely requires a simple majority for the winner to be declared elected, but Nigeria retains the distribution requirement for the second round too, which creates the possibility of a third round. If this were to take place in practice it could have implications both for the length of the election period and for the financial and administrative resources required.

Distribution requirements introduce strategic imperatives for candidates. In Kenya, to be elected president a candidate has to receive a plurality overall and at least 25 per cent of the vote in at least five out of the eight provinces. Even so, throughout the 1990s a divided opposition allowed Daniel Arap Moi to remain president with less than an absolute majority of the vote.

Electing an Upper House

189. Not all legislatures consist only of one chamber; particularly in larger countries, many are bicameral. Most second chambers (often called upper houses or senates) exist for one or both of two reasons. The first is to provide a different type of representation or represent different interests, most often the regions or provinces of a country. The second is to act as a 'house of review', to provide a brake or delay against impetuous decisions in a lower chamber. The powers of upper houses are often less than those of lower chambers, especially when they are chambers of review. Around the world, about two-thirds of all countries have unicameral legislatures, while the remaining one-third have some kind of second chamber.

190. The structures of these vary widely, but in general the most common use of second chambers is in federal systems to represent the constituent units of the federation. For example, the states in the USA and Australia, the Länder in Germany and the provinces in South Africa are all separately represented in an upper house. Typically, this involves a weighting in favour of the smaller states or provinces, as there tends to be an assumption of equality of representation between them. In addition, many second chambers feature staggered elections: half the chamber is elected every three years in Australia and Japan; one-third of the chamber is elected every second year in the USA and India, and so on.

191. Some countries whose upper houses are 'houses of review' place special restrictions on them. In Thailand, for example, the Senate is now elected, but senators are prohibited from belonging to a political party or campaigning for election.

192. A less common type of alternative representation is the deliberate use of the second chamber to represent particular ethnic, linguistic, religious or cultural groups. A second chamber may also deliberately contain representatives of civil society. In Malawi, for instance, the constitution provides for 32 of the 80 senators to be chosen by elected senators from a list of candidates nominated by social 'interest groups'. These groups are identified as women's organizations, the disabled, health and education groups, the business and farming sectors, the trade unions, eminent members of society and religious leaders. The much-maligned British House of Lords is occasionally defended on the grounds that it contains individuals with specific policy expertise who can check government legislation drawn up by generalist politicians. Similarly, second chambers in countries like Fiji and Botswana are used to represent traditional chiefs, although these are appointed in the first case and elected in the second.

193. Because of these variations, many second chambers are partly elected, indirectly elected or unelected. Of those that are elected, most jurisdictions have chosen to reflect the different roles of the two houses by using different electoral systems for the upper

house and the lower house. In Australia, for example, the lower house is elected by a majoritarian system (AV) while the upper house, which represents the various states, is elected using a proportional system (STV). This has meant that minority interests which would normally not be able to win election to the lower house still have a chance of gaining election, in the context of state representation, in the upper house. In Indonesia, the lower house is elected by List PR, while the upper house uses SNTV to elect four representatives from each province. In Colombia, while both houses are elected by PR, the Senate is elected from one nationwide district, thus making it more likely that small parties and minority interests will be represented in that chamber.

Different Tiers of Governance

194. As noted above, the requirements for designing an electoral system vary depending on the type of body to be elected and its function and powers. When a body is designed to serve supranational, provincial or local interests, the considerations involved in the choice of system are different from those involved when designing national legislative bodies.

Electing Supranational Bodies

195. Supranational bodies with significant decision-making power encompassing a number of countries, such as the European Parliament, are as yet a rarity but may become more commonplace with the globalization of politics and the aggregation of interests at a regional level. The EU has adopted, and now made effective, a requirement for all member states to adopt a proportional system for elections to the European Parliament: 23 member states use List PR, and two (the Republic of Ireland and Malta) use STV. Seats are allocated to member states not purely in proportion to population but by a tiered system which gives equal numbers of representatives to countries of approximately equal size but also over-represents smaller countries.

196. The designers of such systems give greater priority to choosing systems which produce regional and partisan balance than to localized geographical representation. The European Parliament has 732 MEPs (Members of the European Parliament) representing over 500 million people, which makes small district connections between voter and representative impossible.

197. While the European Parliament is a supranational body, it has not yet achieved a separate electoral identity in the minds of voters, even though citizens of one member state are also allowed to be a candidate in another member state. Elections to it are seen for the most part as contests between the national political parties in each member state. It is probably generally true that existing national political parties will play a major role in the development of supranational electoral systems and that dominant regional traditions at national level (in the case of the European Parliament, PR) may dominate at supranational level also.

THE EUROPEAN PARLIAMENT:
Elections to
a Supranational Body

Andrew Ellis and Stina Larserud

In June 2004 the citizens of 25 European countries went to the polls to elect their representatives to the European Parliament. Many were doing so for the first time, while others were in countries with experience of up to five previous elections to the Parliament. In 2004, all were conducting their elections under a proportional electoral system.

The first piece of legislation covering elections to the European Parliament came in 1976, when the Act Concerning the Election of the Representatives of the Assembly by Direct Universal Suffrage was agreed. As the name implies, this act determined the principles for direct elections of the representatives from each member state. In the early days of the EU, the members of the European Parliament were nominated by the legislature in each member state, with no direct input from the electorate. The passing of the 1976 act meant that from then on the members would be elected by direct universal suffrage in each member state; and in 1979 the first European Parliament elections were held in the then nine member states—Belgium, Denmark, France, the Federal Republic of Germany, Italy, Luxembourg, the Netherlands, the Republic of Ireland and the United Kingdom—resulting in a total of 410 elected members.

The act of 1976 determined many things regarding the elections, such as the length of the parliamentary term and the eligibility of candidates, but did not in itself determine the actual electoral system to be used in these elections. It did, however, give the European Parliament the task of drawing up a proposal for a uniform electoral procedure. Until such a procedure came into force, the act left the electoral procedures to the national provisions of the member states.

As most member states at the time were using a PR system of one form or another to elect their legislatures, either alone or as one component of the electoral system, the choice of which electoral system to use for the European Parliament was a simple one. Belgium, Denmark, the Federal Republic of Germany, Italy, Luxembourg and the Netherlands were already familiar with the List PR system in one form or another, and all their representatives were therefore elected under a List PR system (except for the one representative of Greenland, included within the representation of Denmark, who was elected by FPTP until Greenland left the European Community in 1985). The Republic of Ireland chose to elect its representatives using its preferential STV system. There were only two exceptions: the UK with its FPTP electoral system and France with its Two-Round system for national elections were both unfamiliar with the PR system.

The UK simply copied the electoral system used for the elections to the House of Commons and applied it to the European Parliament elections as well. This system suited the two largest parties, Labour and the Conservatives, very well, and made it difficult for any third party to enter the arena. Resistance against a representative holding a dual mandate also contributed to the adoption of FPTP for European Parliament elections in the UK. If serving in both the European Parliament and the British Parliament simultaneously were to be prohibited, as some British politicians wanted, and some form of PR were also to be adopted, party lists would be likely to be made up of unknown candidates not elected to any other national or local body, which would carry the risk of undermining the perceived importance of the elections. A candidate-centred, single-member district system, where candidates would be closer to their electorate, was thought to be a better solution.

None of this thinking applied to Northern Ireland. Concern to ensure the representation of majority and minority communities, combined with the fact that the parties of England, Scotland and Wales do not normally contest elections there, resulted in the use of STV for Northern Ireland's three seats. An attempt was made to challenge in the courts the use of FPTP for European Parliament elections in England, Scotland and Wales on the basis of the requirement contained in the act for a uniform electoral procedure to be proposed, but this was unsuccessful. The system used in England, Scotland and Wales only changed in 1999 when the European Parliamentary Elections Act was passed, as the UK anticipated the changes that would be forced on it as the process which led to the 2002 Council decision (see below) got under way. From 1999 onwards, the UK joined the other member states in the use of a PR system, choosing List PR with closed lists and regional electoral districts.

In France—despite its using TRS for the elections to the national legislature—a closed List PR system with one national district was adopted as early as 1977, before the first European Parliament elections in 1979. The reasons for this were many. One of the main advantages of a plurality/majority system—the formation of stable majority governments—was clearly not relevant for these elections, and the proportional representation of all political parties was seen as a much more important criterion for the design of the electoral system. The nationwide district in combination with a 5 per cent threshold was thought of as providing a balance between a high level of proportionality on the one hand, and the desire to exclude parties with little support on the other. The ability to fill vacant seats between elections with the next person on the list, thus eliminating the need to hold by-elections, was another advantage that led to the adoption of the List PR system. After five elections, the wish to strengthen the relationship between voters and representatives, and the desire for greater geographical representation (a disproportionate number of those elected had been residents of Paris), led to the nationwide district being abandoned before the election in 2004. It was replaced by eight multi-member districts for the election of France's 78 representatives to the European Parliament.

The next piece of important legislation on the European Parliament elections was concluded in 2002 with the Council Decision 8964/02 amending the Act Concerning the Election of the Representatives of the Assembly by Direct Universal Suffrage—an amendment to the 1976 act. Twenty-six years after the establishment of provisions for direct elections, this decision specified a common electoral system family for European Parliament elections for all member states. Article 1 reads: 'In each Member State, members of the European Parliament shall be elected on the basis of proportional representation, using the list system or the single transferable vote.' For the 2004 elections, all 25 member states thus used a PR electoral system.

While all these systems belong to the same family, they also differ in some respects. Twenty-three countries (Austria, Belgium, Cyprus, the Czech Republic, Denmark, Estonia, Finland, France, Germany, Greece, Hungary, Italy, Latvia, Lithuania, Luxembourg, the Netherlands, Poland, Portugal, Slovakia, Slovenia, Spain, Sweden and the UK) use List PR, while Malta and the Republic of Ireland use the Single Transferable Vote. This difference may be expected, since the List PR system makes up at least a part of the electoral system for the national legislatures of 21 of the 23 countries (France and the UK being the exceptions), while the Republic of Ireland and Malta both use STV for their national elections.

In the 23 countries using List PR, some used closed lists, while others have chosen open lists—a choice which in most cases mirrors that made for national elections, although Greece is one exception. Equally, some member states, especially the smaller ones, elect their members from one national district, while others have set up a number of districts at regional level.

The threshold for gaining representation in the different member states also varies. The 2002 decision allows for the individual countries to determine the threshold, but sets the ceiling for any formal threshold at 5 per cent. Some countries, for example Cyprus, Hungary and Sweden, use formal thresholds, again for the most part mirroring their use at national level (although Belgium, which uses a formal threshold for national elections, does not do so for European Parliament elections). Not only the formal thresholds, but also the actual level of support needed to gain representation—natural thresholds—vary significantly between member states. The reason for the variations in thresholds is found in the combination of the number of representatives to be elected from each country and the level at which the electoral districts are defined (more specifically, the number of representatives to be elected from each district). Italy, with one nationwide district and 78 representatives to elect, has a very low effective threshold of under 1 per cent, while the four electoral districts and 13 representatives of the Republic of Ireland mean that a successful candidate under STV will need to win a much higher proportion of the vote. In 2004, the winning candidates in Ireland received between 12.9 and 25.9 per cent of the first-preference votes in their district.

While a common electoral system family is now specified for European Parliament elections, there is little sign of any momentum for further integration. Although party groups are formed within the European Parliament, there is no sign that national parties are willing to relinquish any significant leading role to pan-European parties. There is thus every likelihood that decisions about electoral system details will remain in the hands of national politicians, influenced by their own interests and their existing national traditions.

Debate seems more likely to centre on the low voter turnout in European Parliament elections, which remains a major concern of the EU member states. Despite the use of a PR system in all countries—an electoral system family which is usually linked to a higher voter turnout than other systems—turnout is still strikingly low. At the 2004 elections, the 15 countries that were members before enlargement in 2004 had an average turnout of 52.9 per cent, and the 10 new member states an even lower figure of 40.2 per cent. It appears that as long as the electorate sees European Parliament elections as being secondary, with little clarity as to what changes result when representation changes at elections, interest and turnout will remain low. The electoral systems used are not seen as a controversial element, and there is very little serious debate about their amendment. It is therefore likely that the electoral systems will remain fairly constant in the near future.

Electing Federal/State Assemblies and Autonomous Jurisdictions

198. The legislatures of regions or states within a federation may use the same electoral system as the national legislature (symmetry), as happens in South Africa's closed-list PR system, or they may use different systems (asymmetry), as in the UK, where the Scottish Parliament and the National Assembly for Wales are elected by MMP and the national legislature is elected by FPTP. The system for a state legislature may give primacy to the inclusion of minority groups within its borders or balance between urban and rural interests. The more autonomy a region has, the less the pressure for its electoral arrangements to mirror those of other states or provinces. The very fact of its being an autonomous jurisdiction implies that its attributes and needs are quite distinct from those of other areas.

Electing Local Authorities

199. Any of the electoral systems outlined in this Handbook can be used at the local or municipal government level, but often there are a number of special considerations arising from the particular role of local government. In particular, because local government is more about the 'nuts and bolts' issues of everyday life, geographical representation is more often given primacy. The use of local elections as a step towards democratization is an example of this (see the case study on China).

200. Single-member districts can be used to give every neighbourhood a say in local affairs, especially where political parties are weak or non-existent. Where these districts are small, they are usually highly homogeneous. This is sometimes seen to be a good thing, but if diversity within a local government district is required the 'spokes of a wheel' principle of districting can be applied. Here, district boundaries are not circles drawn around identifiable neighbourhoods but are segments of a circle centring on the city centre and ending in the suburbs. This means that one district includes both the urban and the suburban voters, and makes for a mix of economic class and ethnicity.

201. In contrast, the municipalities in some countries which use PR systems for local government have one single-list PR district which can proportionally reflect all the different political opinions in the municipality. In order to achieve this, however, specific space may need to be made for representatives of local associations who are not driven by party-political ideology to nominate lists, and perhaps also for independents to be nominated as single-person lists.

202. It is also true that the choice of local electoral system may be made as part of a compromise involving the system for the national legislature. For example, in some newly democratizing countries such as Congo (Brazzaville) and Mali, tradition and the French influence have resulted in a Two-Round System for the national legislature, while a desire to be inclusive and more fully reflect regional and ethnic loyalties resulted in the choice of PR for municipal elections.

CHINA:
Village Committee Elections:
First Steps on a Long March?

Dong Lisheng and Jørgen Elklit

With the 'household contract responsibility system' introduced in the Chinese countryside in the late 1970s, farmers began to produce for their families. As production was decentralized, the collective-oriented organization of the People's Communes became outdated.

The earliest villagers' committees (VCs) emerged in the Guangxi Autonomous Region in 1980–1. Formed without the knowledge of the local authorities, these organizations were created by village elders, former cadres and community-minded villagers. The intention was to address a decline in social order and a broader political crisis as production brigades and teams stopped functioning at the grass-roots level. Within months, local officials had reported this development to the central government. The National People's Congress (NPC) leaders encouraged experiments with this new form of organization.

In 1982, VCs were written into the constitution as elected mass organizations of self-government (article 111). In contrast to the relationship between the commune and production brigade or production team, the newly restored township—the lowest level of government—does not lead the VC but only exercises guidance over it. Another difference is the introduction of direct election by all eligible voters. In 1987, the Provisional Organic Law of Villagers' Committees was passed, setting out general principles for direct elections to VCs and defining the tasks and responsibilities of the VCs. Implementation of the law, including the enactment of detailed regulations, was left to the provincial and lower-level authorities. The quality of elections and overall implementation varied considerably, and after ten years perhaps only 25 per cent of the more than 658,000 villages (the latest figure, for the end of 2002) in China had experienced direct elections in full accordance with the law.

In 1998, the NPC made the Organic Law permanent. The law has clarified and improved some aspects of the prescribed election procedures and strengthened the rules on transparency and popular control of VCs. The permanent law is seen by many as a political and legal consolidation of the village election process, but its full implementation remains a challenge—perhaps even more so after the introduction of more demanding standards, for instance, in relation to secret polling booths and the direct nomination of candidates. The quality of elections across the country still varies considerably.

The VC members are elected for three years, with no limit on the number of terms for which a person can be re-elected. The VCs usually consist of between three and seven members, one of whom is chair and one or two vice-chairs. Although there is variation from province to province, VCs generally oversee all the administrative matters of a village, including budget management, public utilities, dispute resolution, public safety, social order and security, health issues and local business management. A large village can consist of more than 10,000 people, while small ones might only have several hundred. The 'average village' has 1,000–2,000 inhabitants.

VCs report to the Village Assembly or the Village Representative Assembly. As the former meet only once or twice a year, the latter, composed of 25–50 people from the village and selected by Villagers' Small Groups, play a greater role in decision making and in the supervision of the VCs. A Village Election Committee administers village elections.

Village elections have now been held in all 31 provinces, autonomous regions and municipalities. By 2003, the provinces of Fujian and Liaoning, two front-runners in this regard, had completed eight and seven elections, respectively, and 19 provinces had held between four and six elections. At least one province held its first village elections as late as 2000. There is no single election day for all VC elections across the country. During a province's designated election year, the counties and townships within the province together decide the election days for the villages within their jurisdictions.

Each election adheres to the same basic framework. The first step in the process is the registration of voters, which is handled by the Village Election Committee. A list of registered voters must be prepared and publicly displayed 20 days prior to the election. Voters are allowed to challenge the registration lists. Except for those who have been deprived of political rights, all those aged 18 or above enjoy the right to vote and to be elected without regard to ethnicity, race, sex, profession, family background, religious belief, level of education, property or period of residence in the community. One important challenge is the large number of voters whose residence registrations are in their 'home village', but who live and work a long distance away, often in a major urban area. It is difficult or impossible for most such voters to get back to their village on election day. At the same time, they cannot attend the elections in the cities in which they work and reside. Therefore they cannot actually exercise their right to vote.

Following voter registration, candidates are nominated directly by villagers. In most provinces, the requirement is to have only one more candidate than there are seats to be filled as chair, deputy chair, and ordinary members. In recent years, nominations in some provinces have been organized through villagers attending either a meeting of the Village Assembly or a meeting of the Villagers' Small Group, while the latest development in other provinces is to have no pre-election nomination. In these areas, voters receive either a blank piece of paper or a blank ballot paper with only the different positions indicated above the relevant columns. If the election fails to produce a new committee or to fill all positions it de facto becomes a first-round election, and a run-off election follows.

The final election must be direct. The use of secret ballots and polling booths (or rooms) is mandatory in most provinces. There are three voting styles: (a) mass voting, where all voters go to a central voting place in the morning, vote, and remain there until the end of the count; (b) individual voting throughout the course of the day of the election; and (c) proxy or absentee voting, or 'roving boxes'. Most of the provinces use mass voting. The ballot papers used contain names of candidates listed under the post for which they are standing; and the voting is done by the voter marking the names of the candidates he or she wishes to elect. The voter can mark as many candidates as there are posts (one chair, one or two vice-chairs, and a number of committee members) in the village. For an election to be considered valid an absolute majority of eligible voters must cast their ballots and winning candidates are required to get 50 per cent of the vote plus one. When no candidate receives a majority, a run-off election is held within three days. In run-off elections, candidates are only required to receive 33 per cent of all votes cast. Winners take up their positions immediately.

Village elections are important in that the election law mandates the basic norms of a democratic process—secret ballot, direct election and multiple candidates (even though their numbers are very restricted). Other elections in China have yet to implement these norms. The progress made in relation to VC elections has raised expectations as to whether and when direct elections will work their way up from the village to the township, county, and even higher levels of government. Each round of VC elections also strengthens local capacity to administer electoral processes.

An assessment of the significance of China's village elections has much to do with the question whether such 'limited democracy' can lead to genuine democracy. There are different ways of assessing how democratic elections are. The three universal criteria of free, fair and meaningful elections are appropriate terms of reference. China does not meet any recognized standards of free and fair elections in choosing its national parliament and local councils, and in many cases elected village leaders do not exercise as much authority as the Chinese Communist Party (CCP) secretaries do. However, just because the village elections are not fully free or fair, and some VCs do not command complete authority, it cannot be concluded that they are completely unfree, unfair, or meaningless. Elections should not be evaluated against some absolute standard but rather viewed as positioned on a democratic continuum.

The VC elections have produced a ripple effect as village CCP branch elections in some cases have invited ordinary villagers to cast a vote of confidence, and some experiments with elections of township government leaders have taken place. China's democratization now appears to require that the top leadership's political decisions find an echo at the grass roots. After two decades of continuously improved direct elections at the village level, elections at higher levels of government appear technically feasible; the question is whether and how there will be further change in the direction of democratization.

大关庄村第五届村委会选举选票

职务	主任候选人		副主任候选人			委员候选人									
姓名	关利泽	李少顺	李少顺	关利泽	勾井仕	李桂芬	关真宝	勾井仕	李少顺	关真奎	刘万喜	关利泽	关真国		

说明：1. 主任应选1人，副主任应选1人，委员应选3人，超过应选人数的选票无效。

2. 同意的在候选人姓名下方空格内划"○"；不同意的划"×"，另选他人在空格内写上另选人的姓名，并在其姓名下方空格内划"○"，未划符号的无效。

3. 不许提同一候选人担任两种或两种以上职务，否则该候选人的赞成票无效。

Chinese village election ballot paper

203. The debate between parliamentarism and presidentialism in national constitutions has a counterpart in discussion of the structure of local government. Directly elected governors and mayors who head executive authorities that are separate from the elected local legislative body are becoming more popular worldwide, at the expense of elected authorities with collective committee structures directly responsible for services. The range of systems for electing governors and mayors is in principle the same as that for the direct election of presidents, and parallels may also be drawn when considering the issues surrounding the relationship between the electoral system and the legislative–executive relationship at local level.

Electoral Systems and Political Parties

204. Different kinds of electoral system are likely to encourage different kinds of party organization and party system. While it is important for party systems to be as representative as possible, most experts favour systems which encourage the development of parties based on broad political values and ideologies and specific policy programmes, rather than narrow ethnic, racial or regional concerns. As well as reducing the threat of societal conflict, parties which are based on these broad 'cross-cutting cleavages' are more likely to reflect national opinion than those that are based predominantly on sectarian or regional concerns.

205. Highly centralized political systems using closed-list PR are the most likely to encourage strong party organizations; conversely, decentralized, district-based systems like FPTP may have the opposite effect. But there are many other electoral variables that can be used to influence the development of party systems. For example, new democracies like Russia and Indonesia have attempted to shape the development of their nascent party systems by providing institutional incentives for the formation of national rather than regional political parties (see the case study on Indonesia). Other countries such as Ecuador and Papua New Guinea have used party registration and funding requirements to achieve similar objectives. Access to public and/or private funding is a key issue that cuts across electoral system design, and is often the single biggest constraint on the emergence of viable new parties.

Just as electoral system choice will affect the way in which the political party system develops, the political party system in place affects electoral system choice. Existing parties are unlikely to support changes that are likely to seriously disadvantage them, or changes that open the possibility of new, rival parties gaining entry to the political party system, unless there is a strong political imperative. The range of options for electoral system change may thus be constrained in practice.

206. Different kinds of electoral system also result in different relationships between individual candidates and their supporters. In general, systems which make use of single-member electoral districts, such as most plurality/majority systems, are seen as encouraging individual candidates to see themselves as the delegates of particular geographical areas and beholden to the interests of their local electorate. By contrast,

systems which use large multi-member districts, such as most PR systems, are more likely to deliver representatives whose primary loyalty lies with their party on national issues. Both approaches have their merits, which is one of the reasons for the rise in popularity of mixed systems that combine both local and national-level representatives.

207. The question of accountability is often raised in discussions of political parties and electoral systems, especially in relation to individual elected members. The relationships between electors, elected members and political parties are affected not only by the electoral system but also by other provisions of the political legislative framework such as term limits, provisions regulating the relationship between parties and their members who are also elected representatives, or provisions barring elected members from changing parties without resigning from the legislature.

208. The freedom for voters to choose between candidates as opposed to parties is another aspect of accountability. Many countries in recent years have therefore introduced a greater element of candidate-centred voting into their electoral systems, for example, by introducing open lists in PR elections.

Direct Democracy Options

209. This Handbook covers issues of electoral system design for the election of representatives at all levels. When considering the question of accountability, however, a broader framework may be necessary which also takes into account the role of institutions of direct democracy. The use of referendums is becoming more common worldwide. Switzerland has a long history of use of the citizens' initiative, a procedure which enables legislative proposals to be submitted by groups of citizens to popular vote. While Venezuela is the only country which provides for a recall vote against a directly elected president, such votes can be demanded against legislators and/or regional and local office holders in some presidential systems and many US states.

CHAPTER 5

CHAPTER 5

5. Cost and Administrative Implications of Electoral Systems

210. IN ANY COUNTRY, THE LOGISTICS CAPACITY AND THE AVAILABILITY OF SKILLED HUMAN resources may constrain the available options for electoral system choice, as may the amount of money available. Even when donor funding is available, issues of the long-term sustainability of electoral system choice are important.

This does not, however, mean that the most straightforward and least expensive system is always the best choice. It may well be a false economy, as a dysfunctional electoral system can have a negative impact on a country's entire political system and on its democratic stability.

Any choice of electoral system has a wide range of administrative consequences, including those addressed in the following paragraphs.

211. *The Drawing of Electoral Boundaries.* Any single-member district system requires the time-consuming and expensive process of drawing boundaries for relatively small constituencies. The way in which they are demarcated will depend on issues such as population size, cohesiveness, 'community of interest' and contiguity. Furthermore, this is rarely a one-off task, as boundaries have to be adjusted regularly to take population changes into account. FPTP, AV and TRS systems produce the most administrative headaches on this score. The BV, PBV, SNTV, LV and STV systems also require electoral districts to be demarcated but are somewhat easier to manage because they use multi-member districts, which will be fewer in number and larger. Drawing districts for an element of a mixed system poses similar challenges.

212. When multi-member districts are used, it is possible to avoid the need to adjust boundaries by changing the number of representatives elected in each electoral district—a method of particular value when established units such as provinces are used as electoral districts. List PR systems are often the cheapest and easiest to administer because they use either one single national constituency, which means that

no boundaries need be drawn at all, or very large multi-member districts which dovetail with pre-existing state or provincial boundaries. Recent UN-sponsored elections in Sierra Leone in 1996, Liberia in 1997 and Kosovo in 2001 were all conducted under a national List PR system, partly because the displacement of people and the lack of accurate census data meant that electoral authorities did not have the population data necessary to draw smaller districts.

213. *The Registration of Voters.* Voter registration is the most complex and controversial, and often least successful, part of electoral administration. By its nature it involves collecting in a standardized format specific information from a vast number of voters, and then arranging and distributing these data in a form that can be used at election time—moreover, in such a way as to ensure that only eligible electors engage in the voting process and to guard against multiple voting, personation and the like. The political sensitivity of these matters and the laborious nature of the task itself mean that voter registration is often one of the most expensive and time-consuming parts of the entire electoral process.

214. Voter registration requirements are influenced by the design of the electoral system. A system which uses single-member districts usually requires that each voter must be registered within the boundaries of a specified district. This means that FPTP, AV, TRS and BC (when using single-member districts) are the most expensive and administratively time-consuming systems in terms of voter registration, alongside Parallel and MMP systems which contain single-member districts. The fewer, multi-member districts of the BV, PBV, SNTV and STV systems make the process a little easier, while large-district List PR systems are the least complicated. Arrangements for registration for out-of-country voting may be particularly difficult.

The simplicity of List PR in this context has been a contributing factor in its adoption in some major transitional elections, such as South Africa's first democratic elections in 1994. It should be emphasized, however, that variations in electoral systems have only a minor impact on the often extremely high cost of voter registration.

215. *The Design and Production of Ballot Papers.* Ballot papers should be as friendly as possible to all voters in order to maximize participation and reduce the number of spoilt or 'invalid' votes. This often entails the use of symbols for parties and candidates, photographs, and colours; a number of interesting ballot paper examples are illustrated in this Handbook. FPTP and AV ballot papers are often easiest to print and, in most cases, have a relatively small number of names. TRS ballot papers are similarly easy, but in many cases new ballot papers have to be printed for the second round of voting, thus effectively doubling the production cost; and consideration also has to be given to allowing sufficient time to print the papers for the second ballot. Parallel and MMP systems often require the printing of at least two ballot papers for a single polling day, and use two (or more) very different electoral systems, with logistical implications for the training of election officials and the way in which people vote. SNTV, BV, BC and STV ballot papers are more complex than FPTP ballot papers because they

will have more candidates, and therefore more symbols and photographs (if these are used). Lastly, List PR ballot papers can span the continuum of complexity. They can be very simple, as in a closed-list system, or quite complex in a free-list system such as Switzerland's.

216. *Voter Education.* Clearly the nature of, and the need for, voter education will vary dramatically from society to society, but when it comes to educating voters on how to fill out their ballot papers, there are identifiable differences between the different systems. The principles behind voting under preferential systems such as AV, STV or Borda Count are quite complex, and if they are being used for the first time voter education needs to address this issue, particularly if the voter is obliged to number all candidates in order of preference, as is the case in Australia. The increasing use of mixed systems, many of which give voters two ballot papers, also creates an additional level of complexity for voters. By contrast, the principles behind single-vote systems such as FPTP, PBV or SNTV are very easy to understand. The remaining systems fall somewhere in between these two extremes (see Table 8).

217. *Number of Polling Days.* FPTP, AV, BV, SNTV, List PR, Borda Count and STV all generally require just one election on one day, as do Parallel and MMP systems. Two-Round systems are more costly and difficult to administer because they often require the whole electoral process to be re-run a week or a fortnight after the first round.

218. *By-elections.* If a seat becomes vacant between elections, List PR systems often simply fill it with the next candidate on the list of the party of the former representative, thus eliminating the need to hold another election. However, plurality/majority systems often have provisions for filling vacant seats through a by-election. When other systems are in use, either approach may be possible: under STV, the Republic of Ireland holds by-elections for vacant seats in the legislature, but Australia does not do so for Senate vacancies. It is also possible to avoid by-elections by electing substitutes at the same time as the ordinary representatives, as is done for example in Bolivia.

By-elections are smaller and therefore less costly than normal elections, but in some countries they will nevertheless put a significant burden on the budget, and seats are sometimes left vacant for long periods because of a lack of capacity to arrange by-elections. This is an especially salient problem in some countries in Southern Africa where the HIV/AIDS epidemic often leads to a large number of vacant seats between elections.

In some circumstances, by-elections can have a wider political impact than merely replacing individual members, and are seen to act as a mid-term test of the performance of the government. In addition, if the number of vacancies to be filled during a parliamentary term is large this can lead to a change in the composition of the legislature and an altered power base for the government.

219. *The Count.* FPTP, SNTV and simple closed-list PR systems are easiest to count, as only one vote total figure for each party or candidate is required to work out the results. The BV and LV systems require the polling officials to count a number of votes on a single ballot paper, and Parallel and MMP systems often require the counting of two ballot papers. AV, BC and STV, as preferential systems requiring numbers to be marked on the ballot, are more complex to count.

Table 8: Potential Cost and Administrative Implications of 12 Electoral Systems

	Drawing Electoral Boundaries	Voter Registration	Ballot Paper Design and Production	Voter Education	Number of Polling Days	By-elections	The Count
FPTP	High	High	Low	Low	Low	High	Low
BV	Medium	Medium	Medium	Medium	Low	High	Medium
TRS	High	High	High	Medium	High	High	Medium
AV	High	High	Low	High	Low	High	Medium
PBV	Medium	Medium	Low	Low	Low	Low	Low
List PR	Low	High	Medium	Medium	Low	Low	Low
STV	Medium	Medium	Medium	High	Low	High	High
Parallel	Medium	High	Medium	Medium	Medium	Medium	High
MMP	Medium	High	Medium	High	Medium	Medium	High
BC	Medium	High	Medium	High	Low	High	Medium
SNTV	Medium	Medium	Medium	Low	Low	High	Low
LV	Medium	Medium	Medium	Medium	Low	High	Medium

Key: 🙂 = Low cost and complexity; 😐 = Medium cost and complexity; ☹️ = High cost and complexity.

220. *Sustainability.* The stresses which any electoral system places on a country's administrative capacity will be determined primarily by history, context, experience and resources, but Table 7 does offer some clues to the potential costs of various systems. A cursory glance shows that List PR systems, especially national closed-list systems, score well when it comes to being cheap to run and requiring few administrative resources. So does PBV. Next come SNTV and LV systems, followed by BV and FPTP; and a little further down by the AV, STV, Parallel, Borda Count and MMP systems. The system which is most likely to put pressure on any country's administrative capacity is the Two-Round System.

CHAPTER 6

CHAPTER 6

6. Advice for Electoral System Designers

221. ONE OF THE CLEAREST CONCLUSIONS TO BE DRAWN FROM THE COMPARATIVE study of electoral systems is simply the range and utility of the options available. Often, designers and drafters of constitutional, political and electoral frameworks simply choose the electoral system they know best—often, in new democracies, the system of the former colonial power if there was one—rather than fully investigating the alternatives. Sometimes the elements of a peace settlement or external pressures constrain the options available.

The major purpose of this Handbook is to provide some of the knowledge for *informed* decisions to be made. The Handbook does not necessarily advocate wholesale changes to existing electoral systems; in fact, the comparative experience of electoral reform to date suggests that moderate reform, building on those parts of an existing system which work well, is often a better option than jumping to a completely new and unfamiliar system.

222. There is much to be learned from the experience of others. For example, a country with an FPTP system which wishes to move to a more proportional system while still retaining the geographical link to constituents might want to consider the experience of New Zealand, which adopted an MMP system in 1993, or Lesotho, which did so in 2002. A similar country which wants to keep single-member districts but encourage inter-group accommodation and compromise could evaluate the experience of AV in the Oceania region (Fiji or Papua New Guinea in particular). Any deeply divided country that wishes to make the transition to democracy would be well advised to consider both the multi-ethnic power-sharing government the List PR electoral system in South Africa has facilitated and the more troubled history of the Northern Ireland Assembly elected by STV. Lastly, a country which simply wishes to reduce the cost and instability created by a TRS system for electing a president could examine the AV option used by the Republic of Ireland. In all these cases, the choice of electoral system has had a clear impact on the politics of that country.

223. The following guidelines summarize the advice contained in this Handbook.

Keep It Simple and Clear

224. Effective and sustainable electoral system designs are more likely to be easily understood by the voter and the politician. Too much complexity can lead to misunderstandings, unintended consequences, and voter mistrust of the results.

Don't be Afraid to Innovate

225. Many of the successful electoral systems used in the world today themselves represent innovative approaches to specific problems, and have been proved to work well. There is much to learn from the experience of others—both neighbouring countries and seemingly quite different cases.

Pay Attention to Contextual and Temporal Factors

226. Electoral systems do not work in a vacuum. Their success depends on a happy marriage of political institutions and cultural traditions. The first point of departure for any would-be electoral system designer should be to ask: What is the political and social context I am working within? The second might be: Am I designing a permanent system or one which needs to get us through a transitional period?

Don't Underestimate the Electorate

227. While simplicity is important, it is equally dangerous to underestimate the voters' ability to comprehend and successfully use a wide variety of different electoral systems. Complex preferential systems, for example, have been used successfully in developing countries in the Asia–Pacific region, while the experience of many recent elections in new democracies has underlined the important distinction between 'functional' literacy and 'political' literacy. Even in very poor countries, voters often have, and wish to express, relatively sophisticated orderings of political preferences and choices.

Err on the Side of Inclusion

228. Wherever possible, whether in divided or relatively homogeneous societies, the electoral system should err on the side of including all significant interests in the legislature. Regardless of whether minorities are based on ideological, ethnic, racial, linguistic, regional or religious identities, the exclusion of significant shades of opinion from legislatures, particularly in the developing world, has often been catastrophically counterproductive.

Process is a Key Factor in Choice

229. The way in which a particular electoral system is chosen is also extremely important in ensuring its overall legitimacy. A process in which most or all groups are included, including the electorate at large, is likely to result in significantly broader acceptance of the end result than a decision perceived as being motivated by partisan self-interest alone. Although partisan considerations are unavoidable when discussing the choice of electoral systems, broad cross-party and public support for any institution is crucial to its being accepted and respected. The reform of the New Zealand electoral system from FPTP to MMP, for example, involved two referendums which served to legitimize the final outcome. By contrast, the French Socialist government's decision in 1986 to switch from the existing Two-Round System to PR was widely perceived as being motivated by partisan considerations, and was quickly reversed as soon the government lost power in 1988.

Build Legitimacy and Acceptance Among All Key Actors

230. All groupings which wish to play a part in the democratic process should feel that the electoral system to be used is fair and gives them the same chance of electoral success as anyone else. The paramount aim should be that those who 'lose' the election cannot translate their disappointment into a rejection of the system itself or use the electoral system as an excuse to destabilize the path of democratic consolidation. In 1990 in Nicaragua, the Sandinistas were voted out of the government but accepted the defeat, in part because they accepted the fairness of the electoral system. Cambodia, Mozambique and South Africa were able to end their bloody civil wars through institutional arrangements which were broadly acceptable to all sides.

Try to Maximize Voter Influence

231. Voters should feel that elections provide them with a measure of influence over governments and government policy. Choice can be maximized in a number of different ways. Voters may be able to choose between parties, between candidates of different parties, and between candidates of the same party. They may also be able to vote under different systems when it comes to presidential, upper house, lower house, regional and local government elections. They should also feel confident that their vote has a genuine impact on the formation of the government, not just on the composition of the legislature.

But Balance That Against Encouraging Coherent Political Parties

232. The desire to maximize voter influence should be balanced against the need to encourage coherent and viable political parties. Maximum voter choice on the ballot paper may produce such a fragmented legislature that no one ends up with the result they were hoping for. There is widespread agreement among political scientists that broadly-based, coherent political parties are among the most important factors in promoting effective and sustainable democracy.

Long-Term Stability and Short-Term Advantage Are Not Always Compatible

233. When political actors negotiate over a new electoral system they often push proposals which they believe will advantage their party in the coming elections. However, this can often be an unwise strategy, particularly in developing nations, as one party's short-term success or dominance may lead to long-term political breakdown and social unrest. For example, in negotiations prior to the transitional 1994 election, South Africa's ANC could reasonably have argued for the retention of the existing FPTP electoral system, which would probably have given it, as by far the largest party, a seat bonus over and above its share of the national vote. That it argued for a form of PR, and thus won fewer seats than it could have under FPTP, was a testament to the fact that it saw long-term stability as more desirable than short-term electoral gratification.

234. Similarly, electoral systems need to be responsive enough to react effectively to changing political circumstances and the growth of new political movements. Even in established democracies, support for the major parties is rarely stable, while politics in new democracies is almost always highly dynamic and a party which benefits from the electoral arrangements at one election may not necessarily benefit at the next.

Don't Think of the Electoral System as a Panacea for All Ills

235. While it is true that if one wants to change the nature of political competition the electoral system may be the most effective instrument for doing so, electoral systems can never be the panacea for all the political ills of a country. The overall effects of other variables, particularly a country's political culture, usually have a much greater impact on its democratic prospects than institutional factors such as electoral systems. Moreover, the positive effects of a well-crafted electoral system can be all too easily submerged by an inappropriate constitutional dispensation, the dominance of forces of discord internally, or the weight of external threats to the sovereignty of the country.

But Conversely Don't Underestimate its Influence

236. Throughout the world the social constraints on democracy are considerable, but they still leave room for conscious political strategies which may further or hamper successful democratization. Electoral systems are not a panacea, but they are central to the structuring of stability in any polity. Skilful electoral system engineering may not prevent or eradicate deep enmities, but appropriate institutions can nudge the political system in the direction of reduced conflict and greater government accountability. In other words, while most of the changes that can be achieved by tailoring electoral systems are necessarily at the margins, it is often these marginal impacts that make the difference between democracy being consolidated or being undermined.

Be Mindful of the Electorate's Willingness to Embrace Change

237. Electoral system change might seem a good idea to political insiders who understand the flaws of the existing system, but unless proposals for reform are presented in an appropriate way the public may well reject tinkering with the system, perceiving reform to be nothing more than a case of politicians altering the rules for their own benefit. Most damaging are situations when the change is seen to be a blatant manoeuvre for political gain (as was the case in Chile in 1989, in Jordan in 1993, and in Kyrgyzstan on several occasions since 1995 (see the case study)), or when the system alters so frequently that the voters do not quite know where they are (as some observers have argued is the case in Bolivia).

And Don't Assume that Defects can Easily be Fixed Later

238. All electoral systems create winners and losers, and therefore vested interests. When a system is already in place, these are part of the political environment. At a time of change, however, it may be unwise to assume that it will be easy to gain acceptance later to fix problems which arise. If a review of the system is intended, it may be sensible for it to be incorporated into the legal instruments containing the system change.

Avoid Being a Slave to Past Systems

239. Nevertheless, all too often electoral systems that are inappropriate to a new democracy's needs have been inherited or carried over from colonial times without any thought as to how they will work within the new political realities. Almost all the former British colonies in Asia, Africa and the Pacific, for example, adopted FPTP systems. In many of these new democracies, particularly those facing ethnic divisions, this system proved utterly inappropriate to their needs. Similarly, it has been argued that many of the former French colonies in West Africa which retained the TRS system (such as Mali) suffered damaging polarization as a result; and many post-communist regimes retain minimum turnout or majority requirements inherited from the Soviet era. One of the fascinating things about the map which comes with this Handbook is that in many ways it mirrors a map of the world's colonies 100 years ago, with many former British colonies using FPTP, those countries under French influence using TRS, and the former Belgian and Dutch colonies often opting for a version of the List PR systems used in continental Europe—although it is true to say that over time this is changing.

Assess the Likely Impact of Any New System on Societal Conflict

240. As noted at the very start of this Handbook, electoral systems can be seen not only as mechanisms for choosing legislatures and presidents but also as a tool of conflict management within a society. Some systems, in some circumstances, will encourage parties to make inclusive appeals for support outside their own core support base. Unfortunately, it is more often the case in the world today that the presence of

inappropriate electoral systems serves actually to exacerbate negative tendencies which already exist, for example, by encouraging parties to see elections as 'zero-sum' contests and thus to act in a hostile and exclusionary manner to anyone outside their home group. When designing any political institution, the bottom line is that, even if it does not help to reduce tensions within society, it should, at the very least, not make matters worse.

Try and Imagine Unusual or Unlikely Contingencies

241. Too often, electoral systems are designed to avoid the mistakes of the past, especially the immediate past. Care should be taken in doing so not to overreact and create a system that goes too far in terms of correcting previous problems. Furthermore, electoral system designers would do well to pose themselves some unusual questions to avoid embarrassment in the long run. What if nobody wins under the system proposed? Is it possible that one party could win all the seats? What if you have to award more seats than you have places in the legislature? What do you do if candidates tie? Might the system mean that, in some districts, it is better for a party supporter not to vote for their preferred party or candidate?

A Design Checklist

☐ Is the system clear and comprehensible?
☐ Has context been taken into account?
☐ Is the system appropriate for the time?
☐ Are the mechanisms for future reform clear?
☐ Does the system avoid underestimating the electorate?
☐ Is the system as inclusive as possible?
☐ Was the design process perceived to be legitimate?
☐ Will the election results be seen as legitimate?
☐ Are unusual contingencies taken into account?
☐ Is the system financially and administratively sustainable?
☐ Will the voters feel powerful?
☐ Is a competitive party system encouraged?
☐ Does the system fit into a holistic constitutional framework?
☐ Will the system help to alleviate conflict rather than exacerbate it?

The Electoral Systems of 213 Independent Countries and Related Territories (2004)

Country or Territory [1]	Electoral System for National Legislature [2]	Electoral System Family	Legis- lature Size — Total Number of Directly Elected Representatives	Legis- lature Size — Total Number of Voting Members	Number of Tiers	Electoral System for President
AFGHANISTAN	SNTV	Other	249	249	1	TRS
ALBANIA	MMP (FPTP & List PR)	Mixed	140 [0]	140	2	-
ALGERIA	List PR	PR	389 [P]	389	1	TRS
ANDORRA	Parallel (List PR & PBV)	Mixed	28	28	2	-
ANGOLA	List PR	PR	220	220	2	TRS
ANGUILLA	FPTP	Plurality/Majority	7	11	1	-
ANTIGUA AND BARBUDA	FPTP	Plurality/Majority	17	17	1	-
ARGENTINA	List PR	PR	257	257	1	TRS [L]
ARMENIA	Parallel (FPTP & List PR)	Mixed	131	131	2	TRS
ARUBA	List PR	PR	21	21	1	-
AUSTRALIA	AV	Plurality/Majority	150	150	1	-
AUSTRIA	List PR	PR	183	183	3	TRS
AZERBAIJAN	Parallel (TRS & List PR)	Mixed	125	125	2	TRS [3]
BAHAMAS	FPTP	Plurality/Majority	40	40	1	-
BAHRAIN	TRS	Plurality/Majority	40	40	1	-
BANGLADESH	FPTP	Plurality/Majority	300	300	1	-
BARBADOS	FPTP	Plurality/Majority	30	30	1	-
BELARUS	TRS	Plurality/Majority	110	110	1	TRS
BELGIUM	List PR	PR	150	150	1	-
BELIZE	FPTP	Plurality/Majority	29	29	1	-

[1] Territories are included where they have no direct representation in a legislature of the country with which they are associated.

[2] For countries with bicameral legislatures, system for the lower house.

[3] A qualified majority of two-thirds is required for a candidate to be elected in the first round.

Country or Territory	Electoral System for National Legislature	Electoral System Family	Legis-lature Size — Total Number of Directly Elected Representatives	Legis-lature Size — Total Number of Voting Members	Number of Tiers	Electoral System for President
BENIN	List PR	PR	83	83	1	TRS
BERMUDA	FPTP	Plurality/Majority	36	36	1	-
BHUTAN	'N'	-	-	-	-	-
BOLIVIA	MMP (FPTP&List PR)	Mixed	130	130	2	TRS [4]
BOSNIA AND HERZEGOVINA	List PR	PR	42	42	1	FPTP
BOTSWANA	FPTP	Plurality/Majority	57	62	1	-
BRAZIL	List PR	PR	513	513	1	TRS
BRITISH VIRGIN ISLANDS	FPTP and BV	Plurality/Majority	13	13	2	-
BRUNEI DARUSSALAM	'N'	-	-	-	-	-
BULGARIA	List PR	PR	240	240	1	TRS
BURKINA FASO	List PR	PR	111	111	2	TRS
BURMA [5]	FPTP	Plurality/Majority	485	485	1	
BURUNDI	List PR	PR	81	179 [6]	1	-
CAMBODIA	List PR	PR	123 [P]	123	1	-
CAMEROON	PBV/List PR&FPTP [7]	Plurality/Majority	180	180	'H'	FPTP
CANADA	FPTP	Plurality/Majority	301	301	1	-
CAPE VERDE	List PR	PR	72	72	1	TRS
CAYMAN ISLANDS	BV	Plurality/Majority	15	18	1	-
CENTRAL AFRICAN REPUBLIC	TRS	Plurality/Majority	105	105	1	TRS
CHAD	PBV/List PR&TRS [8]	Plurality/Majority	155 [P]	155	'H'	TRS
CHILE	List PR	PR	120	120	1	TRS
CHINA	'N'	-	-	-	-	-
COLOMBIA	List PR	PR	166 [P]	166	1	TRS
COMOROS	TRS	Plurality/Majority	18	33	1	FPTP [9]
CONGO, REPUBLIC OF THE (BRAZZAVILLE)	TRS	Plurality/Majority	137	137	1	TRS
CONGO, DEMOCRATIC REPUBLIC OF (KINSHASA)	'N'	-	-	-	-	-
COOK ISLANDS	FPTP	Plurality/Majority	24	24	1	-
COSTA RICA	List PR	PR	57	57	1	TRS [L]
CÔTE D'IVOIRE	FPTP and PBV	Plurality/Majority	225	225	'H'	TRS

[4] If no candidate receives an absolute majority of the vote in the first round, the top two candidates are put to the National Assembly for a vote.

[5] The UN name is Myanmar.

[6] Forty representatives have been appointed for a transitional period.

[7] PBV in the multi-member districts if a list gains an absolute majority of the votes, otherwise List PR.

[8] PBV in the multi-member districts if a list gains an absolute majority of the votes, otherwise List PR.

[9] The federal presidency rotates between the three main islands. A first round of elections is held on the island which currently holds the presidency and the three top candidates move on to a second round in which the voters on all three islands are entitled to vote.

Country or Territory	Electoral System for National Legislature	Electoral System Family	Legis-lature Size — Total Number of Directly Elected Representatives	Legis-lature Size — Total Number of Voting Members	Number of Tiers	Electoral System for President
CROATIA	List PR	PR	151	151	1	TRS
CUBA	TRS	Plurality/Majority	609	609	1	-
CYPRUS	List PR	PR	56	56	1	TRS
CYPRUS (NORTH)	List PR	PR	50	50	1	TRS
CZECH REPUBLIC	List PR	PR	200	200	1	-
DENMARK	List PR	PR	179	179	2	-
DJIBOUTI	PBV	Plurality/Majority	65	65	1	TRS
DOMINICA	FPTP	Plurality/Majority	21	30	1	-
DOMINICAN REPUBLIC	List PR	PR	150^P	150	2	TRS
ECUADOR	List PR	PR	100^P	100	1	TRS^L
EGYPT	TRS [10]	Plurality/Majority	444	454	1	-[11]
EL SALVADOR	List PR	PR	84	84	2	TRS
EQUATORIAL GUINEA	List PR	PR	100	100	1	FPTP
ERITREA	'T'	-	-	-	-	-
ESTONIA	List PR	PR	101	101	2	-
ETHIOPIA	FPTP	Plurality/Majority	547^P	547	1	-
FALKLAND ISLANDS	BV	Plurality/Majority	8	8	1	-
FIJI	AV	Plurality/Majority	71	71	1	-
FINLAND	List PR	PR	200	200	1	TRS
FRANCE	TRS	Plurality/Majority	577	577	1	TRS
GABON	TRS	Plurality/Majority	120	120	1	TRS
GAMBIA	FPTP	Plurality/Majority	48	53	1	TRS
GEORGIA	Parallel (List PR&TRS^L)	Mixed	235	235	2	TRS
GERMANY	MMP (List PR&FPTP)	Mixed	598°	598	2	-
GHANA	FPTP	Plurality/Majority	200	200	1	TRS
GIBRALTAR	LV	Other	15	17	1	-
GREECE	List PR	PR	300	300	2	-
GRENADA	FPTP	Plurality/Majority	15	15	1	-
GUATEMALA	List PR	PR	158^P	158	2	TRS
GUERNSEY	BV	Plurality/Majority	45	47	1	-
GUINEA (CONAKRY)	Parallel (List PR&FPTP)	Mixed	114	114	2	TRS
GUINEA-BISSAU	List PR	PR	102	102	1	TRS
GUYANA	List PR	PR	53	65	1	FPTP
HAITI	TRS	Plurality/Majority	83	83	1	TRS
HOLY SEE (VATICAN CITY)	'N'	-	-	-	-	-

[10] Block Vote in two rounds if necessary.

[11] The president is elected for a five-year term by the legislature and confirmed in a referendum by the people.

Country or Territory	Electoral System for National Legislature	Electoral System Family	Legis-lature Size — Total Number of Directly Elected Representatives	Legis-lature Size — Total Number of Voting Members	Number of Tiers	Electoral System for President
HONDURAS	List PR	PR	128	128	1	FPTP
HUNGARY	MMP (List PR&TRS)	Mixed	386	386	3	-
ICELAND	List PR	PR	63	63	2	FPTP
INDIA	FPTP	Plurality/Majority	543	545	1	-
INDONESIA	List PR	PR	550	550	1	TRS [12]
IRAN, ISLAMIC REPUBLIC OF	TRS [L]	Plurality/Majority	290	290	1	TRS
IRAQ	List PR	PR	275	275	1	-
IRELAND, REPUBLIC OF	STV	PR	166	166	1	AV
ISRAEL	List PR	PR	120	120	1	-
ITALY	MMP (FPTP&List PR)	Mixed	630	630	2	-
JAMAICA	FPTP	Plurality/Majority	60	60	1	-
JAPAN	Parallel (FPTP&List PR)	Mixed	480	480	2	-
JERSEY	BV & FPTP	Plurality/Majority	53	53	3	-
JORDAN	SNTV	Other	104 [13]	110	1	-
KAZAKHSTAN	Parallel (TRS&List PR)	Mixed	77	77	2	TRS
KENYA	FPTP	Plurality/Majority	210	222	1	TRS [14]
KIRIBATI	TRS [15]	Plurality/Majority	40	42	1	FPTP
KOREA, DEMOCRATIC PEOPLE'S REPUBLIC OF	TRS	Plurality/Majority	687	687	1	-
KOREA, REPUBLIC OF	Parallel (FPTP&List PR)	Mixed	299	299	2	FPTP
KUWAIT	BV	Plurality/Majority	50	65	1	-
KYRGYZSTAN	TRS	Plurality/Majority	75	75	1	TRS
LAO PEOPLE'S DEMOCRATIC REPUBLIC	BV	Plurality/Majority	109	109	1	-
LATVIA	List PR	PR	100	100	1	-
LEBANON	BV	Plurality/Majority	128	128	1	-
LESOTHO	MMP (FPTP&List PR)	Mixed	120	120	2	-
LIBERIA	'T'	-	-	-	-	-
LIBYAN ARAB JAMAHIRIYA	'N'	-	-	-	-	-
LIECHTENSTEIN	List PR	PR	25	25	1	-
LITHUANIA	Parallel (TRS&List PR)	Mixed	141	141	2	TRS

[12] 50% +1 of all votes plus a minimum of 20% in half of all provinces is required for a candidate to be elected in the first round.

[13] If at least six women are elected there are 110 directly elected representatives, otherwise up to six women are indirectly elected by an electoral panel.

[14] A minimum of 25% in five of eight regions is required for a candidate to be elected in the first round.

[15] Ordinary TRS in single-member districts and Block Vote with second round if necessary in a few multi-member districts.

Country or Territory	Electoral System for National Legislature	Electoral System Family	Legis- lature Size — Total Number of Directly Elected Representatives	Legis- lature Size — Total Number of Voting Members	Number of Tiers	Electoral System for President
LUXEMBOURG	List PR	PR	60	60	1	-
MACEDONIA, THE FORMER YUGOSLAV REPUBLIC OF	List PR	PR	120	120	1	TRS
MADAGASCAR	FPTP&List PR	Plurality/Majority	160 [P]	160	'H'	TRS
MALAWI	FPTP	Plurality/Majority	193	193	1	FPTP
MALAYSIA	FPTP	Plurality/Majority	219	219	1	-
MALDIVES	BV	Plurality/Majority	42	50	1	- [16]
MALI	TRS [17]	Plurality/Majority	147 [P]	147	1	TRS
MALTA	STV	PR	65	65	1	-
MAN, ISLE OF	BV & FPTP	Plurality/Majority	24	24	'H'	-
MARSHALL ISLANDS	FPTP & BV	Plurality/Majority	33	33	'H'	-
MAURITANIA	TRS	Plurality/Majority	81 [P]	81	1	TRS
MAURITIUS	BV [18]	Plurality/Majority	70	70	1	-
MEXICO	MMP (FPTP&List PR)	Mixed	500	500	2	FPTP
MICRONESIA, FEDERATED STATES OF	FPTP	Plurality/Majority	14	14	2	-
MOLDOVA, REPUBLIC OF	List PR	PR	101	101	1	-
MONACO	Parallel (List PR&BV)	Mixed	24	24	2	-
MONGOLIA	TRS [L]	Plurality/Majority	76	76	1	TRS
MONTSERRAT	TRS [19]	Plurality/Majority	9	11	1	-
MOROCCO	List PR	PR	325	325	2	-
MOZAMBIQUE	List PR	PR	250	250	1	TRS
NAMIBIA	List PR	PR	72	78	1	TRS [20]
NAURU	Modified BC	Other	18	18	1	-
NEPAL	FPTP	Plurality/Majority	205	205	1	-
NETHERLANDS	List PR	PR	150	150	1	-
NETHERLANDS ANTILLES	List PR	PR	22	22	1	-
NEW ZEALAND	MMP (FPTP&List PR)	Mixed	120 [O]	120	2	-
NICARAGUA	List PR	PR	90	92	2	TRS [L]
NIGER	List PR&FPTP [21]	PR	83	83	'H'	TRS

[16] The president is elected for a five-year term by Parliament and confirmed in a referendum by the people.

[17] PBV system with provisions for second round if necessary.

[18] Eight seats are reserved for the highest-polling unsuccessful candidates or 'best losers' from those predefined communities which are under-represented after the allocation of the first 62 seats.

[19] Block vote with second round if at least 6% support for candidates is not reached.

[20] There are provisions for repeated rounds if no candidate receives an absolute majority of the votes.

[21] Eight representatives are elected in single-member national minority districts.

Country or Territory	Electoral System for National Legislature	Electoral System Family	Legis-lature Size — Total Number of Directly Elected Representatives	Legis-lature Size — Total Number of Voting Members	Number of Tiers	Electoral System for President
NIGERIA	FPTP	Plurality/Majority	360	360	1	TRS [22]
NIUE	FPTP & BV	Plurality/Majority	20	20	2	-
NORWAY	List PR	PR	165	165	1	-
OMAN	FPTP	Plurality/Majority	83	83	1	-
PAKISTAN	Parallel (FPTP&List PR)	Mixed	342	342	2	-
PALAU	FPTP	Plurality/Majority	16	16	1	TRS [23]
PALESTINE	BV	Plurality/Majority	89	89	1	FPTP
PANAMA	List PR & FPTP	PR	78[P]	78	'H'	FPTP
PAPUA NEW GUINEA	AV	Plurality/Majority	109	109	2	-
PARAGUAY	List PR	PR	80	80	1	FPTP
PERU	List PR	PR	120	120	1	TRS
PHILIPPINES	Parallel (FPTP&List PR)[24]	Mixed	[24]260	260	2	FPTP
PITCAIRN ISLANDS	SNTV	Other	4	8	1	-
POLAND	List PR	PR	460	460	1	TRS
PORTUGAL	List PR	PR	230	230	1	TRS
QATAR	'N'	-	-	-	-	-
ROMANIA	List PR	PR	345[P]	345	1	TRS [25]
RUSSIAN FEDERATION	Parallel (List PR&FPTP)	Mixed	450	450	2	TRS
RWANDA	List PR	PR	53	80	1	FPTP
SAINT HELENA	BV & FPTP	Plurality/Majority	12	14	'H'	-
SAINT KITTS AND NEVIS	FPTP	Plurality/Majority	10	15	1	-
SAINT LUCIA	FPTP	Plurality/Majority	17	17	1	-
SAINT VINCENT AND THE GRENADINES	FPTP	Plurality/Majority	15	21	1	-
SAMOA	FPTP & BV	Plurality/Majority	49	49	'H'	-
SAN MARINO	List PR	PR	60	60	1	-
SAO TOME AND PRINCIPE	List PR	PR	55	55	1	TRS
SAUDI ARABIA	'N'	-	-	-	-	-
SENEGAL	Parallel (PBV&List PR)	Mixed	120	120	2	TRS
SERBIA & MONTENEGRO	T' [26]	-	126	126	-	-
SEYCHELLES	Parallel (FPTP&List PR)	Mixed	34	34	2	TRS
SIERRA LEONE	List PR	PR	112	124	1	TRS [27]

[22] An absolute majority or at least 25% in two-thirds of the states is required for a candidate to be elected in the first round.

[23] The first round acts as a primary election from which the top two candidates move on to a second round regardless of level of support.

[24] Number of seats varies between 208 and 260 depending on outcome of election. A sectoral interest group or marginalized group which polls over 2% receives a maximum of three additional seats. Established political parties cannot benefit from this provision. Not all additional list seats are necessarily filled.

[25] Support from 50% of the electorate is required for a candidate to be elected in the first round.

[26] At the time of writing no federal electoral law was in place although elections are held in the constituent republics.

[27] A qualified majority of 55% is required for a candidate to be elected in the first round.

Country or Territory	Electoral System for National Legislature	Electoral System Family	Legislature Size — Total Number of Directly Elected Representatives	Legislature Size — Total Number of Voting Members	Number of Tiers	Electoral System for President
SINGAPORE	PBV & FPTP	Plurality/Majority	84 [28]	94	'H'	FPTP
SLOVAKIA	List PR	PR	150	150	1	TRS
SLOVENIA	List PR	PR	90	90	2	TRS
SOLOMON ISLANDS	FPTP	Plurality/Majority	50	50	1	-
SOMALIA	'T'	-	-	-	-	-
SOUTH AFRICA	List PR	PR	400	400	2	-
SPAIN	List PR	PR	350	350	1	-
SRI LANKA	List PR	PR	225	225	2	SV
SUDAN	FPTP	Plurality/Majority	270	360	1	TRS
SURINAME	List PR	PR	51	51	1	-
SWAZILAND	FPTP	Plurality/Majority	55	65	1	-
SWEDEN	List PR	PR	349	349	2	-
SWITZERLAND	List PR	PR	200	200	1	-
SYRIAN ARAB REPUBLIC	BV	Plurality/Majority	250	250	1	- [29]
TAIWAN	Parallel (SNTV&List PR)	Mixed	225	225	2	FPTP
TAJIKISTAN	Parallel (TRS&List PR)	Mixed	63	63	1	TRS
TANZANIA, UNITED REPUBLIC OF	FPTP	Plurality/Majority	231	295	1	TRS
THAILAND	Parallel (FPTP&List PR)	Mixed	500	500	2	-
TIMOR-LESTE	Parallel (List PR&FPTP)	Mixed	88	88	2	TRS
TOGO	TRS	Plurality/Majority	81	81	1	TRS
TOKELAU	'T'	-	-	-	-	-
TONGA	BV	Plurality/Majority	9	30	1	-
TRINIDAD AND TOBAGO	FPTP	Plurality/Majority	36	36	1	-
TUNISIA	Parallel (PBV&List PR)	Mixed	189 [P]	189	2	FPTP
TURKEY	List PR	PR	550	550	1	-
TURKMENISTAN	TRS	Plurality/Majority	50	50	1	TRS
TURKS & CAICOS ISLANDS	FPTP	Plurality/Majority	13	18	1	-
TUVALU	BV	Plurality/Majority	15	15	1	-
UGANDA	FPTP	Plurality/Majority	214	295	1	TRS
UKRAINE	Parallel (List PR&FPTP)	Mixed	450	450	2	TRS
UNITED ARAB EMIRATES	'N'	-	-	-	-	-
UNITED KINGDOM OF GREAT BRITAIN AND NORTHERN IRELAND	FPTP	Plurality/Majority	659	659	1	-

[28] The number of appointed opposition members may vary from election to election from none to three depending on the number of seats won by opposition parties. The president may also appoint a maximum of nine additional representatives.

[29] The president is elected for a five-year term by Parliament and confirmed in a referendum by the people.

Country or Territory	Electoral System for National Legislature	Electoral System Family	Legis-lature Size — Total Number of Directly Elected Representatives	Legis-lature Size — Total Number of Voting Members	Number of Tiers	Electoral System for President
UNITED STATES OF AMERICA	FPTP	Plurality/Majority	435	435	1	FPTP [30]
URUGUAY	List PR	PR	99	99	1	TRS
UZBEKISTAN	TRS	Plurality/Majority	250	250	1	TRS
VANUATU	SNTV	Other	52	52	1	-
VENEZUELA	MMP (FPTP&List PR)	Mixed	165[P]	165	3	FPTP
VIET NAM	TRS [31]	Plurality/Majority	498	498	1	-
YEMEN	FPTP	Plurality/Majority	301	301	1	TRS
ZAMBIA	FPTP	Plurality/Majority	150	158	1	FPTP
ZIMBABWE	FPTP	Plurality/Majority	120	150	1	TRS

[30] President is elected by an absolute majority of an electoral college. The members of the electoral college are elected on the state level, and the candidate with the plurality of the vote in a given state normally receives all of that state's electoral votes.

[31] Block Vote in two rounds if necessary.

Key:

D: Distribution requirements apply.

H: Hybrid system. Electoral system family classification by the system under which the largest number of seats in the legislature is elected.

L: Lower level of support than 50% +1 required for a candidate to be elected in first round.

N: No provisions for direct elections.

O: Actual size of legislature may vary between elections because of provisions for overhang mandates.

P: Legislature size varies based on population size.

SV: Supplementary Vote.

T: Country or territory in transition: new electoral system not decided at time of publication.

FPTP – First Past the Post
TRS – Two Round System
AV – Alternative Vote
BV – Block Vote
PBV – Party Block Vote
Parallel – Parallel System
MMP – Mixed Member Proportional
List PR – List Proportional Representation
STV – Single Transferable Vote
SNTV – Single Non-Transferable Vote
LV – Limited Vote
Modified BC – Modified Borda Count

Annex B

Glossary of Terms

Absentee voting – Another term for *remote voting.*

Additional Member System – Another term for a *Mixed Member Proportional system.*

Alternative Vote (AV) – *A candidate-centred, preferential plurality/majority* system used in *single-member districts* in which voters use numbers to mark their preferences on the ballot paper. A candidate who receives an absolute majority (50 per cent plus 1) of valid first-preference votes is declared elected. If no candidate achieves an absolute majority of first preferences, the least successful candidates are eliminated and their votes reallocated until one candidate has an absolute majority of valid votes remaining.

Apparentement – A term of French origin for a provision which can be included in *List Proportional Representation (List PR)* systems which enables two or more parties or groupings which fight separate campaigns to reach agreement that their votes will be combined for the purpose of seat allocation. See also *Lema* and *Stembusaccoord.*

Average district magnitude – For a country, local authority or supranational institution, the number of representatives to be elected divided by the number of *electoral districts.* See also *District magnitude.*

Ballotage – Another term for a *two-round system,* used primarily in Latin America.

Ballot structure – The way in which electoral choices are presented on the ballot paper, in particular whether the ballot is *candidate-centred* or *party-centred.*

Bicameral legislature – A legislature made up of two houses, usually known as an *upper house* and a *lower house.*

Block Vote (BV) – A *plurality/majority* system used in *multi-member districts* in which electors have as many votes as there are candidates to be elected. Voting is *candidate-centred*. The candidates with the highest vote totals win the seats.

Borda Count (BC) – A *candidate-centred preferential* system used in either *single-* or *multi-member districts* in which voters use numbers to mark their preferences on the ballot paper and each preference marked is then assigned a value using equal steps. For example, in a ten-candidate field a first preference is worth one, a second preference is worth 0.9 and so on, with a tenth preference worth 0.1. These are summed and the candidate(s) with the highest total(s) is/are declared elected. See also *Modified Borda Count*.

Boundary delimitation – The process by which a country, local authority area or area of a *supranational institution* is divided into *electoral districts.*

Candidate-centred ballot – A form of ballot in which an elector chooses between candidates rather than between parties and political groupings.

Circonscription – The term most frequently used for *electoral* district in francophone countries. See Electoral *district.*

Closed list – A form of List PR in which electors are restricted to voting only for a party or political grouping, and cannot express a preference for any candidate within a party list. See also *Open list* and *Free list.*

Communal roll – A register of electors for which the qualification for registration is a determinable criterion such as religion, ethnicity, language or gender. All electors who meet the criterion may be entered in the communal roll automatically, or each such elector may be able to choose whether or not to be entered. This register is used for the election of representatives of the group defined by the criterion from *electoral districts* specified for that purpose.

Compensatory seats – The *List PR* seats in a *Mixed Member Proportional* system which are awarded to parties or groupings to correct disproportionality in their representation in the results of the elections held under the first part of the *MMP* system, normally under a *plurality/majority* system.

Constituency – A synonym for *electoral district* used predominantly in some anglophone countries. See *Electoral district.*

Contiguous district – An *electoral district* that can be enclosed in a single continuous boundary line.

Cross-cutting cleavages – Political allegiances of voters which cut across ethnic, religious and class divisions in a society.

Cumulation – The capacity within some *electoral systems* for voters to cast more than one vote for a favoured candidate.

Democratic consolidation – The process by which a country's political institutions and democratic procedures become legitimized, stable and broadly accepted by both political actors and the wider population.

D'Hondt Formula – One of the options for the series of divisors used to distribute seats in List *PR* systems which adopt the *Highest Average Method*. The votes of a party or grouping are divided successively by 1, 2, 3... as seats are allocated to it. Of the available formulas, D'Hondt tends to be the most favourable to larger parties. See also *Sainte-Laguë Formula*.

Distribution requirements – The requirement that to win election a candidate must win not merely a specified proportion of the vote nationally but also a specified degree of support in a number of different states or regions.

District – Used in this Handbook to mean *electoral district*.

District magnitude – For an *electoral district*, the number of representatives to be elected from it. See also *Average district magnitude*.

Droop Quota – A variant of *quota* used in *proportional representation systems* which use the *Largest Remainder Method*, defined as the total valid vote divided by the number of seats to be filled in the *electoral district* plus one. Also known as *Hagenbach-Bischoff Quota*. See *Quota (a)*. See also *Hare Quota* and *Imperiali Quota*.

Elector – A person who is both qualified and registered to vote at an election.

Electoral district – One of the geographic areas into which a country, local authority or *supranational institution* may be divided for electoral purposes. See also *Circonscription, Constituency, Electorate (b)* and *Riding*. An electoral district may elect one or more representatives to an elected body. See *Single-member district* and *Multi-member district*.

Electoral formula – That part of the *electoral system* dealing specifically with the translation of votes into seats.

Electoral law – One or more pieces of legislation governing all aspects of the process for electing the political institutions defined in a country's constitution or institutional framework.

Electoral management body (EMB) – The organization tasked under *electoral law* with the responsibility for the conduct of elections. The EMB in most countries consists either of an independent commission appointed for the purpose or of part of a specified government department.

Electoral regulations – Rules subsidiary to legislation made, often by the *electoral management body,* under powers contained in the *electoral law* which govern aspects of the organization and administration of an election.

Electoral system – That part of the electoral law and regulations which determines how parties and candidates are elected to a body as representatives. Its three most significant components are the *electoral formula,* the *ballot structure* and the *district magnitude.*

Electorate – May have one of two distinct meanings:
a. The total number of *electors* registered to vote in an *electoral district.*

b. A synonym for *electoral district* used predominantly in some anglophone countries. See *Electoral district.*

External voting – A mechanism by which voters who are permanently or temporarily absent from a country are enabled to cast a vote, also called *out-of-country voting.*

First Past The Post (FPTP) – The simplest form of *plurality/majority electoral system,* using *single-member districts* and *candidate-centred* voting. The winning candidate is the one who gains more votes than any other candidate, even if this is not an absolute majority of valid votes.

Free list – A form of *List PR* in which voters may vote for a party or grouping and in addition for one or more candidates, whether or not those candidates are nominated by that party or grouping. Also known as *panachage.* See also *Closed list* and *Open list.*

Gerrymandering – The deliberate manipulation of *electoral district* boundaries so as to advantage or disadvantage a particular political interest.

Hagenbach-Bischoff Quota – Another term for the *Droop Quota.*

Hare Quota – A variant of *quota* used in *proportional representation systems* which use the *Largest Remainder Method,* defined as the total valid vote divided by the number of seats to be filled in the *electoral district.* See *Quota (a).* Also known as Hare-Niemeyer. See also *Droop Quota* and *Imperiali Quota.*

Heterogeneous district – An *electoral district* in which, either by design or as a result of the operation of other criteria for *boundary delimitation,* the *electorate* manifests social, ethnic, religious or linguistic diversity.

Highest Average Method – A principle for converting votes into seats in *List PR* systems. One seat is allocated in a *district* at each of a series of counts to the party or grouping with the highest vote total. When a seat is allocated, the original vote of the party that wins it is reduced by division. The most common series of divisors used are *D'Hondt* and *Sainte-Laguë*. The Highest Average Method tends to be more favourable to larger parties than its alternative, the *Largest Remainder Method*.

Homogeneous district – An *electoral district* in which, either by design or as a result of the operation of other criteria for *boundary delimitation*, the *electorate* manifests substantial social, ethnic, religious or linguistic uniformity.

Hybrid System – The result of dividing a country into two or more non-overlapping areas, in each of which a different *electoral system* is used.

Imperiali Quota – A variant of *quota* used in *proportional representation systems* which use the *Largest Remainder Method*, defined as the total valid vote divided by the number of seats to be filled in the *electoral district* plus two. See also *Droop Quota* and *Hare Quota*.

Index of disproportionality – A figure which is designed to measure the degree of deviation from proportionality in the allocation of seats to parties or groupings which participated in an election. It is most commonly defined as the square root of the sum of the squares of the differences for each party or grouping between the percentage of votes received and the percentage of seats gained.

Invalid votes – Votes which cannot be counted in favour of any participant in an election due to accidental or deliberate errors of marking by the voter.

Largest Remainder Method – A principle for converting votes into seats in *List PR* systems. After parties and groupings have been allocated seats in an *electoral district* because they have received full *quotas (a)* of votes, some seats will be unfilled, and some votes remain—for each party, less than a full *quota (a)*. The remaining seats are then awarded to parties and groupings in order of the number of left-over votes they possess. The Largest Remainder Method tends to be more favourable to smaller parties than the alternative approach, the *Highest Average Method*.

Lema – A term used in Latin America for an umbrella list including two or more sub-lists which receive votes separately but whose votes are counted together for the purposes of seat allocation in some *List PR* systems. See also *Apparentement* and *Stembusaccoord*.

Limited Vote (LV) – An *electoral system* used in *multi-member districts* in which electors have more than one vote, but fewer votes than there are candidates to be elected. The candidates with the highest vote totals win the seats, in the same way as in a *Block Vote* system and in *SNTV*.

List Proportional Representation (List PR) – A system in which each participant party or grouping presents a list of candidates for an *electoral district*, voters vote for a party, and parties receive seats in proportion to their overall share of the vote. Winning candidates are taken from the lists. See *Closed list, Open list* and *Free list*.

Lower house – One of the two chambers in a *bicameral legislature*, usually seen as comprising 'the representatives of the people'. It is the more powerful chamber when the powers of the two chambers are unequal.

Majoritarian – Designed to produce an absolute majority (50 per cent plus 1) of votes.

Malapportionment – The uneven distribution of voters between *electoral districts*.

Manufactured majority – An election result, more commonly found where a *plurality/ majority* system is used, in which a single party or coalition wins less than 50 per cent of the valid votes but an absolute majority of the seats in an elected body.

Member state – A country which is a member of a *supranational institution*, for example the European Union.

Mixed Member Proportional (MMP) – A *mixed system* in which all the voters use the first *electoral system,* usually a *plurality/majority system,* to elect some of the representatives to an elected body. The remaining seats are then allocated to parties and groupings using the second *electoral system,* normally *List PR*, so as to compensate for disproportionality in their representation in the results from the first *electoral system*.

Mixed system – A system in which the choices expressed by voters are used to elect representatives through two different systems, one *proportional representation* system and one *plurality/majority* system. There are two kinds of mixed system: *Parallel systems* and *Mixed Member Proportional systems*.

Modified Borda Count – A *candidate-centred, preferential* system used in either *single-* or *multi-member districts* in which voters use numbers to mark their preferences on the ballot paper and each preference marked is then assigned a value calculated by using the series of divisors 1, 2, 3 ... . For example, in a ten-candidate field a first preference is worth one, a second preference is worth 0.5, a third preference 0.3333, and so on. These are summed and the candidate(s) with the highest total(s) is/are declared elected. See also *Borda Count*.

Multi-member district – A *district* from which more than one representative is elected to a legislature or elected body. See also *Single-member district*.

Multiple-tier system – An *electoral system* in which two or more sets of representatives are elected to the same chamber by the entire electorate of a country. The multiple tiers may be *electoral districts* defined at different levels within a country, for example, *single-member districts* and regions, or regions and the country as a whole. Systems in which two distinct sets of representatives are elected from the same level are also multiple-tier systems. All *mixed systems* are multiple-tier systems.

One Person One Vote One Value (OPOVOV) – A principle of representation in which each elected representative represents the same number of electors, and under which *malapportionment* is minimized.

Open list – A form of *List PR* in which voters can express a preference both for a party or grouping and for one, or sometimes more, candidates within that party or grouping. See also *Closed list* and *Free list*.

Out-of-country voting – A mechanism by which voters who are permanently or temporarily absent from a country are enabled to cast a vote. See *External voting*. See also *Remote voting*.

Overhang mandate – See *Überhangsmandat*.

Panachage – The term used in francophone countries for the version of *List PR* in which voters may vote for a party or grouping and in addition for one or more candidates, whether or not those candidates are nominated by that party or grouping. See also *Free list*.

Parallel System – A *mixed system* in which the choices expressed by the voters are used to elect representatives through two different systems, usually one *plurality/majority* system and one *proportional representation* system, but where no account is taken of the seats allocated under the first system in calculating the results in the second system. See also *Mixed-Member Proportional*.

Party Block Vote (PBV) – A *plurality/majority* system using *multi-member districts* in which voters cast a single *party-centred* vote for a party of choice, and do not choose between candidates. The party with most votes will win every seat in the *electoral district*.

Party-centred ballot – A form of ballot in which a voter chooses between parties or groupings, rather than individual candidates.

Party magnitude – For an *electoral district*, the average number of representatives elected by each party and grouping. For a country, the average of the party magnitudes for all electoral districts.

Personation – The fraudulent casting of the vote of a registered *elector* by another person.

Plurality/majority systems – Plurality/majority systems are based on the principle that a candidate(s) or party with a plurality of votes (i.e. more than any other) or a majority of votes (i.e. 50 per cent plus one—an absolute majority) is/are declared the winner(s). Such a system may use *single-member districts*—for example, *First Past The Post*, *Alternative Vote* or the *Two-Round System*—or *multi-member districts*—for example, the *Block Vote* and *Party Block Vote*.

Preferential voting systems – Electoral systems in which voters rank parties or candidates on the ballot paper in order of their choice. The *Alternative Vote*, the *Borda Count*, the *Single Transferable Vote* and the *Supplementary Vote* are all examples of preferential voting systems.

Proportional Representation (PR) – An *electoral system* family based on the principle of the conscious translation of the overall votes of a party or grouping into a corresponding proportion of seats in an elected body. For example, a party which wins 30 per cent of the votes will receive approximately 30 per cent of the seats. All PR systems require the use of *multi-member districts*. There are two major types of PR system, *List PR* and the *Single Transferable Vote (STV)*.

Quota – May have one of two distinct meanings:
a. The number of votes which guarantees a party or candidate to win one seat in a particular *electoral district* in a *proportional representation* system. There are three variants in common use, the *Hare, Droop* (or *Hagenbach-Bischoff*) and *Imperiali* quotas.

b. A number of seats in an elected body or a proportion of candidates nominated by a party or grouping which are required by law to be filled by representatives of a particular kind; most commonly used to ensure the nomination and election of a minimum number of women.

Regional fiefdom – A situation in which one party wins all, or nearly all, of the seats in a particular geographic region of a country.

Remote voting – A mechanism by which voters are enabled to cast a vote which does not involve their attendance at a polling station on the day or days fixed for voting. See also *Out-of-country voting*.

Reserved seats – Seats in which a determinable criterion such as religion, ethnicity, language or gender is a requirement for nomination or election.

Riding – A synonym for electoral district used in some countries. See *Electoral district*.

Sainte-Laguë Formula – one of the options for the series of divisors used to distribute seats in *List PR* systems which adopt the *Highest Average Method*. The votes of a party or grouping are divided successively by 1, 3, 5... as seats are allocated to it. See also *D'Hondt Formula*.

Single-member district – An electoral district from which only one member is elected to a legislature or elected body. See also *Multi-member district*.

Single Non-Transferable Vote (SNTV) – An *electoral system* in which voters cast a single *candidate-centred* vote for one candidate in a *multi-member district.* The candidates with the highest vote totals are declared elected.

Single Transferable Vote (STV) – A *preferential candidate-centred proportional representation system* used in *multi-member districts.* Candidates that surpass a specified *quota* (see *Quota (a)*) of first-preference votes are immediately elected. In successive counts, votes are redistributed from least successful candidates, who are eliminated, and votes surplus to the *quota* are redistributed from successful candidates, until sufficient candidates are declared elected.

Spoilt votes – See *Invalid votes.*

State – Used in this Handbook to denote a sub-national unit of a country, often in the context of a federal constitution.

Stembusaccoord – A term of Dutch origin for a provision which can be included in *List PR* systems which enables two or more parties or groupings which are fighting separate campaigns to reach agreement that their votes will be combined for the purpose of seat allocation. See also *Apparentement* and *Lema.*

Supplementary Vote – A *candidate-centred, preferential plurality/majority* system, similar to the *Alternative Vote.* If no candidate achieves an absolute majority of first preferences, all candidates except the two leading candidates are eliminated and their votes reallocated according to the second, third and so on preferences expressed. The candidate with the highest number of votes is declared elected.

Supranational institution – an organization created by a number of countries by treaty where power is held by independent appointed officials or by representatives elected by the legislatures or people of the member states.

Threshold – The minimum level of support which a party needs to gain representation in the legislature. A threshold may be a formal threshold, which is a figure laid down in the constitution or the law, usually in the form of a percentage of the valid votes cast, or an effective or natural threshold, which is a mathematical property of the electoral system in use.

Two-Round System (TRS) – A *plurality/majority* system in which a second election is held if no candidate achieves a given level of votes, most commonly an absolute majority (50 per cent plus one), in the first election round.

A *Two-Round System* may take a majority-plurality form, in which it is possible for more than two candidates to contest the second round. An example is the French system, in which any candidate who has received the votes of over 12.5 per cent of the registered electorate in the first round can stand in the second round. The candidate who wins the highest number of votes in the second round is then declared elected, regardless of whether they have won an absolute majority. Alternatively, a *Two-Round System* may take a majority run-off form, in which only the top two candidates in the first round contest the second round.

Überhangsmandat – An additional seat in a legislature which results in an *MMP* system when a party or grouping wins more seats in a region under the first, usually *plurality/majority,* electoral system than the number to which it would be entitled in total on the basis of its proportion of the vote. Also known as *excess mandate* or *overhang mandate.*

Upper house – One of the two chambers in a *bicameral legislature,* often seen either as containing 'the representatives of regions/federal states' or as 'a chamber of review'. The less powerful chamber when the powers of the two chambers are unequal.

Wasted votes – Valid votes which do not ultimately count towards the election of any candidate or party.

Annex C

Further Reading

Amy, Douglas, *Real Choices: New Voices: The Case for PR Elections in the United States* (New York: Columbia University Press, 1993)

Andrews, Josephine T. and Jackman, Robert, 'Strategic Fools: Electoral Rule Choice Under Extreme Uncertainty', *Electoral Studies*, 24/1 (2005), pp. 65–84

Barkan, Joel D., 'Elections in Agrarian Societies', *Journal of Democracy*, 6 (1995), pp. 106–116

Birch, Sarah, 'Single-Member District Electoral Systems and Democratic Transition', *Electoral Studies*, 24/2 (June 2005), pp. 281–301

Bogdanor, Vernon, *What is Proportional Representation?* (Oxford: Martin Robertson, 1984)

—and David Butler (eds), *Democracy and Elections* (Cambridge: Cambridge University Press, 1983)

Colomer, Josep (ed.), *Handbook of Electoral System Choice* (Basingstoke: Palgrave, 2004)

— 'It's Parties That Choose Electoral Systems (or Duverger's Laws Upside Down)', *Political Studies*, 53 (2005), pp. 1–21

Dahl, Robert, *On Democracy* (New Haven, Conn.: Yale University Press, 1998)

Downs, Anthony, *An Economic Theory of Democracy* (New York: Harper and Row, 1957)

Duverger, Maurice, *Political Parties: Their Organization and Activity in the Modern State* (New York: John Wiley, 1954)

Elklit, Jørgen and Nigel S. Roberts, 'A Category of its Own? Four PR Two-Tier Compensatory Member Electoral Systems in 1994', *European Journal of Political Research*, 30 (1996), pp. 217–240

Farrell, David M., *Electoral Systems: A Comparative Introduction* (London and New York: Palgrave, 2001)

Finer, S. E. (ed.), *Adversary Politics and Electoral Reform* (London: Anthony Wigram, 1975)

Gallagher, Michael, 'Comparing Proportional Representation Electoral Systems: Quotas, Thresholds, Paradoxes, and Majorities', *British Journal of Political Science,* no. 22 (1992), pp. 469–496

Golder, Matt, 'Democratic Electoral Systems Around the World 1946–2000', *Electoral Studies*, 24/1 (2005), pp. 103–121

Grofman, Bernard and Arend Lijphart (eds), *Electoral Laws and their Political Consequences* (New York: Agathon Press, 1986)

Grofman, Bernard, Arend Lijphart, Robert McKay and Howard Scarrow (eds), *Representation and Redistricting Issues* (Lexington, Md.: Lexington Books, 1982)

Guinier, Lani, *The Tyranny of the Majority* (New York: Free Press, 1994)

Hermens, Ferdinand, *Democracy or Anarchy? A Study of Proportional Representation,* 2nd edn (New York: Johnson Reprint Corporation, 1972)

Horowitz, Donald L., 'Democracy in Divided Societies', *Journal of Democracy,* 4 (1993), pp. 18–38

— 'Electoral Systems: A Primer for Decision Makers', *Journal of Democracy,* 14 (2003), pp. 115–127

Jones, Mark P., *Electoral Laws and the Survival of Presidential Democracies* (Notre Dame, Ind.: University of Notre Dame Press, 1995)

Lakeman, Enid, *How Democracies Vote* (London: Faber and Faber, 1974)

Lardeyret, Guy, 'The Problem with PR', *Journal of Democracy,* 2 (1991), pp. 30–35

LeDuc, Lawrence, Richard G. Niemi and Pippa Norris (eds), *Comparing Democracies 2: Elections and Voting in Global Perspective* (Thousand Oaks, Calif.: Sage, 2002)

Lijphart, Arend, 'Constitutional Design for Divided Societies', *Journal of Democracy,* 15/2 (2004)

—*Patterns of Democracy* (New Haven, Conn.: Yale University Press, 1999)

—and Bernard Grofman (eds), *Choosing an Electoral System: Issues and Alternatives* (New York: Praeger, 1984)

Lovenduski, Joni and Pippa Norris (eds), *Gender and Party Politics* (London: Sage, 1993)

Mackie, Thomas and Richard Rose, *The International Almanac of Electoral History* (Washington, DC: Congressional Quarterly Press, 1991)

Mackie, Thomas and Richard Rose, *A Decade of Election Results: Updating the International Almanac. Studies in Public Policy* (Glasgow: Centre for the Study of Public Policy, University of Strathclyde, 1997)

Mainwaring, Scott and Matthew Shugart, *Presidentialism and Democracy in Latin America* (Cambridge: Cambridge University Press, 1997)

Miragliotta, Narelle L., 'Little Differences, Big Effects: An Example of the Importance of Choice of Method For Transferring Surplus Votes in PR-STV Voting Systems', Representation, 41/1 (2004) [2005], pp. 15–23

Moser, Robert G. and Ethan Scheiner, 'Mixed Electoral Systems and Electoral System Effects: Controlled Comparison and Cross-National Analysis', *Electoral Studies: An International Journal,* 23/4 (December 2004), pp. 575–600

Nishikawa, Misa and Erik S. Herron, 'Mixed Electoral Rules' Impact on Party Systems', *Electoral Studies: An International Journal,* 23/4 (December 2004), pp. 753–768

Nohlen, Dieter, *Elections and Electoral Systems* (Delhi: Macmillan, 1996)

—(ed.), *Enciclopedia Electoral Latinamericana y del Caribe* (San José, Costa Rica: Instituto Interamericano de Derechos Humanos (IIDH)/CAPEL, 1993)

—et al., *Elections in Africa* (Oxford and New York: Oxford University Press, 1999)

—et al., *Elections in the Asia–Pacific Region* (Oxford and New York: Oxford University Press, 2001)

Norris, Pippa, *Electoral Engineering: Voting Rules and Political Behaviour* (Cambridge: Cambridge University Press, 2004)

Pitkin, Hanna F., *The Concept of Representation* (Berkeley, Calif.: University of California Press, 1967)

Rae, Douglas W., *The Political Consequences of Electoral Laws* (New Haven, Conn.: Yale University Press, 1967)

Reilly, Ben, *Democracy in Divided Societies* (Cambridge: Cambridge University Press, 2001)

—'The Global Spread of Preferential Voting: Australian Institutional Imperialism?', *Australian Journal of Political Science,* 39/2 (July 2004), pp. 253–266

Reynolds, Andrew (ed.), *The Architecture of Democracy* (Oxford: Oxford University Press, 2001)

—*Electoral Systems and Democratization in Southern Africa* (Oxford: Oxford University Press, 1999)

Rule, Wilma and Joseph Zimmerman (eds), *Electoral Systems in Comparative Perspective: Their Impact on Women and Minorities* (Westport, Conn.: Greenwood, 1994)

Sartori, Giovanni, *Comparative Constitutional Engineering: An Inquiry Into Structures, Incentives, and Outcomes* (New York: Columbia University Press, 1994)

Shugart, Mathew S. and John Carey, *Presidents and Assemblies: Constitutional Design and Electoral Dynamics* (Cambridge: Cambridge University Press, 1992)

Shugart, Mathew S. and Martin P. Wattenberg, *Mixed-Member Electoral Systems: The Best of Both Worlds?* (Oxford: Oxford University Press, 2004)

Sisk, Timothy D., *Power Sharing and International Mediation in Ethnic Conflicts* (Washington, DC: United States Institute of Peace Press, 1996)

Taagepera, Rein and Matthew S. Shugart, *Seats and Votes: The Effects and Determinants of Electoral Systems* (New Haven, Conn.: Yale University Press, 1989)

Annex D

Electoral Systems' Impact on the Translation of Votes into Seats

Example 1

Here is a hypothetical election (of 25,000 votes contested by two political parties) run under two different sets of electoral rules: a plurality/majority FPTP system with five single-member districts, and a List PR system with one large district.

	Electoral Districts							Seats Won	
	1	2	3	4	5	Total	%	FPTP	List PR
Party A	3 000	2 600	2 551	2 551	100	10 802	43	4	2
Party B	2 000	2 400	2 449	2 449	4 900	14 198	57	1	3
Total	5 000	5 000	5 000	5 000	5 000	25 000	100	5	5

Key: FPTP = First Past The Post; List PR = List Proportional Representation system using the Largest Remainder Method of seat allocation with a Hare Quota.

Party A receives far fewer votes than Party B (43 per cent as opposed to 57 per cent), but under an FPTP system it wins four of the five seats available. Conversely, under a List PR system Party B wins three seats against two seats for Party A. This example may appear extreme but similar results occur quite regularly in plurality/majority elections.

Example 2

In the second example the two hypothetical electoral systems remain the same but there are now five parties contesting the election and the distribution of the votes is changed.

	Electoral Districts							Seats Won	
	1	2	3	4	5	Total	%	FPTP	List PR
Party A	2 000	2 000	2 000	200	50	6 250	25	3	1
Party B	500	500	500	3 750	500	5 750	23	1	1
Party C	500	250	750	1 000	3 000	5 500	22	1	1
Party D	1 000	500	1 700	25	1 025	4 250	17	0	1
Party E	1 000	1 750	50	25	425	3 250	13	0	1
Total	5 000	5 000	5 000	5 000	5 000	25 000	100	5	5

Key: FPTP = First Past The Post; List PR = List Proportional Representation system using the Largest Remainder Method of seat allocation with a Hare Quota.

Under the List PR system every party wins a single seat despite the fact that Party A wins almost twice as many votes as Party E. Under an FPTP system the largest party (A) would have picked up a majority of the five seats with the next two highest-polling parties (B and C) winning a single seat each. The choice of electoral system thus has a dramatic effect on the composition of the legislature and, by extension, the government in a parliamentary system.

Example 3

In the third example there are again two parties competing; but there are now 50,000 votes and ten seats to be allocated. The two electoral systems are a Parallel (five List PR seats and five FPTP seats) system, and an MMP (five List PR seats and five FPTP seats) system.

	Electoral Districts								Seats Won	
	1	2	3	4	5	National District 5 Seats	Total	%	Parallel	MMP
Party A	2 600	2 600	2 600	2 600	3 100	13 500	27 000	54	Party A total: 8 (FPTP: 5 and List PR: 3)	Party A total: 5 (FPTP: 5 and List PR: 0)
Party B	2 400	2 400	2 400	2 400	1 900	11 500	23 000	46	Party B total: 2 (FPTP: 0 and List PR: 2)	Party B total: 5 (FPTP: 0 and List PR: 5)
Total	5 000	5 000	5 000	5 000	5 000	25 000	50 000	100	10	10

Key: Parallel = Parallel system with the elements List PR and FPTP; MMP = Mixed Member Proportional system with the elements List PR and FPTP. (The List PR systems use the Largest Remainder Method of seat allocation with a Hare Quota.)

Under the Parallel system Party A wins eight seats and Party B gets the remaining two seats. All five of the FPTP seats and three of the five List PR seats go to Party A, which thus wins a total of 80 per cent of the seats with 54 per cent of the vote. Under the MMP system, with the List PR element compensating for the disproportionality under the FPTP element, the same vote distribution gives both parties five seats each. In this example, under MMP, Party A wins all five of the FPTP seats and hence all the five List PR seats are allocated to Party B.

The result of the MMP system is a much more proportional 50 : 50 per cent seat distribution with a 54 : 46 per cent vote distribution compared to the outcome of the election under the Parallel system. This clearly shows the difference between the List PR element simply running parallel to the plurality/majority system on the one hand, and actually compensating for the disproportionalities produced by it on the other.

Annex E

Boundary Delimitation

These two figures are designed to illustrate the principle that there is no independent approach to boundary delimitation. Like many other facets of electoral system design, apparently technical methods and decisions inevitably have political consequences, and those with political interests can be expected to argue for solutions which are politically beneficial to them.

The figures show the results of two different approaches to boundary delimitation in an area which contains a town and surrounding countryside. The total population qualifies the area for two seats in the legislature. Forty per cent of the population live in the town, and 60 per cent in the countryside. (These numbers may equally refer to the total electorate, which is also used as the basis of seat entitlement in some countries.)

For the sake of simplicity, it is assumed that everyone in the town votes for the Workers' Party, and everyone in the countryside votes for the Farmers' Party. The real world is obviously more complex, but this does not change the principles of the mathematics.

In Model 1, the Doughnut principle, the town is retained as a single community in one relatively homogeneous SMD, to which a small amount of adjacent countryside is added to equalize the electorates of the two districts. Most of the countryside makes up a homogeneous second SMD. The result is victory in the town district for the Workers' Party, and victory in the countryside district for the Farmers' Party.

In Model 2, the Burger principle, the area is divided along the river which runs through the centre of it. Two heterogeneous SMDs are created, one containing the northern half of the town and the surrounding northern countryside, the other the southern half of the town and the surrounding southern countryside. In both districts, the Farmers' Party gains victory by 60 per cent to 40 per cent and is given both seats.

Unsurprisingly, the Workers' Party will attempt to persuade the delimitation authority of the technical virtues of homogeneity and the unity of the town, while at the same time the Farmers' Party will be arguing the case for heterogeneity and the undesirability of a seat with a hole in it!

Town and Country: Two Seats
Model 1: Doughnut

Everyone in town votes Workers' Party
Everyone outside votes Farmers' Party

	District A:	Workers 80%
		Farmers 20%
	District B:	Farmers 100%
	Result:	Workers 1 seat
		Farmers 1 seat

Town and Country : Two Seats
Model 2: Burger

Everyone in town votes Workers' Party
Everyone outside votes Farmers' Party

	District A:	Workers 40%
		Farmers 60%
	District B:	Workers 40%
		Farmers 60%
	Result:	Farmers 2 seats

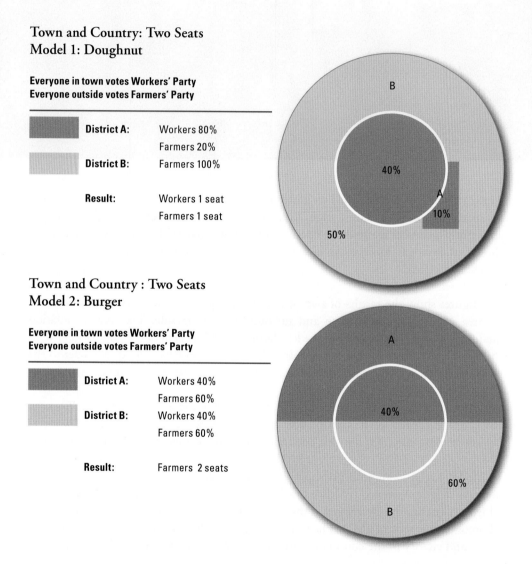

About the Authors

Andrew Reynolds

Andrew Reynolds, Associate Professor of Political Science at the University of North Carolina, Chapel Hill, received his MA from the University of Cape Town and his PhD from the University of California, San Diego. His research and teaching focus on democratization, constitutional design and electoral politics. He has worked for the United Nations, the International Institute for Democracy and Electoral Assistance (IDEA), the UK Department for International Development, the US State Department, the National Democratic Institute, the International Republican Institute, and the Organization for Security and Co-operation in Europe (OSCE). He has also served as a consultant on issues of electoral and constitutional design for Afghanistan, Angola, Burma, Fiji, Guyana, Indonesia, Iraq, Jordan, Liberia, the Netherlands, Northern Ireland, Sierra Leone, South Africa, Sudan and Zimbabwe.

He has received research awards from the US Institute of Peace (USIP), the National Science Foundation, and the Ford Foundation. Among his books are *The Architecture of Democracy: Constitutional Design, Conflict Management, and Democracy* (Oxford University Press, 2002), *Electoral Systems and Democratization in Southern Africa* (Oxford University Press, 1999), *Election '99 South Africa: From Mandela to Mbeki* (St Martin's Press, 1999), and *Elections and Conflict Management in Africa* (co-edited with Tim Sisk, USIP, 1998). His articles have appeared in journals including *World Politics, Legislative Studies Quarterly, Democratization, the Journal of Democracy, Politics and Society, the Journal of Commonwealth and Comparative Politics* and *the Political Science Quarterly.*

Ben Reilly

Benjamin Reilly is a senior lecturer in the Asia Pacific School of Economics and Government at the Australian National University. He has previously been a democratic governance adviser at the United Nations Development Programme (UNDP) in New York, a research fellow at the Australian National University, and a senior programme officer at International IDEA. His work focuses on political institutions, democratization and conflict management, and he has advised numerous governments and international organizations on these issues. He is currently working on a new book on democracy, ethnicity and governance in the Asia–Pacific region.

His books include *Democracy in Divided Societies: Electoral Engineering for Conflict Management* (Cambridge University Press, 2001), *Electoral Systems and Conflict in Divided Societies* (US National Research Council, 1999), *Democracy and Deep-Rooted Conflict: Options for Negotiators* (International IDEA, 1998), and the *International IDEA Handbook of Electoral System Design* (International IDEA, 1997). He has also published in academic journals such as the *Journal of Democracy*, the *International Political Science Review*, *International Security*, *The National Interest*, *Party Politics*, *Electoral Studies*, the *Australian Journal of Political Science*, the *Australian Journal of International Affairs*, *International Peacekeeping*, *Commonwealth and Comparative Politics*, *Representation*, *Asian Survey*, *Pacifica Review*, *Pacific Affairs*, the *Journal of Pacific History* and the *Pacific Economic Bulletin*. He has a PhD in political science from the Australian National University.

Andrew Ellis

Andrew Ellis is currently the head of the Electoral Processes Team at International IDEA in Stockholm. He has wide experience as a technical adviser on electoral and institutional matters in democratic transitions. He acted as senior adviser for the National Democratic Institute (NDI) in Indonesia from 1999 to 2003, working with members of the Indonesian legislature on constitutional amendment and reform of electoral and political laws, and with non-governmental organizations (NGOs) and political commentators. His other recent assignments include acting as chief technical adviser to the Palestinian Election Commission under the European Commission's support for all aspects of the preparation of the first Palestinian elections in 1996, and design and planning for the Commission's electoral assistance programme in Cambodia for the 1998 elections.

He was formerly Vice Chair and subsequently Secretary General of the UK Liberal Party and Chief Executive of the UK Liberal Democrats, stood four times for the UK Parliament, and was an elected member of a major local authority.

José Antonio Cheibub

José Antonio Cheibub, PhD, University of Chicago, 1994 is associate professor of political science and director of undergraduate studies for the International Studies Program at Yale University. His research and teaching interests are in comparative politics, political economy and democratic institutions. He is the co-author of *Democracy and Development: Political Institutions and Well-Being in the World, 1950–1990* (Cambridge University Press, 2000) and co-editor of *The Democracy Sourcebook* (MIT Press, 2003), and is currently completing a book on *The Stability of Democracy under Parliamentarism and Presidentialism.*

Karen Cox

Karen Cox is a PhD candidate at the University of Virginia specializing in comparative and Japanese politics. She has conducted research as a Japan Foundation doctoral fellow at the University of Tokyo. Her publications include 'Interaction Effects in Mixed-Member Electoral Systems: Theory and Evidence from Germany, Japan, and Italy' (with Leonard Schoppa, in *Comparative Political Studies,* November 2002).

Dong Lisheng

Dong Lisheng is professor and assistant director of the Institute of Political Science of the Chinese Academy of Social Sciences. He was an expert employed by the Chinese Ministry of Civil Affairs for its cooperative programme with the UNDP on China's Villagers' Committee elections from 1996 to 2001. Currently he is a member of the Steering and Advisory Committee of the EU–China Training Programme on Village Governance (2003–2006). He has been appointed the Chinese Co-Director of the EU–China European Studies Centres Programme (February 2004–January 2009). His publications include electoral training handbooks for village committees.

Jørgen Elklit

Jørgen Elklit is a professor of political science at the University of Aarhus, Denmark. His professional interests include electoral systems and electoral administration in emerging democracies and elsewhere. Since 1990 he has undertaken a number of election- and democratization-related consultancies in Asia, Europe and Africa. He was also a member of the 1994 Independent Electoral Commission (IEC) in South Africa. His most recent assignments have been to Afghanistan, South Africa, China and Lesotho. His most recent book is a survey of members of Danish political parties (*Partiernes medlemmer,* co-edited with Lars Bille, Aarhus Universitetsforlag, 2003).

Michael Gallagher

Michael Gallagher is an associate professor in the Department of Political Science, Trinity College, University of Dublin. He is co-editor of *The Politics of Electoral Systems* (Oxford University Press, 2005), *Politics in the Republic of Ireland,* 4th edn (co-edited, Routledge, 2005), and *The Referendum Experience in Europe* (Macmillan and St Martin's Press, 1996), and co-author of *Representative Government in Modern Europe,* 4th edn (McGraw Hill, 2006).

Allen Hicken

Allen Hicken is an assistant professor of political science and South-East Asian politics at the University of Michigan and a faculty associate at the Center for Southeast Asian Studies and the Center for Political Studies. He studies political institutions and political economy in developing countries. His primary focus is on political parties and party systems in developing democracies and their role in policy making. His regional specialty is South-East Asia. He has worked or carried out research in Thailand, the Philippines and Cambodia.

Carlos Huneeus

Carlos Huneeus is associate professor of political science at the Instituto de Estudios Internacionales at the Universidad de Chile and executive director of Corporation CERC. His most recent books include *El régimen de Pinochet* [Pinochet's regime] (Editorial Sudamericana, 2000) and *Chile, un país dividido* [Chile, a divided country] (Catalonia, 2003).

Eugene Huskey

Eugene Huskey is William R. Kenan, Jr professor of political science and Russian studies at Stetson University in Florida. His books and articles examine politics and legal affairs in the Soviet Union and the post-Soviet states of Russia and Kyrgyzstan. Among his works are articles on the 1990, 1995 and 2000 elections in Kyrgyzstan.

Stina Larserud

Stina Larserud is the researcher for the *Electoral System Design: The New International IDEA Handbook,* working as part of the Electoral Processes Team at International IDEA in Stockholm. She holds a Master's degree in political science from Uppsala University in comparative politics and institutional design, and acts as a member of a polling station commission at elections in Sweden.

Vijay Patidar

Vijay Patidar is a member of the senior civil service of India (Indian Administrative Service) and has specialized in elections at national and provincial level in India and also internationally. He has served as joint chief electoral officer of the state of Madhya Pradesh, as a consultant in the electoral components of four UN peacekeeping missions and as head of the Election Team at International IDEA.

Nigel S. Roberts

Nigel S. Roberts is an associate professor of political science at the Victoria University of Wellington. Together with Jonathan Boston, Stephen Levine and Elizabeth McLeay, he was for eight years a member of a research team funded by the New Zealand Foundation for Research, Science and Technology that studied the administrative and political consequences of the introduction of proportional representation in *New Zealand.* His most recent book is *New Zealand Votes: The General Election of 2002* (co-editor, Victoria University Press, 2003).

Richard Vengroff

Richard Vengroff, professor of political science at the University of Connecticut, is the author or editor of seven books, more than 70 articles in scholarly journals, and edited volumes. His current research is devoted to issues of democratic governance, decentralization and electoral reform. His two most recent grants deal with democratic transitions and Islam, and with sub-national democratic reform in five East European countries.

Jeffrey A. Weldon
Jeffrey A. Weldon is a professor of political science at the Instituto Tecnológico Autónomo de México (ITAM) and currently a visiting fellow at the Center for US-Mexican Studies at the University of California, San Diego. He has been an adjunct fellow at the Center for Strategic and International Studies (CSIS) since 2001. He has published extensively on the Mexican Congress and the Mexican electoral system.

Annex G

Acknowledgements

A great number of individuals and organizations have contributed to this new Handbook. Members of electoral management bodies, legislatures and embassies worldwide have provided information on a wide range of issues. In addition, we would like to thank the following, who have given generously of their time, ideas and insights as the framework of the book has come together:

José Maria Aranaz, Shem Baldeosingh, Julie Ballington, Brigalia Bam, Virginia Beramendi-Heine, Sarah Birch, André Blais, Neven Brandt, Nadja Braun, Ingrid Bäckström-Vose, Nicholas Cottrell, Bikash Dash, Asha Elkarib, Jørgen Elklit, Arpineh Galfayan, Guido Galli, Maria Gratschew, Lisa Hagman, Donald L. Horowitz, Torquato Jardim, Eve Johansson, Subhash Kashyap, Anna Katz, Therese Pearce Laanela, Lotta Lann, Stephen Levine, Arend Lijphart, Johan Lindroth, Alonso Lujambio, Valentí Martí, Simon Massey, Richard Matland, Andres Mejia-Acosta, Marcel Mikala, José Molina, Simon-Pierre Nanitelamio, Paolo Natale, Sa Ngidi, Pippa Norris, Simon Pachano, Vijay Patidar, Carina Perelli, Colville Petty, Joram Rukambe, Andrew Russell, Matthew Shugart, Olga Shvetsova, Timothy D. Sisk, Bruno Speck, Antonio Spinelli, Sara Staino, Michael Steed, Thorvald Stoltenberg, Markku Suksi, Kate Sullivan, Jan Sundberg, Rein Taagepera, Maja Tjernström, Daniel Zovatto and the British Columbia Citizens' Assembly on Electoral Reform.

Thanks also go to IDEA's Publications Manager, Nadia Handal Zander.

Above all, we would like to express our thanks to Stina Larserud. She has held together the mass of material, text and technical detail necessary to support the Handbook through its many phases and drafts. We could not have asked for a better or more committed researcher and editorial anchor.

Andrew Reynolds
Ben Reilly
Andrew Ellis
February 2005

About International IDEA

Created in 1995, the International Institute for Democracy and Electoral Assistance (IDEA), an intergovernmental organization with member states from all continents, has a mandate to support sustainable democracy worldwide. IDEA operates at an interface between those who analyse and monitor trends in democracy and those who engage directly in political reform or act in support of democracy at home and abroad. IDEA works with both new and long-established democracies, helping to develop and strengthen the institutions and culture of democracy. It operates at an international, regional and national level, working in partnership with a range of institutions.

IDEA aims to:

- Assist countries in building capacity to develop and strengthen democratic institutions
- Provide a forum for dialogue between academics, policy makers and practitioners around the world
- Synthesize research and field experience, and develop practical tools to help improve democratic processes
- Promote transparency, accountability and efficiency in election management
- Facilitate in-country democracy assessment, monitoring and promotion by local citizens.

The International Institute for Democracy and Electoral Assistance (IDEA)
Strömsborg, S-103 34 Stockholm, Sweden
Tel: +46 8 698 3700
Fax: +46 8 20 24 22 E-mail: info@idea.int
Web site: www.idea.int

Index

D

E

T